READY STEADY COOK™

365

READY STEADY COOK™

365

A recipe for every day of the year

BBC BOOKS

This book is based on the television series *Ready Steady Cook*, produced for
BBC Daytime by Endemol UK plc

1 3 5 7 9 10 8 6 4 2

Published in 2009 by BBC Books, an imprint of Ebury Publishing.
A Random House Group Company

Recipes © Endemol UK plc and the contributors
Some of the recipes in this book previously appeared in:
Ready Steady Cook 1 & 2 (1996); *Fast Meals for Two* (1998); *The Big Ready
Steady Cook Book* (1997); *Ready Steady Cook: The Top 100 Recipes* (2003);
The Ten-Minute Cookbook (2006)

Food photography © BBC Worldwide Limited 2009
Cover photography and pp. 2, 18, 22, 36, 47, 64 top right and bottom, 71, 77, 100,
112, 122 top and bottom right, 127, 159, 169, 173, 180, 212, 230, 236 by Philip
Webb pp. 6, 8, 11, 15, 31, 42, 53, 58, 64 top left, 81, 86, 92, 96, 105, 122 bottom
left, 131, 136, 147, 154, 162, 177, 183, 186, 191, 205, 226 by Steve Lee
pp. 60, 109, 118, 142, 196, 201. 218, 222 by Julie Piddington

The Random House Group Limited Reg. No. 954009

Addresses for companies within the Random House Group can be found at
www.randomhouse.co.uk

A CIP catalogue record for this book is available from the British Library.

ISBN 978 1 84 607801 9

Limited supports The Forest Stewardship Council (FSC),
rest certification organization. All our titles that are printed
ved FSC certified paper carry the FSC logo. Our paper
can be found at www.rbooks.co.uk/environment

Commissioning editor: Muna Reyal
Project editor: Caroline McArthur
Designer: Carl Hodson
Proofreader: Catherine Ward
Production: Antony Heller

origination by: Pixel Envy S.r.l Verona Italy
nd bound in Singapore by Tien Wah Press

Front cover photograph: Warm Chorizo and Chickpea Salad with Roasted Red
Peppers, page 135. Back cover photographs: Seared Prawn Cocktail, page 14;
Pan Fried Seabass with Asparagus and Baby Plum Tomatoes, page 95; Stuffed
Field Mushrooms, page 132; Hot Chocolate with Marshmallows, page 235

contents

Introduction

Ready Steady Cook has been inspiring the nation to cook quick, simple and mouth-watering dishes in minutes for over 15 years. Its success comes from watching well-loved chefs cook up culinary feasts that you can recreate yourself at home. This new collection will become, like the programme, a long-term favourite in your kitchen – it presents a different dish for every day of the year, with 365 of the very best recipes created on the show.

Organised into spring, summer, autumn and winter, RSC 365 will help you follow the seasons and eat the best ingredients at the best times of the year. Each part is split into chapters with starters, light meals, accompaniments, vegetarian, poultry and game, meat, fish and seafood, desserts and drinks and cocktails. Some of the recipes can be cooked in 20 minutes, while others can be whipped up in ten – and we've selected particular recipes to suit special occasions such as Mothering Sunday, Valentine's Day and Halloween.

You'll find a wonderful variety of flavours and styles, from dishes from the East, such as Miso mullet and Oriental style sesame duck, to the West – Quick lamb cobbler and Chocolate drop scones, for example; from the north – Fillet steak with whisky sauce – to the south – Pea and onion bhajis; European classics such as Lemon and Parmesan risotto and Sausage cassoulet, and tangy American treats like Quesadilla triangles and Cajun-style salmon. You'll find modern twists on traditional favourites such as Toad in the hole with venison sausages and Caramelized ground rice pudding, plus good old-fashioned Sausages and mash with onion gravy, and Rhubarb and stem ginger crumble.

Ready Steady Cook's fresh and fun approach to cooking has proved that cooking on a budget can be tasty and healthy all year round. It has inspired its viewers to get creative in the kitchen and not to be afraid of using new ingredients to cook delicious, affordable meals quickly and easily. 365 is the perfect recipe book for dipping into, and we haven't limited the dishes to specific days of the year. Simply pick the recipes that suit the ingredients you have in your storecupboard, or that are available in your local supermarket and cook yourself a tasty seasonal treat that's as quick and easy to cook as it is to eat.

SPRING

CASHEL BLUE CHEESE SOUFFLÉS

These rich little soufflés are much simpler to make than they appear.
You could use any soft blue cheese, such as Gorgonzola or Dolcelatte.

Serves 2

25g (1oz) unsalted
butter, plus extra for
greasing

25g (1oz) plain flour

120ml (4fl oz) milk

2 eggs

50g (2oz) Cashel Blue
cheese

salt and freshly
ground black pepper

Preheat the oven to 220°C/425°F/gas 7. Lightly butter the insides of two 120ml (4fl oz) ramekins. Melt the butter in a small pan, stir in the flour and cook over a low heat for 1 minute. Remove from the heat and gradually add the milk, little by little, stirring well after each addition. Return to the heat and cook for 4–5 minutes until smooth and shiny, stirring occasionally.

Allow the white sauce to cool slightly, then separate the eggs; place the egg whites in a bowl and set aside. Crumble the Cashel Blue cheese into the white sauce and stir in the egg yolks to combine. Season to taste. Using an electric beater, whisk the egg whites until stiff peaks form. Beat a third of the egg whites into the Cashel Blue mixture until just blended, then add the rest and gently fold in.

Divide the mixture between the prepared ramekins and place them on a baking sheet. Bake for 8–10 minutes until cooked through, well risen and golden brown – avoid opening the oven door during cooking time. Transfer the soufflés onto serving plates and serve immediately – they don't hang around!

SPINACH AND PARMESAN FILO TARTS

If you don't have cooking rings for this dish, a four-hole Yorkshire
pudding tin is a useful substitute.

Serves 2

4 sheets filo pastry,
thawed if frozen

50g (2oz) butter,
melted

225g (8oz) baby
spinach leaves

225ml (8fl oz)
double cream

2 egg yolks

100g (4oz) freshly
grated Parmesan

50g (2oz) pine nuts

salt and freshly
ground black pepper

Preheat the oven to 220°C/425°F/gas 7. Place two 10cm (4in) metal cooking rings on a large non-stick baking sheet. Cut down each filo sheet into a square of approximately 15cm (6in). Brush with melted butter and layer two in each ring at an angle to each other to form a crown. Press down firmly into the ring and bake for 2–3 minutes until crisp and lightly golden.

Meanwhile, put the spinach and remaining butter in a small pan and wilt, draining off any excess liquid. Place the cream, egg yolks and Parmesan in a bowl and whisk to combine. Season to taste and fold in the spinach.

Remove the filo cases from the oven and divide the spinach mixture between them. Bake for another 4–5 minutes until the tarts are just set and the filo is golden brown.

Meanwhile, toast the pine nuts in a dry frying pan for a few minutes, tossing to ensure they cook evenly. Remove the cooked tarts from the oven, transfer to warmed plates and scatter over the toasted pine nuts to serve.

SCRAMBLED EGGS IN SHELLS WITH CAVIAR AND SMOKED SALMON

3

Serve this with toast soldiers spread with butter. Long thin slices of toasted flavoured breads also make a nice change: try herby focaccia, black olive or sun-dried tomato ciabatta, or cheese and onion loaf.

Serves 2

2 large eggs

a knob of unsalted butter

1 tbsp soft cream cheese

1 tsp Dijon mustard

1 tsp caviar

salt and freshly ground black pepper

thin strips of smoked salmon and snipped fresh chives, to garnish

Carefully crack the top off each egg and drain into a bowl, reserving the shell. Season the eggs and lightly beat together with a fork.

Melt the butter in a heavy-based pan over a low heat. Swirl the butter around the sides of the pan so that it coats the sides. Add the beaten eggs and cook over a medium heat for 2 minutes, or until the eggs are half set, stirring all the time.

Take the pan off the heat, add the cream cheese and mustard and keep stirring, returning to the heat if necessary, until the eggs are soft and creamy.

Spoon the scrambled eggs back into the shells, and set into egg cups, then top each one with half a teaspoon of caviar. Garnish with a swirl of smoked salmon and a sprinkling of chives.

SMOKED SALMON WITH BAKED EGGS

4

A simple but effective meeting of three ingredients. Serve with buttered toast soldiers for a retro feel.

Serves 2

25g (1oz) butter

225g (8oz) smoked salmon slices (about 8 in total)

225ml (8fl oz) double cream

4 eggs

freshly ground black pepper

crusty bread, to serve

Preheat the oven to 220°C/425°F/gas 7. Grease 2 small gratin dishes with the butter. Ruffle up the salmon slices and divide them between the dishes.

Drizzle the double cream on top of the salmon and then break two eggs into each dish. Add a good grinding of black pepper and bake for 6–8 minutes or until the whites of the eggs are just set but the yolks are still runny.

Transfer the gratin dishes directly onto plates and arrange some crusty bread alongside to serve.

SEARED GRAVADLAX AND HERB SALAD WITH HORSERADISH DRESSING

This horseradish dressing is easy to prepare and keeps for several weeks in the fridge.

Serves 2

about 2 tbsp olive oil

4 slices gravadlax

75g (3oz) mixed herb salad

juice of ½ a lemon, pips removed

FOR THE HORSERADISH DRESSING

2 tbsp creamed horseradish

100ml (3½fl oz) olive oil

a squeeze of lemon juice

1 tbsp snipped fresh chives

freshly ground black pepper

Heat a large griddle pan. To make the dressing, whisk the creamed horseradish into the olive oil in a small bowl. Stir in the lemon juice to taste with the chives and season with pepper.

Brush the heated griddle pan with 1 tablespoon of the olive oil and then add the slices of gravadlax. Chargrill for a minute or so on each side.

Place the herb salad in a bowl and dress with the remaining olive oil and enough lemon juice to barely coat the leaves. Divide between plates and top with the seared gravadlax. Add a squeeze of lemon juice, drizzle over the horseradish dressing and serve at once.

SMOKED SALMON PÂTÉ WITH TOASTED RYE BAGELS

Chewy toasted bagels are perfect spread thickly with this delicious pâté. You can use any type available, but rye varieties have a particular affinity with the smoked salmon.

Serves 2

2 rye bagels

100g (4oz) smoked salmon slices

75g (3oz) soft cream cheese

2 tbsp Greek yoghurt

½ teaspoon creamed horseradish

a few drops of Tabasco sauce

freshly ground black pepper

2 tiny fresh dill sprigs, to garnish

2 lemon wedges, to serve

Preheat the grill. Cut the rye bagels in half and toast under the grill for 2–3 minutes.

To make the pâté, roughly chop the smoked salmon and place in a mini food-processor with the cream cheese, Greek yoghurt, horseradish and Tabasco. Season generously with pepper and whizz until smooth.

Spoon the smoked salmon pâté into individual ramekins and smooth over with a palette knife. Garnish with a dill sprig and set on plates. Arrange the rye bagels and lemon wedges alongside to serve.

PRAWN WONTONS WITH CHILLI JAM

This starter is ideal with a drink (preferably a glass of bubbly). The wontons are simple to make and taste far superior to ready-made versions.

Serves 2

sunflower oil, for deep-frying

6 raw, peeled tiger prawns, cleaned

2 spring onions, chopped

1 mild red chilli, seeded and chopped

2½cm (1in) piece fresh root ginger, peeled and chopped

2 garlic cloves, chopped

12 wonton wrappers, thawed if frozen

1 egg, beaten

1 tbsp chopped fresh coriander

½ tsp sesame seeds

FOR THE CHILLI JAM

1 mild red chilli, seeded and chopped

2 spring onions, sliced

1 tsp freshly grated root ginger

1 tbsp sesame seeds

a drizzle of sesame oil

a drizzle of dark soy sauce

1 tbsp clear honey

juice of 1 lime

salt and freshly ground black pepper

Preheat a deep-fat fryer or fill a deep-sided pan one-third full with oil and heat to 190°C/375°F. The oil should be hot enough so that when a bread cube is added, it browns in 40 seconds.

Place the prawns in a food-processor with the spring onions, chilli, ginger and garlic. Season and blitz until the mixture is well combined.

Place a teaspoon of the prawn mixture in the middle of a wonton wrapper, brush the sides with beaten egg and fold over to form a triangle. Repeat until you have 12 wontons in total. Deep-fry the wontons in the hot oil for 2–3 minutes until cooked through and golden brown.

Meanwhile, make the chilli jam: place the chilli, spring onions, ginger, sesame seeds, sesame oil, soy sauce, honey and lime juice in a mini food-processor and blitz for a few seconds until well combined.

Drain the cooked wontons well on kitchen paper and arrange on warmed plates with individual bowls of the chilli jam. Garnish with coriander and a sprinkling of sesame seeds.

SEARED PRAWN COCKTAIL

You could use tiger prawns or Dublin Bay prawns (langoustines) for this dish. (See illustration, back cover.)

Serves 4

2 tbsp mayonnaise

2 tbsp Greek yoghurt

1 tbsp tomato ketchup

½ tsp clear honey, or sugar to taste

a dash of Worcestershire sauce

a few drops of Tabasco sauce

a pinch of medium curry powder

juice of 1 lime

225g (8oz) raw, peeled prawns, cleaned (such as Dublin Bay or tiger)

1 tbsp sunflower oil

a pinch of dried crushed chillies

2 little Gem lettuces, shredded

1 firm ripe avocado

salt and freshly ground black pepper

4 lime wedges, to garnish

To make the dressing, mix together the mayonnaise, Greek yoghurt, tomato ketchup, honey or sugar, Worcestershire sauce, Tabasco and curry powder. Add a squeeze of lime and season.

Heat a heavy-based pan. Pat dry the prawns on kitchen paper and tip into a bowl. Add the oil and crushed chillies, season and toss until well combined. Add to the pan and sear over a high heat for 1–2 minutes until opaque in colour and just cooked through. Add a good squeeze of lime juice, tossing to coat, and remove from the heat.

Put the shredded lettuce in the bottom of serving dishes. Cut the avocado in half and remove the stone. Peel off the skin and chop or slice the flesh, then scatter over the lettuce. Arrange the seared prawns on top and drizzle over the cocktail dressing. Garnish with lime wedges to serve.

THAI FRAGRANT CHICKEN SOUP

Once you've mastered the basic method for this soup you can experiment with a choice of ingredients. For a special occasion try a mixture of scallops, mussels and squid. Thai basil is available in Asian supermarkets and often has a slight red tinge. You could substitute with a mixture of ordinary basil and coriander.

Serves 2

1 tbsp olive oil

1 shallot, finely chopped

1 red chilli, finely chopped

40g (1½oz) chestnut mushrooms, thinly sliced

50g (2oz) chicken fillet, shredded

450ml (¾ pint) chicken stock

1 lemongrass stalk, trimmed and bruised

2 kaffir lime leaves

25g (1oz) fresh Thai basil

juice of 1 lime

Heat the olive oil in a pan. Add the shallot and sauté for 2 minutes until softened but not coloured. Stir in the chilli and mushrooms and sauté for another 2 minutes.

Tip the shredded chicken fillet into the pan and continue to cook for 2–3 minutes or until the chicken is sealed and just tender. Pour in the chicken stock and add the lemongrass and kaffir lime leaves. Bring to the boil, then simmer for 8 minutes or until the flavours are well combined and the soup has slightly reduced.

Just before serving, quickly shred the Thai basil leaves, discarding the stalks, and stir into the soup with the lime juice. Remove from the heat and ladle into Thai-style bowls. Serve immediately.

SMOKED MACKEREL AND WATERCRESS PÂTÉ

Avoid mackerel that's been dyed with tartrazine – easy to spot as the fish will have a golden-yellow tinge to it.

Serves 2

1 small French baguette

2 tbsp extra-virgin olive oil

25g (1oz) walnut halves

75g (3oz) smoked mackerel fillet

25g (1oz) watercress, well picked over, tough stalks removed, plus extra to garnish

1 tbsp Dijon mustard

25g (1oz) butter, softened

juice of ½ lemon

4 tbsp crème fraîche

salt and freshly ground black pepper

Preheat the oven to 180°C/350°F/gas 4. Cut the baguette into slices, drizzle with half of the olive oil and arrange on a baking sheet. Place in the oven for about 8 minutes or until crisp and golden.

Place the walnuts in a dry frying pan and lightly toast, tossing occasionally to ensure that they cook evenly. Tip out onto a flat plate and leave to cool completely, then roughly chop.

Strip the mackerel flesh from the skin, discarding the skin, and place the flesh in a food-processor. Add the watercress, mustard, butter, lemon juice and remaining olive oil. Blend until smooth and then season to taste.

Divide half of the mackerel mixture between two 6cm (2¼ in) metal cooking rings that have been set on plates and scatter the walnuts on top. Cover with the remaining mackerel mixture and then carefully spread over a layer of crème fraîche to come up to the top of each cooking ring. Garnish with the watercress and serve at once with the toasts piled high to the side.

ASPARAGUS WRAPPED IN PANCETTA

This is best during asparagus season, which runs for approximately eight weeks starting in May.

Serves 2

14 asparagus spears

14 thin slices pancetta (Italian streaky bacon)

1 tbsp olive oil

FOR THE BLUSHED CHIVE DIP

100g (4oz) soft cream cheese

2 tbsp Greek yoghurt

6 sun-blushed tomatoes

a small bunch of fresh chives, snipped

salt and freshly ground black pepper

Heat a griddle pan until very hot. Trim the asparagus spears and blanch in a pan of boiling water for 2–3 minutes until just tender. Drain and quickly refresh under cold running water, then pat dry on kitchen paper.

Wrap each of the asparagus spears in a slice of pancetta and arrange on a plate. Drizzle with olive oil and season. Add the wrapped asparagus spears to the heated griddle pan and cook for 3–4 minutes until crisp and lightly golden, turning regularly.

Meanwhile, place the cream cheese in a mini food-processor with the yoghurt, sun-blushed tomatoes, chives and seasoning. Blend until smooth.

Arrange stacks of the asparagus wrapped in pancetta on warmed plates and serve with the dip at once.

SMOKED CHICKEN GOUJONS WITH GARLIC AIOLI

If you haven't got time to make your own aioli, beat the garlic into a good-quality shop-bought mayonnaise with a couple of tablespoons of extra-virgin olive oil.

Serves 2

sunflower oil, for deep-frying

225g (8oz) cooked smoked chicken breast, skinned

100g (4oz) self-raising flour

1 egg yolk

150ml (¼ pint) sparkling water

1 baby Cos lettuce

a squeeze of lemon juice

a little extra-virgin olive oil

FOR THE GARLIC AIOLI

1 egg yolk

1 tsp Dijon mustard

1 garlic clove, crushed

½ tsp white wine vinegar

50ml (2fl oz) sunflower oil

50ml (2fl oz) extra-virgin olive oil

salt and freshly ground black pepper

Preheat a deep-fat fryer or fill a deep-sided pan one-third full with the sunflower oil and heat to 180°C/350°F.

To make the aioli, beat the egg yolk in a bowl with the mustard, garlic, vinegar, two teaspoons of water and seasoning, until thickened. Mix the oils together in a jug and add to the egg yolk mixture, drop by drop, whisking constantly. After adding two tablespoons of oil the mixture should be quite thick. Add the remaining oil more quickly, a teaspoon at a time, whisking constantly. Season to taste, then transfer to a plastic squeezy bottle.

To make the goujons, cut the chicken breast into long, thin strips. Place the flour, egg yolk and sparkling water in a large bowl and quickly whisk together to form a smooth batter. Dip the chicken strips into the batter, shake off any excess and drop into the heated oil. Deep-fry for 2–3 minutes until crisp and golden brown.

Shred the lettuce and lightly dress the leaves with lemon juice and a little extra-virgin olive oil. Season to taste and place a pile in the middle of each plate. Pile the crispy smoked chicken goujons on top and drizzle around the aioli to serve.

SESAME, SOY AND LIME CHICKEN SKEWERS

These skewers are full of fresh, clean flavours; the sauce is similar to teriyaki, but not quite as sweet.

Serves 2

225g (8oz) skinless chicken fillet, cut into 2cm (¾ in) cubes

1 red romero pepper, halved, seeded and cut into 2cm (¾ in) pieces

1 small courgette, sliced on the diagonal

1 small red onion, cut into 2cm (¾ in) pieces

juice of 1 lime

2 tbsp dark soy sauce

juice of ½ orange

1 tbsp sesame oil

a pinch of caster sugar

1 x 250g (9oz) packet cooked basmati rice

Heat a flat griddle pan until very hot. Meanwhile, place the chicken in a large bowl with the red pepper, courgette and onion pieces. Add the lime juice, soy sauce, orange juice, sesame oil and sugar. Toss until well combined and then thread onto six 15cm (6in) bamboo skewers.

Add the chicken skewers to the heated griddle pan and sear on all sides for about 1 minute, then reduce the heat and cook for another minute or so on each side until the chicken and vegetables are cooked through and tender.

Meanwhile, place the remaining marinade in a small pan and cook for about 5 minutes until well reduced and sticky. Heat the rice according to the packet instructions. Divide between warmed plates and arrange the chicken skewers to the side. Drizzle over the reduced marinade and serve at once.

EGGS BENEDICT ROYALE

The secret to a trouble-free beurre blanc is to keep the sauce at the right temperature. To test it, stick your finger in – it should feel warm, not hot.

Serves 2

½ tsp white wine vinegar

2 large eggs

1 soft white muffin, halved

olive oil, for cooking

4 smoked salmon slices (about 100g/4oz in total)

fresh dill sprigs, to garnish

FOR THE BEURRE BLANC

100ml (3½fl oz) double cream

25g (1oz) unsalted butter

juice of ½ lemon

2 tsp Dijon mustard

a dash of Tabasco sauce

salt and freshly ground black pepper

Preheat the grill. To make the beurre blanc, place the cream, butter, lemon juice, mustard and Tabasco in a small pan. Heat for 3–4 minutes, whisking until the sauce is thick and glossy. Season to taste and keep warm.

Meanwhile, heat a large pan of boiling water with the vinegar. When the water is bubbling, break the eggs in, then move the pan to the edge of the heat and simmer gently for 3 minutes.

Toast the muffin halves for 3–4 minutes under the hot grill until lightly golden. Heat a non-stick frying pan, add a film of oil and lightly sear the smoked salmon for up to 1 minute on each side.

Remove the poached eggs with a slotted spoon, drain on kitchen paper and trim down any ragged edges. Put a muffin half on each of 2 warmed plates and arrange the salmon on top. Top with a poached egg and either spoon over the beurre blanc or serve it on the side. Garnish with dill and black pepper and serve at once.

GUINNESS PANCAKES WITH CRISPY BACON AND CHEDDAR

Use a good-quality, heavy-based, non-stick frying pan to make pancakes so that the heat is conducted evenly.

Serves 2

100g (4oz) plain flour

1 tsp baking powder

½ tsp fresh thyme leaves

2 eggs

150ml (¼ pint) Guinness

2 tbsp sunflower oil

a knob of unsalted butter

6 rindless bacon rashers (dry-cure, if possible)

50g (2oz) freshly grated mature Cheddar

2 tbsp chopped mixed fresh herbs (such as chives, flat-leaf parsley and basil)

salt and freshly ground black pepper

Preheat the grill and heat a heavy-based frying pan. Sift the flour into a bowl with the baking powder and a pinch of salt, then stir in the thyme. Break the eggs into a jug with the Guinness and lightly whisk to combine. Make a well in the centre of the flour and quickly add enough of the Guinness mixture to make a smooth batter – the consistency of thick cream.

Add 1 tablespoon of oil to the heated pan and ladle in spoonfuls of the pancake batter, allowing them to spread out to about 7½ cm (3in) in diameter. Reduce the heat and cook for 2–3 minutes until small bubbles appear on the surface. Flip and cook for another 1–2 minutes until the pancakes are lightly golden. Stack on a plate and keep warm. Repeat until you have 8–10 pancakes.

Meanwhile, heat a separate frying pan and add the remaining oil and butter. Fry the bacon until crisp, turning once. Mix together the cheese and herbs. Arrange the pancakes on a baking sheet, scatter over the cheese mixture and season with pepper. Place under the grill until just beginning to melt, then transfer to warmed serving plates and top with the bacon to serve.

FONTINA CHEESE SCONES

To help them stay moist and fluffy, cover the cooked scones immediately with a clean tea towel as they cool on the wire rack. (See illustration, page 8.)

Makes 6

100g (4oz) plain flour, plus extra for dusting

a good pinch of salt

1 tsp baking powder

25g (1oz) unsalted butter

50g (2oz) finely grated fontina cheese

85ml (3fl oz) milk

beaten egg, to glaze (optional)

butter, to serve

Preheat the oven to 220°C/425°F/gas 7. Sift the flour, salt and baking powder into a bowl. Rub in the butter and stir in the Fontina cheese, then make a well in the centre and add enough of the milk to quickly mix to a soft dough.

Turn the dough out on to a lightly floured surface and knead briefly, then roll out to a 1cm (½ in) thickness. Cut into 6 rough square shapes and arrange slightly apart on a non-stick baking sheet dusted with flour. Brush the tops with the beaten egg, if liked, and bake for 8–10 minutes until well-risen and golden brown.

Transfer the cooked scones to a wire rack, cover with a clean tea towel and leave to cool. Serve with a small pot of butter so that guests can help themselves.

SALMON MILLEFEUILLES

These salmon stacks with new potatoes and spiced courgettes
make a great brunch dish on a warm spring day.

Serves 2

225g (8oz) puff
pastry, thawed if
frozen

1 egg yolk, lightly
beaten

4 tbsp olive oil

225g (8oz) new
potatoes, scrubbed
and thinly sliced

2 x 175g (6oz)
boneless salmon
steaks

1 small onion, finely
chopped

1 courgette, diced

1 tsp wholegrain
mustard

¼ tsp ground cumin

¼ tsp cayenne

300ml (½ pint) fish or
chicken stock

50g (2oz) unsalted
butter

3 tbsp white wine

1 tsp Dijon mustard

2 tbsp chopped fresh
basil

salt and freshly
ground black pepper

Preheat the oven to 220°C/425°F/gas 7. Roll out the pastry to
5mm (¼ in) thick. Using a 5cm (2in) pastry cutter, stamp out 6
circles. Transfer to a baking sheet, brush with egg yolk and bake
for 10–15 minutes until well risen.

Fry the potatoes for 10–15 minutes in 2 tablespoons of the hot
oil, turning occasionally. Roll each steak into a round, secure with
cocktail sticks and fry in 1 tablespoon of oil for 8 minutes, turning once. Remove the sticks and cut in half horizontally.

Remove the pastry from the oven. Lower the temperature to
200°C/400°F/gas 6. Cook the onion and courgette in the
remaining oil for 2 minutes. Stir in the wholegrain mustard,
cumin and cayenne. Season and cook for 5 minutes. Spoon into
a buttered 10cm (4in) ramekin. Cook in the oven for 5 minutes.

Bring the stock to the boil in a pan. Boil rapidly for 5 minutes
until reduced by a third. Whisk in the butter, wine and mustard.
Simmer for 3 minutes then stir in the chopped basil and season.
Stack up the salmon and pastry rounds, spoon the potatoes onto
the side, turn out the timbale on top and drizzle with the sauce.

GARLIC MUSHROOM PARCELS

There is no need to wash commercially produced mushrooms.
Just a quick wipe with a damp cloth will do if needed.

Serves 2

1 x 375g (13oz)
packet ready-rolled
puff pastry, thawed if
frozen

plain flour, for
dusting

2–3 tbsp mild
wholegrain mustard

1 tbsp olive oil and a
knob of unsalted
butter, for frying

1 small onion, finely
chopped

2 garlic cloves,
crushed

225g (8oz) chestnut
mushrooms, sliced

a small bunch of
fresh flatleaf parsley,
roughly chopped

a squeeze of lemon
juice

1 egg, beaten

150ml (¼ pint) double
cream

sea salt and freshly
ground black pepper

fresh flat-leaf parsley
sprigs, to garnish

Preheat the oven to 220°C/425°F/gas 7. Unroll the pastry on
and brush over 1 heaped tablespoon of mustard. Fold the pastry
in half to enclose the mustard and roll out again as thinly as
possible. Cut out two 25cm (10in) squares and leave to rest.

Heat the oil and butter in a frying pan. Add the onion, garlic and
mushrooms and fry until softened. Stir in the parsley, season and
add a squeeze of lemon juice. Take off the heat and cool slightly.

Pile the mushrooms into the middle of the pastry squares. Draw
up the edges of each square and squeeze them together to seal.
Trim the tops flat. Turn them over and gently press into lightly
oiled 10cm (4in) fluted tartlet or Yorkshire pudding tins. Brush
with beaten egg, sprinkle with salt and bake on a baking sheet in
the oven for 8–10 minutes or until puffed up and golden brown.

Place the cream in a small pan with 2 teaspoons of mustard.
Season and heat gently to thicken. Remove the tartlet tins from
the oven and carefully turn out the parcels. Arrange them on
serving plates, drizzle around the sauce and garnish with
parsley sprigs to serve.

SUN-BLUSHED TOMATO SALAD WITH BACON AND POACHED EGG

The poached eggs can be cooked in advance and plunged into ice-cold water until needed. You just slip them into hot salted water when ready to serve.

Serves 2

1 ciabatta loaf

5 tbsp olive oil, plus extra for brushing

1 small red onion, sliced

75g (3oz) rindless streaky bacon rashers, chopped

1 garlic clove, chopped

50g (2oz) Cambozola cheese, rind removed, diced

juice of ½ lemon

3 tbsp milk

a dash of white wine vinegar

2 large eggs

50g (2oz) sun-blushed tomatoes, roughly chopped

1 tbsp chopped fresh flat-leaf parsley

1 tbsp snipped fresh chives

salt and freshly ground black pepper

Preheat the oven to 200°C/400°F/gas 6 and heat a griddle pan until searing hot. Cut the crusts off the ciabatta and cut into 1cm (½ in) cubes. Toss half with 2 tablespoons of olive oil and spread out in a baking tin. Season and cook for 8 minutes until lightly golden, tossing occasionally to ensure they cook evenly.

Brush the pan with oil. Add the onion and bacon. Cook for 3–4 minutes until cooked through and lightly charred. Turn regularly.

Whizz the rest of the bread cubes in a food-processor until you have fine breadcrumbs, add the remaining oil, garlic, Cambozola, lemon juice and milk and blend until smooth. Season to taste.

Boil some water with the vinegar in a large pan until bubbling. Break the eggs into the water, then move the pan to the edge of the heat and simmer gently for 3 minutes. Remove each poached egg with a slotted spoon.

Toss the chargrilled bacon, onion, sun-blushed tomatoes, parsley, chives and croûtons with the dressing and season. Arrange the salad on plates and top each with a poached egg to serve.

ROCKET, RADICCHIO AND PINE NUT SALAD WITH PARMESAN SHAVINGS

The sharp, contrasting flavours of the peppery rocket, bitter radicchio, Parmesan and toasted nuts work a treat.

Serves 2–4

2 tbsp pine nuts

1 small head radicchio

25g (1oz) rocket leaves

1½ tsp balsamic vinegar

1 tsp freshly squeezed lemon juice

3 tbsp extra-virgin olive oil

25g (1oz) piece Parmesan

salt and freshly ground black pepper

Toast the pine nuts in a dry frying pan for 6–8 minutes, tossing occasionally to ensure that they cook evenly. Pour onto a flat plate and spread out to cool.

Meanwhile, cut the radicchio into quarters and remove the white central core; discard. Cut each piece crossways into strips that are roughly the same size as the rocket leaves. Place in a large bowl with the rocket.

Mix the balsamic vinegar with the lemon juice in a small bowl. Whisk in the olive oil and season to taste. Using a potato peeler, pare the Parmesan into thin shavings.

Add the cooled pine nuts to the rocket mixture and pour over enough of the dressing to barely coat the leaves, tossing to combine. Divide between plates and scatter over the Parmesan shavings to serve.

CHICKEN SATAY WITH DIPPING SAUCE AND CUCUMBER SALAD

21

It's always good to be able to do a quick and simple version of a classic dish. You could marinate the chicken for up to 24 hours, if time allows.

Serves 2

2 tbsp dark soy sauce

1 tsp clear honey

1 tsp medium curry powder

225g (8oz) skinless chicken fillets, cut into long strips

4 tbsp rice wine vinegar

2 tbsp caster sugar

½ small cucumber, peeled, halved, seeded and thinly sliced

FOR THE DIPPING SAUCE

2 tbsp crunchy peanut butter

2 tsp dark soy sauce

1 tsp light muscovado sugar

juice of ½ lime

120ml (4fl oz) coconut milk

½ mild red chilli, seeded and finely diced

2 tbsp chopped fresh coriander

salt and freshly ground black pepper

Heat a griddle pan until very hot. Whisk together the soy sauce, honey and curry powder. Season with pepper and add the chicken pieces. Leave to marinate for 2 minutes.

Thread the chicken pieces onto six 15cm (6in) bamboo skewers and arrange on the griddle pan. Cook for 4–6 minutes until completely tender and cooked through, turning once or twice.

Meanwhile, prepare the cucumber salad. Place the vinegar in a bowl and stir in the sugar and a good pinch of salt until dissolved. Tip in the cucumber, stirring to combine, and set aside to allow the flavours to develop.

To make the dipping sauce, put the peanut butter in a bowl and stir in the soy sauce, light muscovado sugar and lime juice. Gradually whisk in the coconut milk until you have achieved a smooth sauce. Stir in the chilli and coriander, then divide between individual dipping bowls.

Divide the cucumber salad between serving bowls. Arrange the skewers on plates with both bowls to the side and serve at once.

CRUNCHY FISH FINGERS WITH YOGHURT DIP

22

These fish fingers are much healthier and better-tasting than shop-bought.

Serves 2

sunflower oil, for deep-frying

50g (2oz) toasted natural breadcrumbs

2 tbsp freshly grated Parmesan

2 eggs

2 tbsp milk

25g (1oz) seasoned flour

225g (8oz) lemon sole fillets

FOR THE CHILLI-CHIVE YOGHURT DIP

100g (4oz) Greek yoghurt

2 tbsp snipped fresh chives

a squeeze of lime juice

2 tbsp sweet chilli sauce

salt and freshly ground black pepper

2 lime wedges, to garnish

Preheat a deep-fat fryer or fill a deep-sided pan one-third full with oil and heat to 180°C/350°F, or until a bread cube browns in it in 60 seconds.

Place the breadcrumbs and Parmesan in a shallow dish, season and mix well. Beat the eggs and milk together in a separate shallow dish. Put the seasoned flour on a flat plate. Cut the lemon sole into strips, then dust in the flour, tip into the egg and roll in the breadcrumbs. Repeat with the egg and breadcrumbs to double-coat each piece. Deep-fry in batches for 2–3 minutes until cooked through and golden brown. Drain on kitchen paper and keep warm.

To make the dip, combine the yoghurt, chives and lime juice and season well. Divide between dipping bowls and spoon a layer of the sweet chilli sauce on top. Pile the crunchy fish fingers onto warmed plates and serve with a bowl of the chilli-chive yoghurt dip and lime wedges to the side.

CUMIN AND LEMON ROASTED CARROTS

The cumin seeds and chilli combine with the flavour of the carrots to make a delicious side order for roast new season lamb, best enjoyed in spring when carrots are at their sweetest. (See illustration, page 8.)

Serves 4

1 tbsp olive oil

15g (¾ oz) unsalted butter

a pinch of cumin seeds

½ tsp dried chilli flakes

350g (12oz) baby carrots, scrubbed and trimmed

juice of ½ lemon

2 tbsp chopped fresh coriander

salt and freshly ground black pepper

Preheat the oven to 220°C/425°F/gas 7. Heat the oil and butter in a small ovenproof frying pan, then add the cumin seeds and chilli flakes and cook gently for 1–2 minutes until fragrant.

Add the carrots, turning to coat, then season and cook for 2–3 minutes, turning the carrots occasionally. Squeeze the lemon over them, tossing to combine.

Transfer the carrots to the oven and cook for another 10–12 minutes or until cooked through and completely tender. Toss in the coriander and pile into a warmed serving dish to serve.

ROSEMARY NEW POTATOES

Serve these potatoes with succulent lamb or as a side order for a barbecue feast. (See illustration, page 2.)

Serves 2

225g (8oz) new potatoes, scraped or scrubbed

2 tbsp olive oil

2 garlic cloves, finely chopped

2 fresh rosemary sprigs

a knob of butter

salt and freshly ground black pepper

Slice the potatoes and place in a non-metallic bowl with a tablespoon of water. Cover with cling film and then pierce with a fork. Cook on high in the microwave for 3 minutes until almost tender.

Meanwhile, heat a non-stick frying pan. When the potatoes are ready, quickly drain off any excess water and dry on kitchen paper. Add the oil to the frying pan and then tip in the potatoes, garlic and rosemary, tossing to combine. Pan-fry for 3–4 minutes until lightly golden – just be careful not to allow the garlic to burn.

Season the potatoes generously, add the butter, tossing to coat evenly, and then continue to sauté for another minute or two until the potatoes are completely tender and lightly golden. Pile into a warmed dish to serve, discarding any excess oil.

CRUSHED NEW POTATOES WITH SPRING ONIONS

These potatoes are a kind of textured mash that you often see in trendy restaurants, so don't be tempted to make them too smooth.

Serves 2

350g (12oz) tiny baby new potatoes, scraped or scrubbed

50ml (2fl oz) extra-virgin olive oil

2 spring onions, finely chopped

a handful of fresh basil leaves

salt and freshly ground black pepper

Place the potatoes in a large pan of boiling water and bring to the boil. Cover and simmer for about 8 minutes until tender, then drain well.

Warm the olive oil in a small pan with the spring onions until the spring onions have softened but not coloured.

Tip the cooked potatoes into a large bowl. Add the warmed olive oil and spring onion mixture and, with the back of a fork, gently crush each potato until it just splits. Season, and then mix carefully until all the oil has been absorbed. Finely chop the basil and stir through the potatoes. Season to taste and pile into a bowl to serve.

GRATIN DAUPHINOIS

This is comfort cuisine at its best and a great accompaniment to enhance any main course, especially lamb or beef. Just look at the ingredients – you know it's got to be good.

Serves 2

350g (12oz) Jersey Royal new potatoes, scrubbed

150ml (¼ pint) double cream

50g (2oz) unsalted butter

1 garlic clove, peeled

salt and freshly ground black pepper

a few whole chives, to garnish (optional)

Preheat the oven to 220°C/425°F/gas 7. Thinly slice the potatoes using a mandolin cutter, being very careful of your fingers. Place in a small pan with the cream, 25g (1oz) of the butter and the garlic. Season generously and bring to the boil, then reduce the heat and simmer for 4 minutes.

Generously butter two 10cm (4in) cooking rings and place on a baking sheet on squares of buttered foil. Remove the potatoes from the cream mixture with a slotted spoon and layer up in the cooking rings, pressing down with the back of a spoon.

Spoon 1–2 tablespoons of the cream mixture over each filled cooking ring and dot with the rest of the butter. Bake for 12–15 minutes until the potatoes are cooked through and lightly golden. Remove from the oven and carefully take off the cooking rings, then transfer to warmed serving plates. Garnish with the whole chives, if liked, and serve immediately.

LEEKS IN SAUCE

The trick here is not to add the melted butter too fast and also to make sure that the sauce doesn't get too hot, otherwise the yolks will become grainy.

Serves 2

1 leek, halved and cut in half again lengthways

2 egg yolks

1 tsp Dijon mustard

1 tsp white wine vinegar

100g (4oz) butter

1 tbsp chopped fresh herbs, such as parsley, chives or chervil (optional)

salt and freshly ground black pepper

Cook the leeks for 3 minutes in boiling salted water, until just soft.

Put the egg yolks in a bowl, beat in the mustard and vinegar and season with salt and pepper. Melt the butter, but don't let it get too hot as the eggs may scramble, and whisk it into the egg-yolk mixture. Avoid adding the white residue from the butter if you can. Add the herbs, if using. If you wish to thicken the sauce, set the bowl over a pan of simmering water and whisk it.

Drain the leeks and combine with the sauce.

CAULIFLOWER CHEESE MASH

This is great served with ham or bacon, and if you fancy a change from the traditional cheese try using Dijon mustard, chopped capers and flat-leaf parsley instead. This would go perfectly with a gutsy game casserole.

Serves 2–4

1 small cauliflower, broken into small florets

25g (1oz) butter

1 small onion, finely chopped

100g (4oz) finely grated mature Cheddar

85ml (3fl oz) double cream

a pinch of freshly grated nutmeg

salt and freshly ground white pepper

Cook the cauliflower florets for 6–8 minutes in a pan of boiling salted water until tender but not mushy.

Melt the butter in a large pan and gently pan-fry the onion for 4–5 minutes until well softened but not coloured. Transfer to a food-processor and add the Cheddar and cream.

When the cauliflower is cooked, quickly drain and then either blend to a thick purée in the food-processor or mash by hand with a potato masher. Season to taste and stir in the nutmeg. Transfer to a warmed bowl to serve.

CHEESY BROCCOLI SOUFFLÉS WITH MUSHROOM CROÛTES

Cooking this all in 20 minutes for *Ready Steady Cook* was really pushing it but the end result will give you bags of confidence.

Serves 6 as a starter

a little olive oil, for greasing

4 tbsp freshly grated Parmesan

275ml (9fl oz) milk

25g (1oz) butter

25g (1oz) plain flour

¼ tsp freshly grated nutmeg

225g (8oz) broccoli florets, cut into small pieces

3 eggs, separated

150g (5oz) freshly grated Gruyère cheese

FOR THE CROÛTES

25g (1oz) butter

225g (8oz) button mushrooms, sliced

5 tbsp double cream

1 tbsp chopped fresh parsley

3–4 tbsp olive oil

6 slices of French baguette, sliced on the diagonal

FOR THE SAUCE

2 tbsp white-wine vinegar

3 tbsp water

10 peppercorns

3 egg yolks

175g (6oz) unsalted butter, melted

salt and freshly ground black pepper

Preheat the oven to 180°C/350°F/gas 4. Grease 6 ramekins with a little oil and then sprinkle ½ tablespoon of Parmesan into each ramekin, shaking to coat the insides.

In a pan, gently heat the milk; do not allow to boil. Melt the butter in a separate pan, then stir in the flour and cook for 1 minute, stirring continuously. Whisk in the hot milk and slowly bring to the boil, beating until smooth and thickened; season with salt, pepper and nutmeg.

Cook the broccoli in a large pan of boiling salted water for 3–5 minutes until tender; drain well and mash roughly with a fork. Stir the broccoli, egg yolks and Gruyère into the white sauce. In a separate bowl, whisk the egg whites until they form soft peaks, then carefully fold into the sauce. Divide between the 6 ramekins, sprinkle over the remaining Parmesan and bake for 15 minutes until risen and golden.

Meanwhile, make the croûtes. Melt the butter in a frying pan and cook the mushrooms for 5 minutes until tender and golden. Stir in the cream and parsley and add salt and pepper to taste; keep warm. Heat the olive oil in a separate frying pan and cook the bread for 2–3 minutes on each side until golden brown; drain on kitchen paper.

To make the hollandaise sauce, place the white-wine vinegar, water and peppercorns in a small pan and simmer rapidly until the liquid is reduced to about 1 tablespoon. Transfer to a food-processor and whizz until the peppercorns are finely chopped. Add the egg yolks then, with the motor running, very slowly pour in the melted butter to form a smooth, glossy sauce; season with salt to taste.

To serve, arrange the croûtes on a plate and spoon over the mushrooms; top with the hollandaise. Remove the soufflés from the oven and serve both dishes immediately.

NUTTY TOFU BURGERS

Tofu is free of fat and cholesterol, which makes it a miracle food. It provides a healthy alternative source of protein. Marinating it is highly effective.

Serves 2

FOR THE RED PEPPER SAUCE

1 red pepper, seeded and quartered

6 tbsp olive oil

1 tbsp white wine vinegar

FOR THE BURGERS

50g (2oz) cashew nuts

225g (8oz) smoked tofu

1 garlic clove, crushed

2 eggs

a handful of fresh coriander leaves

1 tsp soy sauce

1 tbsp sunflower oil

FOR THE STIR FRY

100g (4oz) long-grain rice

2 tbsp olive oil

3 spring onions, chopped

200g (7oz) mixed baby corn and mangetout, sliced on the diagonal

3 tbsp snipped fresh chives

3 tbsp soy sauce

salt and freshly ground black pepper

fresh coriander and chervil leaves, to garnish

Preheat the oven to 220°C/425°F/gas 7. Cook the rice in a pan of boiling salted water for 12–15 minutes until tender. Drain well.

Roast the peppers skin-side up on a baking sheet for 10–12 minutes. Set aside in a plastic bag while you make the burgers.

Heat a small non-stick frying pan and cook the nuts over a high heat, shaking continuously, until golden brown. Place in a food-processor with the tofu and garlic and whizz until roughly chopped. Add the eggs, coriander and soy sauce and process until the mixture binds together. With floured hands, shape into 4 even-sized burgers. Heat the sunflower oil in a heavy-based frying pan and cook for 2–3 minutes on each side; keep warm.

Skin the pepper and blend the flesh in a clean food-processor until finely chopped. Pour in the olive oil and wine vinegar and whizz until smooth. Season.

Heat the oil in a large frying pan and cook the spring onions, corn and mangetout for 1–2 minutes. Add the cooked rice, chives and soy sauce and stir-fry for a further 3–4 minutes until heated through.

To serve, arrange the burgers on a plate and drizzle around the red pepper sauce. Serve the rice in a separate bowl, garnished with the chervil and coriander.

CHANA DAL

A gastronomic breakthrough! This dish usually takes at least 1½ hours to cook, but this inspired substitute using tinned pease pudding means you can literally make it in minutes!

Serves 2

25g (1oz) unsalted butter

2 tbsp sunflower oil

3 garlic cloves, peeled

1 onion, finely chopped

2 tsp freshly grated root ginger

½ tsp salt

1 tsp ground turmeric

2 green chillies, seeded and finely chopped

1 x 400g (14oz) tin of pease pudding

175ml (6fl oz) hot water

Heat the butter and half the oil in a wok or frying pan. Finely chop 2 garlic cloves and add to the pan with the onion and ginger. Cook for a few minutes until the onion is softened.

Stir in the salt and turmeric, then add the chillies, pease pudding and hot water. Mix well and bring to the boil, then reduce the heat and simmer gently for 5 minutes, stirring occasionally, until slightly thickened.

Meanwhile, heat the remaining oil in a small pan. Thinly slice the remaining garlic clove and add to the pan. Cook for a minute or so until golden brown.

Tip the chana dal into a warmed serving bowl and drizzle over the garlic oil. Serve at once.

CHEESY POLENTA WITH WILTED SPINACH AND ROASTED SHALLOTS

This is a satisfying vegetarian main course.

Serves 2

2 tbsp olive oil, plus a little extra

5 small shallots, peeled and halved

a pinch of caster sugar

a good pinch of fresh soft thyme leaves

225g (8oz) tender young spinach leaves

a pinch of freshly grated nutmeg

200g (7oz) instant polenta

1 garlic clove, crushed

100g (4oz) Cambozola, rind removed, finely diced

salt and freshly ground black pepper

Preheat the oven to 200°C/400°F/gas 6. Heat an ovenproof frying pan and add the olive oil. Sauté the shallots for a couple of minutes until lightly golden. Sprinkle with the sugar and thyme, then season to taste, tossing to coat evenly. Transfer to the oven for another 5 minutes or so until cooked through and tender.

Heat 600ml (1 pint) of water until boiling.

Place a dash of the olive oil in a pan and add the spinach. Season to taste and add a little nutmeg, then stir until just wilted. Drain off any excess moisture and keep warm.

When the water is boiling, add a good pinch of salt and then slowly pour in the polenta in a thin, continuous stream. Add the garlic and continue to stir until the polenta begins to thicken – this should take about 1 minute. Stir in the Cambozola until melted and season to taste.

Divide the cheesy polenta between warmed plates and arrange the spinach and roasted shallots on top to serve.

LEMON, ROCKET AND TALEGGIO PASTA

33

Taleggio is a readily available, creamy, semi-soft Italian rinded cheese.
Be careful not to overcook it or it can become stringy and rubbery.

Serves 2

225g (8oz) fresh
fettuccine pasta

4 tbsp dry white wine

2 garlic cloves, finely
chopped

1 lemon

4 tbsp double cream

40g (1½ oz) rocket
leaves

100g (4oz) taleggio
cheese, rind removed,
cut into cubes

salt and freshly
ground black pepper

Plunge the fettuccine into a large pan of boiling salted water and
cook for 2–3 minutes or according to the packet instructions.
Drain and quickly refresh under cold running water.

Place the wine in a large wide pan with the garlic. Add the
grated rind of the lemon and cook over a gentle heat for 2–3
minutes to allow the liquid to reduce slightly. Add the cream and
season. Cut the lemon in half and add a squeeze of the juice.

Fold in the cooked fettuccine with the rocket and taleggio and
keep over a low heat until the cheese has begun to melt. Divide
between warmed wide-rimmed bowls and serve at once.

TAGLIATELLE WITH MUSHROOMS

34

A word of warning: don't dredge the pasta in flour to prevent it from sticking
in the pasta machine, as the flour turns glue-like when cooked and, ironically,
causes the pasta to stick together.

Serves 2

a knob of butter

2 flat mushrooms,
chopped

1 garlic clove,
crushed

50ml (2fl oz) dry
white wine

85ml (3fl oz) double
cream

a bunch of mixed
fresh soft herbs (such
as basil, flat-leaf
parsley and chives)

1 garlic clove,
chopped

2 tbsp toasted
chopped walnuts

4 tbsp extra-virgin
olive oil

FOR THE PASTA DOUGH

150g (5oz) Italian
'00' flour

1 egg

1 egg yolk

a dash of olive oil

salt and freshly
ground black pepper

Bring a large pan of salted water to the boil. To make the pasta,
place the flour in a food-processor with the egg, egg yolk, olive
oil and a pinch of salt. Blend until the ingredients come together
and resemble a dough.

Turn out onto a floured board and knead for 2 minutes until
smooth and pliable. Roll out with a rolling pin and cut into
2 pieces, then pass through the widest setting of a pasta
machine. Repeat this process, decreasing the roller setting
down grade by grade with each pass, taking it down to the
second-lowest setting. Finally pass through the cutting rollers
to make tagliatelle. Repeat with the remaining piece of dough.

Meanwhile, heat a large frying pan. Add the butter and sauté the
mushrooms and garlic for 3–4 minutes until tender and all the
liquid has evaporated. Season to taste. Pour in the wine and
allow to bubble right down, then stir in the cream and cook for
a minute or so until slightly reduced.

Plunge the tagliatelle into the pan of boiling water and stir once,
then cook for 2 minutes until tender.

To make the herb pesto, strip the herb leaves from the stalks and
place in a mini food-processor with the garlic, walnuts and olive
oil. Blend until smooth. Season to taste.

Drain the pasta and then tip into the mushroom sauce, tossing
to coat. Divide between warmed wide-rimmed bowls and drizzle
over the herb pesto to serve.

ASPARAGUS CREAM PASTA

Supermarkets now offer an incredible selection of freshly prepared pasta, while traditional Italian delis can stock up to a dozen different varieties. Look out for pasta made from durum wheat semolina.

Serves 2

115g (4oz) fine asparagus spears

25g (1oz) unsalted butter

4 spring onions, finely chopped

1 tbsp dry white wine

150ml (¼ pint) double cream

2 tsp wholegrain mustard

3 tbsp snipped fresh chives

225g (8oz) fresh tagliatelle pasta

salt and freshly ground black pepper

freshly grated Parmesan, to garnish (optional)

Cut the asparagus into 4cm (1½ in) lengths. Plunge the stems into a pan of boiling salted water and simmer for 1 minute, then add the tips and cook for another 1 minute until just tender. Drain and quickly refresh under cold running water. Set aside.

Melt the butter in a frying pan and add the spring onions. Sauté for 30 seconds, then add the wine and pour in the cream. Increase the heat, season to taste and simmer for 2–3 minutes or until slightly reduced and thickened. Stir the mustard into the pan with the chives and blanched asparagus. Allow to warm through, stirring.

Meanwhile, bring a large pan of water to a rolling boil. Add the pasta, stir once and simmer for 1–2 minutes or according to the packet instructions. Drain the pasta and quickly refresh under cold running water. Return to the pan and stir in the asparagus cream. Season to taste and divide between warmed wide-rimmed bowls. Scatter over the Parmesan, to garnish, if liked. Serve immediately.

OPEN LASAGNE

This is an unusual but delicious version of a classic lasagne.

Serves 2

150g (5oz) fresh spinach, stalks removed

175g (6oz) fresh lasagne sheets

100ml (3½ fl oz) olive oil

¼ onion, finely chopped

125g (4½ oz) chestnut mushrooms, sliced

a small handful of fresh basil leaves

2 garlic cloves, peeled

1 tbsp freshly grated Parmesan

1 tsp ground turmeric

2 tbsp chopped fresh parsley

salt and freshly ground black pepper

1 tomato, sliced, to garnish

Preheat the oven to 220°C/425°F/gas 7. Place the spinach in a pan with a little salt and pepper. Cover and cook gently for 3–4 minutes until wilted. Drain and keep warm. Cook the pasta in a large pan of boiling water for 3–4 minutes until tender. Drain and cool under cold water.

Heat 2 tablespoons of the olive oil in a large frying pan and cook the onion for 5 minutes until softened. Stir in the mushrooms and cook for a further 2–3 minutes. Season to taste.

Put the basil and garlic in a food-processor and whizz until finely chopped. Add the grated Parmesan and, with the motor running, pour in 150ml (5fl oz) of the oil, processing until well blended. Season to taste. Heat the remaining oil in a separate frying pan and add the turmeric and parsley. Add the pasta sheets and cook for 1–2 minutes, turning frequently until heated through.

To assemble, arrange a layer of fried pasta on a plate, pile on the mushroom mixture and drizzle over half the pesto. Top with a final layer of pasta and pesto and garnish with the tomato.

SPINACH AND GOATS' CHEESE ROULADE

To make this dish in less than ten you've got to work very quickly for the first couple of minutes. The results are worth it and look spectacular.

Serves 2

a knob of butter, plus extra for greasing

100g (4oz) tender young spinach leaves

4 eggs, separated

2 tbsp plain flour

a pinch of English mustard powder

1 tbsp snipped fresh chives

1 tbsp chopped fresh chervil

50g (2oz) soft goats' cheese, finely diced

FOR THE TOMATO SALAD

3 ripe plum tomatoes

2 spring onions, finely chopped

1 tbsp shredded fresh basil

a dash of balsamic vinegar

a good glug of extra-virgin olive oil

salt and freshly ground black pepper

Preheat the oven to 240°C/475°F/gas 9. Grease and line a Swiss roll tin with non-stick parchment paper. Heat the butter in a pan and tip in the spinach. Cook for a minute or so until wilted, stirring occasionally. Season, then drain off any excess moisture.

Whisk the egg whites in a large bowl until you have soft peaks. Sift in the flour and whisk until you have stiff peaks.

Place the egg yolks in a separate bowl and stir in the mustard powder, then fold into the egg white mixture until just combined. Transfer to the Swiss roll tin and smooth over with a spatula.

Sprinkle the herbs over the roulade mixture and then scatter the wilted spinach and goats' cheese on top. Bake for about 8 minutes until cooked through and lightly golden.

To make the tomato salad, cut the tomatoes into wedges and mix with the spring onions, basil, vinegar, olive oil and seasoning.

Remove the roulade from the oven and, using a tea towel, quickly roll up. Cut into slices and serve with the tomato salad.

ASPARAGUS CUSTARDS

These are basically savoury crème caramels with a delicate and fresh flavour. Serve as a starter or as a light supper with a crisp green salad and crusty French bread.

Serves 2

a knob of unsalted butter, for greasing

100g (4oz) asparagus spears

200ml (7fl oz) double cream

1 small garlic clove, crushed

½ tsp snipped fresh chives

½ tsp chopped fresh chervil

1 tsp chopped fresh flat-leaf parsley

2 eggs

salt and freshly ground white pepper

Preheat the oven to 150°C/300°F/gas 2. Butter two 150ml (¼ pint) ramekins. Cut the asparagus leaving a 4cm (1½ in) tip, then cut each tip into 4 lengthways and set them aside. Slice the asparagus stems and plunge into a pan of boiling water for 2 minutes, then drain and refresh under cold running water.

Place the cream in a pan with the garlic and boil to reduce to 150ml (5fl oz). Pour into a food-processor and add the blanched asparagus and all the herbs. Whizz until smooth. Break the eggs into a bowl and lightly whisk, then add the cream mixture and stir until well combined. Season to taste and strain through a sieve into a jug.

Divide the reserved asparagus tips between the ramekins. Pour over the egg and cream mixture and place the ramekins in a small roasting tin. Pour enough boiling water into the tin to come half-way up the sides of the ramekins. Bake for 25–30 minutes until the custards are just set. Remove from the oven, leave to stand for 5 minutes, then unmould to serve.

SUPER-QUICK CHEESE SOUFFLÉS WITH CHICORY AND AVOCADO SALAD

This is a really quick way to make soufflés. The slightly bitter chicory leaves in the salad are perfectly complemented by the creamy avocado.

Serves 2

FOR THE SOUFFLÉS

50g (2oz) butter

150ml (¼ pint) milk

25g (1oz) plain flour

2 eggs, separated

50g (2oz) freshly grated Cheddar or Gruyère cheese

2–3 drops of Tabasco sauce

½ tsp cayenne pepper

salt and freshly ground black pepper

fresh parsley sprigs, to garnish

FOR THE SALAD

1 avocado, stoned and mashed

1 tomato, chopped

2 tbsp chopped fresh coriander

½ onion, chopped

6 chicory leaves

Preheat the oven to 200°C/400°F/gas 6. Melt half of the butter and use it to grease 2 ramekins.

Make a white sauce by mixing the flour, milk and remaining butter in a pan. Bring to the boil, whisking continuously. Simmer for 2 minutes to thicken the sauce. Remove from the heat. Add the egg yolks, cheese, Tabasco, cayenne and seasoning and stir vigorously.

Whisk the egg whites until stiff. Fold a third into the cheese mixture with a metal spoon, then add the remainder. Pour the mixture into the ramekins and bake for 12–14 minutes, until well risen.

Combine the avocado, tomato, coriander and onion in a bowl and season. Separate the chicory leaves. Spoon a tablespoon of the avocado mixture onto each chicory leaf. Put the stuffed chicory leaves on a plate, in a star shape. Serve the soufflés separately, garnished with fresh parsley.

THAI COCONUT STIR FRY

Be warned, this stir fry is incredibly moreish. Don't be surprised if everyone comes back for second helpings.

Serves 2

1 garlic clove, roughly chopped

1 lemongrass stalk, trimmed and roughly chopped

a small bunch of fresh coriander (roots intact, if possible)

a small handful of fresh mint leaves

a pinch of dried crushed chillies

1 tbsp sunflower oil

1 x 250ml (8fl oz) carton coconut cream

2 small carrots, thinly sliced on the diagonal

1 small red pepper, halved, seeded and thinly sliced

75g (3oz) small broccoli florets

50g (2oz) chestnut mushrooms, sliced

1 x 100g (4oz) packet express cooked egg noodles

4 spring onions, shredded

Heat a large pan or wok. Place the garlic in a mini food-processor with the lemongrass, coriander, mint, crushed chillies and oil. Blitz to a fine paste. Add to the heated wok and stir-fry for 1–2 minutes until fragrant.

Pour the coconut cream into the pan and bring to a simmer, then add the carrots, red pepper, broccoli florets and mushrooms. Cook for 4–5 minutes until all the vegetables are tender, stirring occasionally.

Add the noodles to the pan with the spring onions and toss until well combined, then continue to cook for another 1–2 minutes until completely heated through.

CHICKPEA AND POTATO CURRY

This dish uses the distinctive flavours of southern India.

Serves 2

2 tbsp sunflower oil

1 onion, thinly sliced

2 mild green chillies, seeded and finely chopped

2 tbsp hot curry paste (such as Madras)

100ml (3fl oz) hot vegetable stock (from a cube is fine)

1 x 200g (7oz) tin chickpeas, rinsed and drained

225g (8oz) cooked baby potatoes, peeled and quartered

1 tbsp Greek yoghurt

2 naan breads

salt and freshly ground black pepper

chopped fresh coriander, to garnish

Preheat the grill. Heat the oil in a pan and fry the onion and chillies for a few minutes until softened and just beginning to colour, stirring occasionally. Add the curry paste and cook for another minute or so, stirring. Pour in the stock, stir and bring to a simmer. Season to taste.

Add the chickpeas and potatoes to the pan and simmer for a few minutes until heated through, stirring occasionally. Stir in the yoghurt and just warm through.

Meanwhile, sprinkle the naan breads with a little water and arrange on the grill rack. Cook for a few minutes until heated through or according to the packet instructions.

Arrange the naan breads on warmed plates and spoon the chickpea and potato curry on top. Scatter over the coriander to garnish and serve at once.

SPAGHETTI WITH CLAMS

The freshness of the pasta is the key to this recipe.
You could try it with mussels instead of the clams.

Serves 2

8 spring onions

4 tbsp olive oil

1 x 400g (14oz) tin of chopped tomatoes, drained

150ml (¼ pint) water

1 tsp ground turmeric

50g (2oz) butter

250g (9oz) broccoli, cut into small florets

1 fennel bulb, cut into small pieces

1 tbsp chopped fresh sage

225g (8oz) fresh spaghetti

1 x 290g (10oz) tin of clams, drained

salt and freshly ground black pepper

fresh herbs, such as basil and chervil, to garnish

Gently cook the finely sliced spring onions for 2–3 minutes until softened, in 2 tablespoons of olive oil. Pass the chopped tomatoes through a sieve into the pan. Stir in the water and bring to the boil. Stir in the turmeric and half the butter. Whizz with a hand blender until smooth; season and keep warm.

Cook the broccoli and fennel in the remaining olive oil in a hot frying pan for 3–4 minutes, until tender. Drain on kitchen paper. Heat the remaining butter in a separate frying pan and cook the sage leaves for 1 minute until crisp. Drain on kitchen paper.

Cook the spaghetti in a large pan of boiling salted water for 3–4 minutes until tender. Drain and toss with the sage butter. To serve, scatter the fried vegetables and clams over the spaghetti. Top with the tomato sauce and garnish with fresh herbs.

POACHED SALMON WITH FENNEL, SCALLOPS AND WATERCRESS SAUCE

Be careful not to overcook the scallops or they will be tough. They are done when opaque but slightly translucent in the centre.

Serves 2

100g (4oz) Basmati rice

1 fennel bulb, cut into 6–8 wedges

450ml (¾ pint) vegetable stock

75g (3oz) watercress, leaves and stalks separated

2 x 175g (6oz) salmon steaks

2 shallots, finely chopped

40g (1½oz) butter

4 tbsp dry white wine

1 small garlic clove, chopped

1 tsp chopped fresh thyme

1 bay leaf

150ml (¼ pint) double cream

a good squeeze of lemon juice

2 tbsp olive oil

6 spring onions, chopped into 1cm (½ inch) lengths

100g (4oz) scallops

1 tsp balsamic vinegar

salt and freshly ground black pepper

Cook the rice in boiling salted water for 10–12 minutes, until just tender; drain and keep warm. Cook the fennel in boiling salted water for about 6 minutes, until almost tender; drain and set aside.

Heat the stock and watercress stalks almost to boiling point in a pan. Season the salmon and poach in the stock for 7 minutes, until just cooked. Remove from the pan, peel off the skin and keep warm. Boil the stock until reduced by two-thirds. Strain.

Sweat the shallots until softened in 25g (1oz) of melted butter. Add the wine, garlic, thyme, bay leaf and reduced stock and simmer until the liquid has reduced by two-thirds. Remove from the heat, stir in the cream and a handful of watercress leaves. Purée in a liquidizer until smooth. Return to the heat, add the lemon juice and simmer gently for 1–2 minutes.

Heat the remaining butter and half the oil in a pan, and cook the spring onions and fennel for 5 minutes. Slice each scallop into 2 or 3 pieces, add to the pan and cook for ½–1 minute.

Mix the balsamic vinegar, remaining olive oil and salt to make a dressing. Pour onto the remaining watercress and toss well. Arrange on warmed plates to serve.

CHILLI-GLAZED STIR-FRIED PRAWNS

This is a fantastic way to cook tiger prawns – the chilli glaze gives them
a wonderful coating and the pak choi provides much-needed crunch. Serve
with bowls of steaming Thai fragrant rice.

Serves 2

4 tbsp white wine vinegar

2 garlic cloves, crushed

2cm (¾ in) piece of fresh root ginger, peeled and finely grated

1 tsp caster sugar

1 mild red chilli, seeded and finely chopped

1 tbsp sunflower oil

4 spring onions, finely chopped

275g (10oz) raw, peeled tiger prawns, cleaned

1 pak choi, cut on the diagonal into 2½cm (1in) strips

a small handful of torn fresh coriander leaves

Place the vinegar, garlic, ginger and sugar in a small pan with half of the chilli. Bring to the boil, reduce the heat and simmer for 4–5 minutes until well reduced and slightly sticky.

Meanwhile, heat a wok until very hot. Add the sunflower oil and swirl up around the sides, then tip in the remaining chilli with the spring onions and stir-fry for 20 seconds. Add the prawns and pak choi and continue to stir-fry for 2–3 minutes until tender, tossing regularly.

Drizzle the chilli glaze into the wok, tossing to combine, and then scatter over the coriander leaves. When everything is nicely glazed, divide between warmed plates and serve at once.

MISO MULLET

Miso paste works very well as a dressing for red mullet.

Serves 2

4 tbsp olive oil

100g (4oz) long-grain rice

1 tbsp chopped fresh dill

300ml (½ pint) boiling water

1 red mullet, filleted

1 tsp balsamic vinegar

juice of 1 lime

1 tbsp chopped fresh chives

1 x 90g (3½ oz) jar of pickled yellow chillies, drained and roughly chopped

2 red peppers, seeded and sliced

1 Chinese leaf lettuce, shredded

1 lime, halved

FOR THE DRESSING

3 tbsp olive oil

1 tbsp miso paste

juice of 1 lime

1 tbsp balsamic vinegar

1 tbsp caster sugar

½ tbsp chopped fresh coriander

2 tbsp double cream

salt and freshly ground black pepper

Preheat the oven to 200°C/400°F/gas 6. Heat 1 tablespoon of the olive oil in an ovenproof pan. Add the rice and dill, stirring to coat in the oil. Pour over the boiling water and season well. Cook in the oven for 20 minutes until tender.

Diagonally score the fish 3 times on each side. Sprinkle over the balsamic vinegar, lime juice, 1 tablespoon of olive oil, the chives and a little salt and pepper.

To make the dressing, pour the oil into a bowl and whisk in the miso paste. Add half the lime juice, the balsamic vinegar, sugar, coriander and salt and pepper. In a separate bowl, stir together the double cream and remaining lime juice.

Heat 1 tablespoon of olive oil in a wok and stir-fry the chillies and peppers for 5 minutes until softened. Stir in the lettuce and cook for a further 3–4 minutes. Season.

Brush the lime halves with the remaining oil and cook in a hot griddle pan, flesh-side down, for 2–3 minutes until lightly charred. Remove the limes from the pan and add the fish. Cook for 5–6 minutes until golden brown and just cooked. Remove the rice from the oven and spoon into 2 large, buttered ramekins, pressing down well.

To serve, drizzle the dressing over the stir fry, place the fish on top and spoon over the lime cream. Turn out the rice on the side.

HOT-SMOKED SALMON KEDGEREE

Kedgeree originated in India as a peasant dish of rice and peas. The Victorians adapted it by adding smoked finnan haddock and eggs and leaving out the peas. This version uses hot-smoked salmon.

Serves 2

100g (4oz) long-grain rice

2 eggs

50g (2oz) unsalted butter

1 red onion, finely chopped

1 tsp mild curry paste

225g (8oz) honey-roast hot-smoked salmon flakes

2 tbsp chopped fresh flat-leaf parsley

50ml (2fl oz) double cream

salt and freshly ground black pepper

Place the rice in a pan of boiling salted water and simmer for 10–12 minutes until just tender. Drain, then spread out on a baking sheet and allow to cool completely – this will prevent the rice grains sticking together. Cook the eggs in a small pan of simmering water for 10–12 minutes until hard-boiled. Rinse under cold water and crack away the shells, then chop.

Meanwhile, heat the butter in a sauté pan and cook the onion for about 5 minutes until softened but not coloured. Stir in the curry paste and cook for another 30 seconds or so, stirring.

Fold the cooled rice into the onion mixture in the pan along with the salmon and cook for a couple of minutes until just warmed through. Stir in the hard-boiled eggs and parsley and season to taste. Lightly whip the cream in a small bowl and gently fold into the rice mixture. Tip the kedgeree into a warmed serving dish and serve immediately.

TUNA TORTILLA WITH GUACAMOLE

Soft flour tortilla wraps are a healthy and tasty alternative to traditional breads. For a packed lunch, simply spread the tuna mixture all over the tortillas and roll them up.

Serves 2

1 x 200g (7oz) tin of tuna in olive oil, drained

1 x 400g (14oz) tin of cannellini beans, drained and rinsed

2 ripe tomatoes, halved, seeded and diced

2 spring onions, finely chopped

1 tbsp extra-virgin olive oil

4 tbsp Greek yoghurt

2 soft flour tortillas

FOR THE GUACAMOLE

1 small ripe avocado

1 tomato, halved, seeded and diced

2 spring onions, finely chopped

1 garlic clove, crushed

2 tbsp chopped fresh coriander

a pinch of ground cumin

a pinch of ground coriander

juice of 1 lime

2 tbsp extra-virgin olive oil

salt and freshly ground black pepper

Preheat the oven to 220°C/425°F/gas 7. Place the tuna in a bowl with the cannellini beans, tomatoes, spring onions, oil and yoghurt. Season generously and mix well to combine.

Divide the tuna mixture between the 2 tortillas, spooning it into the centre. Fold over the edges to form a neat parcel, then pin in place with wooden cocktail sticks. Arrange the two parcels on a baking sheet and bake for 4–5 minutes until heated through.

Meanwhile, make the guacamole. Cut the avocado in half and remove the stone, then scoop out the flesh into a bowl, reserving the skins. Roughly mash with a fork, then add the tomato, spring onions, garlic, coriander, spices, lime juice and olive oil. Season to taste and mix well to combine. Spoon back into the avocado skins and arrange on plates with the hot tuna tortillas that have been cut on the diagonal to serve.

MONKFISH SKEWERS WITH ASPARAGUS PESTO

48

This pesto would be fantastic folded into noodles, or try stuffing it underneath the skin of a chicken breast before cooking. (See illustration page 8.)

Serves 2

1 tsp cumin seeds

1 tsp medium curry powder

¼ tsp cayenne pepper

1 tsp ground turmeric

350g (12oz) piece of monkfish tail, well trimmed

150g (5oz) Thai jasmine rice

5 lemongrass stalks

50g (2oz) fine asparagus spears

1 garlic clove, chopped

5cm (2in) piece of galangal, peeled and cut into thin slices

1 green chilli, seeded

3 tbsp chopped mixed fresh coriander, chives and parsley

8 tbsp olive oil

8 fresh kaffir lime leaves (optional)

salt and freshly ground black pepper

Toast the cumin seeds in a hot frying pan for ½–1 minute, then blend to a fine powder with the curry powder, cayenne pepper, half the turmeric and seasoning. Cut the monkfish into 12 pieces, place in a shallow non-metallic dish and toss with the spice mixture. Cover with cling film and chill for 10–30 minutes.

Tip the rice into a pan with a tight-fitting lid. Cover with 2½ cm (1in) of water, add a good pinch of salt and the remaining turmeric. Trim the lemongrass stalks, finely chop one and add to the rice, reserving the rest; cover the pan. Boil for 30 seconds, then reduce the heat and simmer gently for 10 minutes. Take off the heat and rest for 5 minutes without lifting the lid.

Chop the asparagus spears into 4cm (1½ in) lengths. Plunge into boiling water and cook for 3–4 minutes. Add the tips and cook for another 2 minutes. Drain and rinse under cold water. Reserve some tips for the garnish. Place the garlic in a food-processor with half of the galangal, the green chilli and herbs. Season and whizz until blended, pouring in enough oil to make a smooth purée. Add the asparagus and blend again briefly.

Preheat a griddle pan until searing hot. Thread the monkfish onto the reserved lemongrass stalks, alternating with kaffir lime leaves and slices of galangal. Brush the griddle pan with oil and cook the kebabs for ½–1 minute on each side until just tender but lightly charred. Serve with the fluffed up rice and asparagus pesto in dipping bowls to the side. Garnish with asparagus tips.

SMOKED SALMON AND SPINACH PUFF PIZZA

49

Try this puff pastry pizza base with diced Mediterranean vegetables or pesto and goats' cheese. (See illustration, page 8.)

Serves 4

350g (12oz) readymade puff pastry, thawed if frozen

a little plain flour, for dusting

50g (2oz) unsalted butter

225g (8oz) fresh spinach, washed

a pinch of freshly grated nutmeg

1 large egg yolk

100g (4oz) smoked salmon slices

4 tbsp double cream

salt

fresh basil leaves, to garnish

Preheat the oven to 220°C/425°F/gas 7. Roll out the pastry on to a 30cm (12in) circle up to 5mm (¼ in) thick. Place on a baking sheet, then press with a pan lid to make an indent, creating a 5mm (¼ in) border. Prick all over with a fork and chill for up to 30 minutes. Bake for 8–10 minutes until lightly golden.

Heat half the butter in a frying pan and cook the spinach for 1–2 minutes, agitating constantly, then season with salt. Drain off any excess liquid and add the remaining butter and nutmeg. Take the pastry out of the oven and brush with egg yolk. Spread over the spinach and arrange the salmon on top. Mix the rest of the egg yolk in a small bowl with the cream, then brush all over the spinach and salmon mixture. Bake for about 5–6 minutes or until puffed and lightly golden. Transfer to a warmed flat serving plate and garnish with the basil leaves.

CRISP FRIED LEMON SOLE WITH HERB VINAIGRETTE

If you fancy a change from lemon sole, use any flat fish, such as plaice or turbot.

Serves 2

2 eggs

2 tbsp milk

25g (1oz) freshly grated Parmesan

2 tbsp chopped mixed fresh herbs (such as flat-leaf parsley, chives and basil)

a pinch of paprika

1 tbsp olive oil

a knob of butter

2 large lemon sole fillets

FOR THE HERB VINAIGRETTE

1 tsp white wine vinegar

a squeeze of lemon juice

2 tbsp extra-virgin olive oil

2 tbsp chopped mixed fresh herbs

salt and freshly ground black pepper

Heat a large frying pan. Break the eggs into a shallow dish and add the milk, Parmesan, herbs and paprika. Season to taste and whisk lightly to combine.

Add the olive oil and butter to the heated frying pan. Dip the lemon sole fillets into the egg mixture until well coated, gently shaking off any excess. Cook for 2–3 minutes on each side until the fish is cooked through and golden brown.

Meanwhile, make the herb vinaigrette. Place the vinegar and lemon juice in a bowl and whisk in a pinch of salt until dissolved. Gradually whisk in the olive oil until emulsified. Season with pepper and stir in the herbs.

Arrange the crisp fried lemon sole on warmed plates and drizzle the herb vinaigrette on top to serve.

THAI SALMON CAKES WITH DIPPING SAUCE

Serve with the dipping sauce, close your eyes and you could be on a street in Bangkok.

Serves 2

600g (1lb 5oz) salmon fillet, skinned and cubed

1 lemongrass stalk, outer leaves removed, finely chopped

50g (2oz) bunch of fresh coriander, roughly chopped, plus extra sprigs to garnish

2 green chillies, seeded and chopped

3 tbsp Thai fish sauce (nam pla)

2 limes

1 garlic clove, crushed

1 tsp sugar

sunflower oil, for shallow-frying

2 tbsp plain flour

Place the salmon in a food-processor with the lemongrass, coriander, chillies and 1 tablespoon of the Thai fish sauce. Grate in the rind from one of the limes and blitz in short bursts until you have achieved a smooth paste. Transfer to a bowl, cover with cling film and chill for 10 minutes to an hour.

To make the dipping sauce, cut the lime that you have grated the rind from in half and squeeze 1 tablespoon of the juice into a small bowl. Add the remaining 2 tablespoons of the Thai fish sauce along with the garlic and sugar.

Heat a frying pan with about 5mm (¼ in) of oil. Divide the mixture into twelve portions, then using slightly wetted hands roll each into a ball. Gently press down each ball to flatten slightly and form a patty. Tip the flour onto a plate and dip in each patty, shaking off any excess.

Fry the salmon cakes in batches for 1–2 minutes on each side until tender and lightly browned. Drain on kitchen paper and arrange on warmed plates. Place a small bowl of the dipping sauce to one side. Garnish with coriander and lime wedges.

COCONUT CRAB AND SPICY STIR FRY

Although this recipe can easily be extended to serve as many as you wish, it makes a lovely treat as a meal for one, with the added advantage that it can be prepared and cooked in minutes.

Serves 1

1 dressed crab

2 tbsp chopped fresh coriander

¼ fresh coconut, grated

½ tsp dried ginger

1 tbsp double cream

1–2 tbsp olive oil

2 garlic cloves, chopped

1 red chilli, seeded and chopped

3 carrots, cut into batons

1 potato, cut into batons

50g (2oz) green beans

1 bunch of spring onions, finely chopped

2 tbsp chopped fresh mint

salt and freshly ground black pepper

lime wedge, to garnish

Preheat the oven to 200°C/400°F/gas 6. Scoop the crab meat out of the shell and mix with half the coriander, the coconut, ginger and double cream. Add salt and pepper to taste, then pile the mixture back into the shell. Bake for 8–10 minutes until golden brown.

Heat the olive oil in a wok or large frying pan and stir-fry the garlic and chilli for 1 minute. Add the carrot, potato and beans and cook for a further 3–4 minutes. Stir in the spring onions, mint and remaining coriander and season with salt and pepper. Continue to cook for a few minutes until the vegetables are tender.

To serve, pile the vegetables onto a plate and place the filled crab on top. Garnish with the lime wedge and serve immediately.

HOT AND SPICY PRONTO PRAWNS

This colourful stir fry of tiger prawns and vegetables is incredibly quick and easy to prepare. Mix and match the vegetables to suit your taste or try adding other fruit such as pineapple.

Serves 2

100g (4oz) couscous

300ml (½ pint) boiling water

2 garlic cloves, crushed

½ tsp ground cumin

1 tbsp chopped fresh coriander

1 tbsp each chopped fresh chives and mint

2 tbsp olive oil

2 tsp freshly grated root ginger

½ Chinese leaf lettuce, finely shredded

½ red pepper, finely chopped

1 bunch of spring onions, thinly sliced

1 small mango, skinned and diced

1 tsp green Tabasco sauce

10 raw, peeled tiger prawns, cleaned

salt and freshly ground black pepper

fresh coriander sprigs, to garnish

Place the couscous in a large heatproof bowl and pour over the boiling water. Set aside for 8 minutes for the grains to absorb the liquid. Stir in half the garlic, the cumin, coriander, chives, mint and salt and pepper. Place two 9cm (3½ in) heart-shaped pastry cutters on a heatproof plate and spoon in the mixture, pressing down well. Sit the plate inside a steamer and cook for 10 minutes.

Meanwhile, heat the olive oil in a wok or large frying pan and stir-fry the remaining garlic, the ginger, Chinese leaf, three-quarters of the pepper, the spring onions, mango and Tabasco sauce over a high heat for 3–4 minutes. Add the prawns and cook for a further 2–3 minutes until they turn pink and the vegetables are tender but still firm. Season to taste.

To serve, carefully transfer the couscous hearts to 2 plates and spoon round the prawn stir fry. Garnish with the reserved red pepper and coriander sprigs.

AROMATIC CHICKEN STIR FRY

You could use any selection of green vegetables, such as asparagus, sugarsnap peas or Chinese cabbage, and blanch them briefly before use.

Serves 4

1 egg white

3 tbsp Chinese rice wine

4 tsp cornflour

450g (1lb) boneless, skinless chicken breasts, cut into 2½ cm (1in) pieces

4 tbsp sunflower oil

2 garlic cloves, finely chopped

2½ cm (1in) piece of fresh root ginger, finely chopped

½ tsp dried chilli flakes

6 spring onions, sliced diagonally into 2½ cm (1in) lengths

150ml (¼ pint) chicken stock

2 tbsp dark soy sauce

a pinch of sugar

225g (8oz) Chinese vegetable medley, cut into 2½ cm (1in) pieces

a good handful of fresh coriander leaves

salt and freshly ground black pepper

oriental noodles, to serve (optional)

Place the egg white in a food-processor with one tablespoon of the Chinese rice wine and a teaspoon of the cornflour. Blend for 1 minute, then pour over the chicken in a non-metallic dish. Cover with clingfilm and set aside for at 10 to 30 minutes.

Place half the oil in a large pan with 1 litre (1¼ pints) of water and bring to the boil. Drop in the chicken with a slotted spoon, stir and cook for 1½ minutes. Drain on kitchen paper.

Heat a wok and swirl in the remaining oil. Add the garlic, ginger, chilli flakes and spring onions and stir-fry for 30 seconds, then add the drained chicken and stir-fry for 1 minute. Pour in the remaining rice wine with the stock, soy sauce and sugar and season generously.

Increase the heat and bring to the boil, then reduce to a simmer, add the vegetables and cook for 1–2 minutes until just tender but still crisp. Mix the remaining cornflour with 1½ tablespoons of water and stir into the wok. Cook for a minute or so until the sauce clears and thickens, then stir in the herbs. Ladle into warmed serving bowls and serve at once with the noodles, if liked.

CHICKEN AND NOODLE GORENG

For authenticity use sambal ulek (Indonesian red chilli paste) and ketjap manis (Indonesian sweet soy sauce).

Serves 2

2 tbsp sunflower oil

2 spring onions, finely chopped

2 tsp freshly grated root ginger

2 garlic cloves, finely chopped

225g (8oz) boneless, skinless chicken thighs, well trimmed and cut into small, thin strips

1 onion, thinly sliced

50g (2oz) baby carrots, thinly sliced on the diagonal

100g (4oz) baby courgettes, trimmed and sliced on the diagonal

100g (4oz) medium egg noodles

1 tbsp dark soy sauce

1 tsp clear honey

¼ tsp chilli powder

¼ tsp ground turmeric

2 tsp chopped fresh coriander

Heat a wok until very hot, then swirl in the oil. Add the spring onions, ginger and garlic to the wok and stir-fry for 20 seconds. Tip in the chicken and continue to stir-fry for 1–2 minutes until it is sealed and lightly golden.

Add the onion, baby carrots and courgettes to the wok and continue to stir-fry for another 3–4 minutes until all the vegetables are just tender, sprinkling over a tablespoon of water if the mixture becomes too dry.

Meanwhile, place the noodles in a pan of boiling water and simmer for 3 minutes or according to the packet instructions. Place the soy sauce, honey, chilli powder, turmeric and coriander in a large bowl and mix until smooth. Drain the noodles and tip them straight into the soy mixture, tossing until evenly coated.

Add the stir-fried chicken and vegetables to the flavoured noodles and mix again until evenly combined. Divide between warmed plates and serve at once.

SPICY SPINACH-STUFFED CHICKEN LEGS

The turmeric-braised potatoes and cumin onions in this dish offer an Indian flavour and are delicious with the spinach-stuffed chicken.

Serves 2

2 eggs

150ml (¼ pint) double cream

75g (3oz) ground almonds

225g (8oz) fresh spinach, stalks removed

3 tbsp sunflower oil

2 chicken legs, thigh bones removed

150ml (¼ pint) chicken stock

2 potatoes, diced

150ml (¼ pint) white wine

5 cardamom pods, cracked

50g (2oz) butter

2 tsp ground turmeric

1 tsp chopped fresh coriander

1 onion, finely chopped

1 tsp ground cumin

salt and freshly ground black pepper

Preheat the oven to 200°C/400°F/gas 6.

In a large bowl, beat together the eggs, cream, ground almonds and plenty of seasoning. Wash the spinach and place in a large pan with a close-fitting lid. Cook gently for 3–4 minutes, shaking the pan occasionally until the spinach has wilted. Drain well then stir into the egg mixture.

Heat 2 tablespoons of oil in a large frying pan and cook the chicken legs for 4–5 minutes, turning occasionally, until well browned. Spoon the stuffing into the cavity left by the bone, then wrap each leg in buttered foil. Place the parcels in an ovenproof dish with 2 tablespoons of the stock and bake for 15–20 minutes until cooked through.

Meanwhile, heat the remaining oil in a separate frying pan and cook the potatoes for 2–3 minutes. Pour over the wine and remaining stock and bring to the boil. Stir in the cardamom pods and simmer for 5–8 minutes until the potatoes are tender. Dice half the butter and whisk it into the potatoes with the turmeric. Stir in the coriander, then taste and adjust the seasoning if necessary.

Meanwhile, heat the remaining butter in a pan and cook the onion for 5 minutes until softened. Add the cumin and cook for a further 5 minutes until golden brown. Season to taste.

To serve, spoon the onion onto a plate and arrange the stuffed chicken legs on top. Spoon around the turmeric potatoes and serve immediately.

WARM CHICKEN LIVER SALAD

Chicken livers are inexpensive, nutritious and delicious. Always trim them to remove any tubes and greenish parts, which may have a bitter taste. Be careful not to overcook them; they should only just cook though or they will be tough and unpalatable.

Serves 2

225g (8oz) chicken livers, trimmed and cut into bite-size pieces

2 rashers smoked back bacon, chopped

1 tbsp balsamic vinegar

1 tbsp olive oil

⅓ small round lettuce

4 radicchio leaves

½ small ripe avocado, peel and cubed

5 yellow or red cherry tomatoes, quartered

¼ small cucumber, cut into ribbons

salt and freshly ground black pepper

sprigs of flat-leaf parsley, to garnish

Fry the chicken-liver pieces, bacon and balsamic vinegar in a tablespoon of olive oil. Season and cook for 4–5 minutes.

To serve, tear up the lettuce leaves and arrange them on a platter with the radicchio leaves, avocado, tomatoes and cucumber. Spoon over the livers and bacon in the centre of the salad and garnish with flat-leaf parsley sprigs.

CHICKEN ESCALOPES WITH LEMON PARSLEY BUTTER

Simple, but very stylish, this dish would be excellent as a main course for a special supper.

Serves 2

50g (2oz) freshly grated Parmesan

50g (2oz) fresh white breadcrumbs

25g (1oz) seasoned flour

2 eggs

2 large boneless, skinless chicken thighs, well trimmed

4 tbsp olive oil

FOR THE LEMON PARSLEY BUTTER

50g (2oz) unsalted butter

juice of ½ lemon

1 tbsp chopped fresh flat-leaf parsley

salt and freshly ground black pepper

Preheat the oven to 200°C/400°F/gas 6 and heat a large ovenproof frying pan. Mix together the Parmesan and breadcrumbs in a shallow dish and season to taste. Place the seasoned flour on a flat plate. Beat the eggs and some seasoning in a shallow bowl.

Place the chicken thighs between 2 pieces of cling film and, using a rolling pin, flatten out to a ½ cm (¼ in) thickness. Toss in the seasoned flour, shaking off any excess, then dip in the beaten egg. Coat in the breadcrumbs, and then repeat with the egg and breadcrumbs.

Add the oil to the heated frying pan and fry the escalopes for 2 minutes on each side until lightly golden. Transfer the frying pan to the oven and continue to cook for another 4 minutes until completely tender and cooked through.

Meanwhile, make the lemon parsley butter. Melt the butter in a small frying pan. Before it begins to brown add the lemon juice and parsley, stirring to combine.

Arrange the escalopes on warmed plates and drizzle the lemon parsley butter on top. Serve at once.

CREAMY CARDAMOM CHICKEN WITH CHILLI FLATBREADS

59

This mildly spiced curry is delicious served with the chilli flatbreads.

Serves 2

2 tbsp sunflower oil

225g (8oz) skinless chicken breast fillets, cut into bite-size pieces

1 red onion, sliced

2 garlic cloves, finely chopped

1 tsp cardamom pods

1 tsp ground turmeric

1 tsp ground coriander

½ tsp ground ginger

100ml (3½ fl oz) hot chicken stock

200ml (7fl oz) double cream

juice 1 lemon

FOR THE CHILLI FLATBREADS

150g (5oz) plain flour, plus extra for dusting

1 tbsp olive oil

finely grated rind of 1 lemon

2 tsp dried crushed chillies

salt and freshly ground black pepper

Heat a large flat griddle pan. Heat the sunflower oil in a sauté pan and sauté the chicken for 1–2 minutes until sealed. Tip in the onion and garlic and cook for 1–2 minutes until golden.

Meanwhile, lightly crush the cardamom pods so that the green husks split open, then remove the little black seeds from inside. Grind these to a fine powder and sprinkle over the chicken and onion mixture along with the turmeric, coriander and ginger. Cook for 1–2 minutes, stirring. Pour the stock into the pan with the cream and lemon juice. Season and cook for another 3 minutes until the chicken is cooked through and the sauce has slightly reduced and thickened.

Place the flour in a bowl with the oil, lemon rind and chilli, and pour in enough water to bind – about 4 tablespoons in total. Shape into a ball, cut in 2 and roll each piece into a 10cm (4in) circle on a lightly floured surface. Cook both flatbreads on the heated griddle for 1 minute on each side. Spoon the chicken into warmed bowls and serve the flatbreads on the side.

CHICKEN IN A CRÈME FRAÎCHE SAUCE

60

This simple dish makes a stylish after-work supper. The crème fraîche gives the sauce a delicious, tangy flavour.

Serves 2

600ml (1 pint) hot chicken stock

4 garlic cloves

3–4 fresh parsley stalks

1 tsp mustard seeds

4 shallots

225g (8oz) potatoes, cut into 5cm (2in) chunks

2 x 175g (6oz) boneless, skinless chicken breasts

100g (4oz) long-grain rice

100g (4oz) crème fraîche

2 tsp Worcestershire sauce

2 tsp Dijon mustard

2 tbsp white wine

75g (3oz) butter

1½ tsp caster sugar

175g (6oz) broccoli florets

salt and freshly ground black pepper

chopped fresh parsley and snipped fresh chives, to garnish

Place the stock, garlic, parsley stalks, mustard seeds and shallots in a pan. Bring to the boil and simmer for 5 minutes. Add the potatoes and cook for 3 minutes. Add the chicken and cook for 10 minutes until both the potatoes and chicken are tender. Drain, reserving the poaching liquid. Discard the parsley stalks.

Cook the rice in a pan of boiling water for 10–12 minutes.

Meanwhile, gently heat the crème fraîche and Worcestershire sauce in a small pan, without letting it boil. Stir in the mustard and wine and simmer for 3 minutes. Gradually whisk in 150ml (¼ pint) of the poaching liquid, reducing between each addition, to give a smooth, glossy sauce. Season to taste.

Melt 25g (1oz) of butter in a large frying pan and cook the poached shallots and potatoes for 3 minutes. Sprinkle over the sugar and cook for a further 3 minutes until tender. Season.

Cook the broccoli in boiling salted water for 3–4 minutes, then drain. Stir the poached chicken into the crème fraîche sauce and gently heat through. Drain the rice and stir in the remaining butter. Serve on warm plates and garnish with the herbs.

CHICKEN AND WATERCRESS PASTA

This dish is packed with flavour and texture but be warned, the portions are pretty generous.

Serves 2

2 x 75g (3oz) boneless, skinless chicken breasts, sliced into 1cm (½in) wide strips

8 tbsp olive oil

3 tbsp chopped, mixed fresh herbs (parsley, basil, coriander and chives)

2 shallots, finely chopped

2 tbsp balsamic vinegar

75g (3oz) watercress

1 small garlic clove, crushed

juice of ½ lemon

1 tsp ground turmeric

250g (9oz) fresh tagliolini tricolore (multi-coloured pasta ribbons)

salt and freshly ground black pepper

TO GARNISH

2 tomatoes, skinned, seeded and finely diced

1 tbsp snipped fresh chives

Place the chicken strips in a large bowl with 2 tablespoons of the olive oil, the chopped herbs and plenty of salt and pepper and toss well together. Heat a large non-stick frying pan and cook the chicken strips for 3–4 minutes, then add the shallots and balsamic vinegar and continue to cook for a further 2–3 minutes until the chicken is cooked through and well browned and the shallots are tender. Season to taste.

Blanch the watercress in a large pan of boiling salted water for 30 seconds, then drain well. Place in a food-processor with 3 tablespoons of olive oil and blend for 1 minute. Add the garlic and lemon juice and whizz again until smooth. Season to taste.

Place 2 tablespoons of the olive oil in a small pan, and stir in the ground turmeric. Heat very gently for 2–3 minutes then strain the oil through muslin or a clean cloth to remove the turmeric.

Cook the pasta in a large pan of boiling salted water for 3–4 minutes until tender. Drain well and toss with the remaining tablespoon of olive oil. Serve in large bowls with the watercress sauce and turmeric oil poured over the top. Garnish with the diced tomatoes and snipped chives.

PARMA-WRAPPED CHICKEN WITH CAMBOZOLA

This would also be delicious served on a bed of creamed sweet potatoes instead of the tomato salad.

Serves 2

2 boneless, skinless chicken thighs, well trimmed

100g (4oz) Cambozola cheese, rind removed and cut into two even-sized pieces

4 thin Parma ham slices

2 tbsp olive oil

25g (1oz) unsalted butter

100ml (3fl oz) double cream

50g (2oz) freshly grated Parmesan

2 plum tomatoes, sliced

1 tsp snipped fresh chives

a few drops of balsamic vinegar

a dash of extra-virgin olive oil

salt and freshly ground black pepper

Preheat the oven to 220°C/425°F/gas 7 and heat an ovenproof frying pan. Open out each chicken thigh and place between 2 pieces of cling film, then flatten with a rolling pin. Add a grinding of black pepper to each one and place a piece of the Cambozola in the middle. Fold over to enclose the filling completely, then wrap each one with 2 slices of the Parma ham.

Add the oil to the heated frying pan and add the chicken parcels. Cook over a high heat for 30 seconds or so on each side to seal completely, then transfer to the oven and cook for another 6–8 minutes or until the chicken is cooked through and tender.

Melt the butter in a small pan. Add the cream and Parmesan and season with pepper. Simmer gently for 3–4 minutes until the Parmesan has melted, stirring occasionally. Keep warm.

Arrange the tomatoes in an overlapping layer round the edge of each serving plate. Scatter over the chives and season generously, then drizzle over a little balsamic vinegar and extra-virgin olive oil. Drizzle the Parmesan cream in the middle of each plate and top with the chicken parcels to serve.

POT-BELLIED CHICKEN

This is a great one-pot dish. You can serve it with mash, but roasted new potatoes or warm crusty bread with a bitter leaf salad also work very well.

Serves 4

3 tbsp wholegrain mustard

1 tbsp clear honey

4 x 85g (3oz) boneless, skinless chicken breasts

12 rindless smoked streaky bacon rashers

2 tbsp olive oil

200ml (7fl oz) white wine

15g (½ oz) bunch of fresh tarragon leaves, roughly chopped

175g (6oz) frozen petit pois

a squeeze of lemon juice

200ml (7fl oz) double cream

salt and freshly ground black pepper

Place the mustard in a small bowl with the honey and mix to form a paste. Spread each chicken breast all over with the mustard paste and then wrap in the streaky bacon rashers – you'll need 3 per fillet.

Heat the oil in a large non-stick frying pan or sauté pan with a lid. Add the wrapped chicken fillets and fry for 2–3 minutes on each side, until well browned all over. Pour in the white wine, add half of the tarragon, cover and cook for 5 minutes.

Remove the lid and scatter the petit pois over the pan, then add a squeeze of lemon juice. Pour over the cream and sprinkle the remaining tarragon on top. Season well and bring to the boil, then simmer for 5 minutes or until the chicken is completely tender and cooked through. Arrange the wrapped chicken fillets in warmed wide-rimmed serving bowls and spoon around some of the sauce to serve.

RABBIT WITH STILTON SAUCE

Easter recipe

This delicious bacon and Stilton sauce will really bring out the delicate flavour of rabbit, served with crisp, deep-fried potatoes.

Serves 2

350g (12oz) boneless, skinless rabbit portions

3 tbsp sunflower oil

½ tsp dried oregano

15g (½ oz) butter

1 small onion, finely chopped

50g (2oz) unsmoked back bacon, cubed

4 tbsp double cream

50g (2oz) Stilton cheese, crumbled

1 tbsp soy sauce

sunflower oil for deep-frying

350g (12oz) potatoes, cut into 2cm (¾ in) cubes

2 carrots

1 tbsp chopped fresh coriander

salt and freshly ground black pepper

sprigs of flat-leaf parsley and chives, to garnish

Put the rabbit portions between 2 sheets of foil or cling film and beat them with a rolling pin until they are just 5 mm (¼ in) thick. Season with pepper and fry in 2 tablespoons of oil for 8 minutes, until cooked through, turning once. Season with salt and oregano.

Meanwhile, heat the remaining tablespoon of oil and the butter in a frying pan, add the onion and bacon and cook for 5 minutes. Stir in the cream, Stilton, soy sauce and black pepper and simmer for 2 minutes.

Heat the oil for deep-frying to 190°C/375°F. Deep-fry the potatoes for 3 minutes, until golden and tender. Drain on absorbent kitchen paper. Cut the carrots into ribbons with a vegetable peeler and blanch them in a pan of boiling water for 2 minutes. Drain and season well.

To serve, put the rabbit on a plate and pour over the Stilton sauce. Put the potatoes and carrots around the rabbit, sprinkle coriander over the carrots and garnish with sprigs of parsley and chives.

FRUIT-FILLED PORK CHOPS

These can be made well in advance and kept covered in the fridge until needed. They would be great with some lightly spiced rice.

Serves 2

50g (2oz) unsalted butter

1 small Granny Smith apple, peeled, cored and diced

¼ tsp medium curry powder

a good pinch of ground cumin

1 small banana, diced

1 heaped teaspoon sultanas

1 tsp chopped fresh flat-leaf parsley

2 x 150g (5oz) pork loin chops, trimmed of excess fat

1 tbsp sunflower oil

450g (1lb) potatoes, cubed

3–4 tbsp Greek yoghurt

salt and freshly ground black pepper

fresh parsley sprigs, to garnish

Preheat the oven to 200°C/400°F/gas 6. Heat a frying pan, add 15g (½ oz) of butter and the apple and cook for 2–3 minutes, then sprinkle with the curry powder and cumin and cook for 30 seconds. Add the bananas, sultanas and parsley and heat through, then toss to combine without breaking up any of the fruit.

Carefully make a deep pocket in the meat side of each pork chop, being careful not to pierce through the flesh. Divide the fruit mixture between the pockets and secure each one with a cocktail stick.

Heat a knob of the butter and the oil in an ovenproof frying pan. Add the stuffed pork chops to the pan and cook over a fairly high heat for 1–2 minutes on each side until sealed and lightly browned. Transfer the pan to the oven and cook the chops for 8–10 minutes or until they are tender and cooked through, then rest for 5 minutes. Remove the cocktail sticks.

Meanwhile, cook the potatoes in a pan of boiling salted water for 10 minutes or until tender. Drain them and mash with a potato masher, then beat in the remaining butter and the yoghurt. Season to taste and divide between 2 serving plates. Arrange the pork chops on top and garnish with parsley sprigs.

PAN-FRIED PORK ESCALOPE WITH MUSTARD AND DILL

Good-quality pork will have a degree of fat that helps soften the meat during cooking.

Serves 2

250g (9oz) baby new potatoes, scraped or scrubbed and cut in half

2 tbsp olive oil

2 pork escalopes

300ml (½ pint) double cream

1 tsp wholegrain mustard

1 tbsp chopped fresh dill

50g (2oz) freshly grated Parmesan

salt and freshly ground black pepper

Cook the potatoes in a pan of boiling salted water for about 8 minutes until tender.

Meanwhile, heat the olive oil in a frying pan. Season the pork escalopes and then sauté for 4–5 minutes until tender, turning once. Remove from the heat and keep warm. Return the frying pan to the heat and deglaze with the cream and mustard. Reduce the heat and continue to cook for a few minutes until nicely reduced and thickened. Season to taste and stir in the dill.

Drain the cooked potatoes and return to the pan, then coarsely crush with a potato masher. Stir in the Parmesan and season with plenty of pepper. Spoon the crushed Parmesan potatoes onto warmed plates and add the pork escalopes. Spoon over the mustard and dill sauce to serve.

GAMMON WITH BROAD BEAN AND POTATO PESTO SALAD

Ham and peas is a traditional flavour combination, which is brought right up to date with this fantastic spicy dish.

Serves 2

450g (1lb) baby new potatoes, scraped or scrubbed and cut in half

225g (8oz) frozen broad beans, thawed

1 small red onion, finely chopped

6 tbsp extra-virgin olive oil

2 garlic cloves, crushed

1 tsp freshly squeezed lemon juice

1 tsp balsamic vinegar

1 small French baguette, sliced on the diagonal

2 x 225g (8oz) raw gammon steaks

15g (½ oz) fresh flat-leaf parsley leaves

1 tsp fresh oregano leaves

1 tinned anchovy fillet, drained and chopped (optional)

40g (1½ oz) piece of Parmesan

sea salt and freshly ground black pepper

fresh basil leaves, to garnish

Preheat the oven to 200°C/400°F/gas 6. Boil the potatoes in salted water for 10–12 minutes and drain. Blanch the beans in boiling water for 30 seconds; drain and refresh. Peel the outer skins and discard. Set the beans and potatoes aside in a bowl.

Fry the onion in 1 tablespoon of oil until softened. Add 1 garlic clove, the lemon juice, balsamic vinegar and 1 tablespoon of oil and combine. Add the bean and potato mixture and stir well.

Place the bread slices on a baking sheet, drizzle with oil, sprinkle with salt and bake for 5 minutes until the crostini are crisp but not coloured. Brush the gammon steaks with olive oil, season with pepper and cook on a griddle for 2 minutes on each side.

Place the parsley in a food-processor with the oregano, anchovy, if using, and remaining garlic, then grate in half of the Parmesan and season to make a pesto. Whizz for 10 seconds, pour in the remaining oil and whizz again. Season. Add 2 heaped table-spoons of the pesto to the beans and potatoes and mix well.

Divide the bean and potato mixture between plates. Place the gammon steaks on top and drizzle around the pesto. Scatter the basil and pare Parmesan shavings on top. Serve with the crostini.

STEAK WITH RED WINE, MASH AND SPINACH

This is a delicious way to serve fillet steak.

Serves 2

350g (12oz) potatoes, cut into 1cm (½ in) cubes

40g (1½ oz) butter

1 tbsp sunflower oil

1 onion, chopped

1½ tsp cornflour

150ml (¼ pint) red wine

250ml (9fl oz) beef stock

1 tsp Worcestershire sauce

¼ tsp English mustard

2 x 100g (4oz) fillet steaks

225g (8oz) spinach, washed and stalks removed

1 tbsp olive oil

1 beefsteak tomato, chopped

1 tbsp mayonnaise

salt and freshly ground black pepper

Cook the potatoes in boiling, salted water for 10 minutes.

Heat 15g (½ oz) of the butter and the sunflower oil in a frying pan and cook the onion for 5 minutes. Put half of the fried onion in another pan, stir in the cornflour and cook for 2 minutes, stirring, until golden. Gradually add the wine, stirring all the time. Add the stock, Worcestershire sauce, mustard and seasoning. Bring to the boil, stirring, and simmer for 10 minutes.

Season the steaks and cook them in a hot griddle pan for 6–8 minutes, turning once. Add the spinach to the remaining onion in the frying pan and cook for 3 minutes, until wilted.

Heat the olive oil in a pan, add the tomato and cook for 2 minutes. Drain the potatoes and mash with the remaining butter, mayonnaise and salt and pepper. Stir in the chopped tomato.

To serve, pile the mashed potatoes onto serving plates, with the steak and spinach. Spoon the sauce around the steak.

FILLET STEAK WITH WHISKY SAUCE AND PAN-FRIED POTATOES

69

This is a simple dish but a real masterpiece. The secret is to crush the peppercorns coarsely in a coffee grinder and then tip them into a fine sieve and shake out all the powder. This is important because otherwise the powder makes the steaks far too spicy.

Serves 2

4 tbsp olive oil

250g (9oz) baby new potatoes, scraped or scrubbed and cut into quarters

2 garlic cloves, chopped

1 onion, thinly sliced

25g (1oz) unsalted butter

2 fillet steaks, about 2½ cm (1in) thick

2 tbsp Dijon mustard

1 tbsp cracked black peppercorns

2 tbsp whisky

85ml (3fl oz) beef stock

50ml (2fl oz) double cream

1 tbsp snipped fresh chives

2 tbsp shredded fresh basil

salt and freshly ground black pepper

steamed mangetout, to serve (optional)

Heat 3 tablespoons of the oil in a wok and sauté the potatoes and garlic for 5 minutes. Add the onion and continue to cook for another 5–10 minutes until the potatoes are cooked through and golden brown, tossing occasionally. Season well and keep hot.

Heat the remaining oil and the butter in a frying pan. Spread each steak with the Dijon mustard and roll in the cracked pepper to coat. Cook for 2–3 minutes on each side, then add the whisky and ignite to flambé.

Transfer the steaks to a warm plate and leave to rest. Pour the stock into the pan and simmer for 4–5 minutes to thicken slightly. Reduce the heat, add the cream and chives and allow to bubble down and warm through. Season to taste.

Arrange each rested steak on a warmed serving plate and spoon over the whisky sauce. Stir the basil into the pan-fried potatoes and spoon onto the plate with some mangetout, if liked.

SEARED CALF'S LIVER WITH BALSAMIC VINEGAR AND ONIONS

The most important thing to remember when cooking liver is to do it quickly, which creates all those wonderful, sweet flavours.

Serves 2

2 tbsp olive oil

50g (2oz) unsalted butter

1 large Spanish onion, thinly sliced

300ml (½ pint) red wine

300ml (1½ pint) beef stock

2 x 175g (6oz) calf's liver slices, each about 1cm (½ in) thick

4 tbsp balsamic vinegar

salt and freshly ground black pepper

Dijon-flavoured mash, to serve (optional)

Heat 1 tablespoon of the oil and half of the butter in a sauté pan. Add the onion and sauté over a high heat for 1–2 minutes until just beginning to soften. Pour in the red wine and let it bubble down for 1 minute, stirring, then add the stock and simmer until the liquid has reduced by four-fifths, stirring occasionally.

When the onions are nearly ready, heat a frying pan over a medium heat until very hot. Add the remaining oil and a knob of the butter, then quickly cook the calf's liver until golden brown but still pink in the middle, turning once – around 2 minutes, but if you prefer it well done cook for slightly longer. Leave to rest in the pan for 1–2 minutes, then season to taste.

Pour the balsamic vinegar into the onion mixture and season, then stir in the remaining butter. Arrange the liver on serving plates with the Dijon mash, if liked. Spoon over the onion gravy.

SPICY LAMB AND FETA SALAD WITH SWEET AND SOUR DRESSING

This is a light and refreshing spring salad with great flavour combinations.

Serves 2

½ tsp each coriander seeds and dried chilli flakes

1 tsp ground turmeric

¼ tsp ground cayenne, paprika and ginger

2 garlic cloves, finely chopped

finely grated rind of 1 orange

1 tbsp clear honey

2 x 150g (5oz) lamb leg steaks

5 tbsp olive oil

2 tsp light muscovado sugar

1 baby red pepper, seeded and diced

1 tbsp balsamic vinegar

4 shredded fresh basil leaves

200g (7oz) feta cheese, cut into cubes

2 tsp freshly squeezed lime juice

150g (5oz) baby spinach leaves

4 spring onions, thinly sliced

salt and freshly ground black pepper

Place the coriander seeds and chilli flakes in a mortar and crush with the pestle. Tip into a shallow dish and stir in the remaining spices, garlic, orange rind and honey. Use to coat the lamb steaks and then bash each one into an escalope using a meat mallet or rolling pin wrapped in cling film. Cut the escalopes into strips, discarding any excess fat.

Heat a wok or sauté pan over a medium heat until searing hot. Add 1 tablespoon of the oil and use to coat the bottom of the pan in a thin film, then tip in the lamb strips. Stir-fry for 5–6 minutes or until tender and caramelized.

Meanwhile, make the dressing. Place the sugar in a small pan and gently melt over a low heat. Stir in the diced pepper and leave to caramelize, tossing occasionally. Pour in 3 tablespoons of the oil and the balsamic vinegar, swirling the pan to combine. Remove from the heat and stir in the basil.

Place the feta in a large bowl. Drizzle over the remaining tablespoon of oil and add the lime juice. Season generously, and gently fold in the spinach and spring onions, then the lamb strips. Arrange on warmed serving plates, drizzle around the dressing and serve at once.

LAMB'S LIVER AND STUFFED TOMATOES

The combination of flavours works really well in this recipe.

Serves 2

600ml (1 pint) lamb stock

4 tbsp white wine

juice and grated rind of 1 orange

1 tbsp olive oil

1 onion, quartered

15g (½ oz) butter

1 baby white cabbage, shredded

1 garlic clove, crushed

1 tsp caraway seeds

2 tbsp double cream

4 tomatoes

350g (12oz) sliced lamb's liver

1 tbsp cornflour

salt and freshly ground black pepper

Place the stock, half the wine and the orange rind and juice in a pan. Bring to the boil and simmer rapidly until reduced by half. Brush a griddle pan or heavy-based frying pan with the olive oil. Add the quartered onion and cook for 8 minutes.

Heat the butter in a large frying pan and cook the cabbage, garlic and caraway seeds for 2 minutes. Add the cream and remaining wine and cook for 3 minutes until the cabbage is tender. Season. Slice the top off each tomato, hollow them out and spoon in the cabbage mixture. Replace the tops.

Dust the liver in a little of the cornflour and add to the onion pan. Cook for 1½ minutes on each side until well browned but still pink in the centre. Remove from the pan and allow to rest.

Dissolve the remaining cornflour in a little water and whisk into the pan of stock. Bring to the boil, stirring continuously until smooth and thickened. Season to taste. To serve, place the liver on a large plate. Arrange the stuffed tomatoes and onions around the plate and pour over the sauce.

LAMB'S KIDNEYS IN A RED WINE SAUCE

In this dish the kidneys are perfectly paired with rice and a tasty red wine and sherry vinegar sauce.

Serves 2

225g (8oz) long-grain rice

250g (9oz) lamb's kidneys

4 tbsp olive oil

a pinch of chilli powder

½ tsp ground ginger

1 red pepper, seeded and roughly chopped

3 shallots, finely chopped

2½cm (1in) piece of fresh root ginger, very thinly sliced

2 tbsp sherry vinegar

2 tbsp red wine

1 tsp soy sauce

1 tsp balsamic vinegar

1–2 tsp caster sugar

salt and freshly ground black pepper

TO GARNISH

1 tbsp chopped fresh parsley

3 spring onions, finely chopped

Cook the rice in a large pan of boiling water for 12–15 minutes.

Blanch the kidneys in a pan of boiling water for 30 seconds. Drain, then cool under cold water. Halve horizontally, peel the outer membrane, cut out the central core and any sinew. Place in a bowl with 1 tablespoon of olive oil, the chilli powder, ground ginger and plenty of salt and pepper. Toss well and set aside.

Blend the red pepper in a food-processor until smooth. Stir into the cooked rice and season to taste; cover and keep warm.

Heat 2 tablespoons of the olive oil in a large frying pan and cook the shallots and sliced ginger for 5 minutes until softened. Stir in the sherry vinegar and red wine, bring to the boil and boil rapidly for 3–4 minutes. Add the soy sauce and balsamic vinegar and season with sugar, salt and pepper; remove from the heat.

Heat the remaining oil in a heavy-based frying pan and cook the kidneys over a high heat for 3–4 minutes on each side until well browned but slightly pink in the centre. Pour over the shallot gravy and mix well. To serve, pile the rice onto a plate and spoon over the kidneys. Garnish with parsley and spring onions.

FRAGRANT LAMB WITH HERBED COUSCOUS

It isn't possible to prepare a tagine in 20 minutes but this is a rather special 'cheat's' version.

Serves 2

225g (8oz) lamb fillet

1 tsp each ground ginger and paprika

1½ tsp ground turmeric

3 tbsp olive oil

1 small onion, finely chopped

2 garlic cloves, finely sliced

200g (7oz) chestnut mushrooms, sliced

½ tsp each dried chilli flakes and ground cumin

100ml (3½ fl oz) chicken stock

FOR THE COUSCOUS

200g (7oz) couscous

3 tbsp extra-virgin olive oil

juice of 1 lemon

300ml (½ pint) chicken stock

a pinch of saffron stamens

2 tbsp chopped fresh flat-leaf parsley and chives

salt and freshly ground black pepper

thick Greek yoghurt and fresh coriander leaves, to garnish

Preheat the oven to 200°C/400°F/gas 6. Trim the excess fat from the lamb. Mix the ginger and paprika and 1 teaspoon of the turmeric, then rub this into the lamb, adding a little salt. Heat 1 tablespoon of the oil in an ovenproof frying pan and brown the lamb on all sides. Transfer to the oven. Cook for 8 minutes until just tender, remove and rest for a couple of minutes.

Sauté the onion, garlic and mushrooms in the remaining oil for 5 minutes, stirring. Season with salt, stir in the remaining turmeric, chilli flakes and cumin and cook for a few minutes.

Mix the couscous with half the olive oil and the lemon juice. Heat 300ml (½ pint) of the stock in a pan with the saffron; season generously. Pour over the couscous and rest in a warm place for 6–8 minutes until all the liquid has been absorbed, stirring occasionally.

Add the remaining stock to the mushroom mixture and increase the heat to reduce the sauce. Slice the lamb and stir it in until just warmed through – do not allow the mixture to reboil. Fluff up the couscous and stir in the remaining oil and the herbs; season. Serve garnished with the yoghurt and coriander.

LAMB KOFTAS

You can cook the koftas under the grill, but soak the bamboo skewers in water first to prevent them from catching alight.

Serves 2

225g (8oz) lean minced lamb

1 garlic clove, roughly chopped

1 tsp hot paprika

½ tsp chilli powder

¼ tsp ground cinnamon

½ tsp ground cumin

¼ tsp ground ginger

1 egg

1 tbsp olive oil

2 white pitta breads

6 tbsp Greek yoghurt

1 small ripe tomato, finely diced

5cm (2in) piece of cucumber, halved, seeded and finely diced

1 tbsp chopped fresh flat-leaf parsley

salt and freshly ground black pepper

2 lemon wedges, to garnish

Heat a large flat griddle pan and preheat the grill. Place the lamb mince in a food-processor with the garlic, paprika, chilli powder, cinnamon, cumin, ginger and egg. Pulse until well combined and divide into 6 portions. Squeeze around six 15cm (6in) bamboo skewers to form kofta shapes.

Add the oil to the griddle pan and cook the koftas for 6–8 minutes, turning every 2 minutes or so to ensure they cook and colour evenly. Meanwhile, grill the pitta breads for 30 seconds on each side until puffed up and lightly golden, then cut in half on the diagonal.

To make the dressing, place the yoghurt in a bowl with the tomato, cucumber and parsley. Season and mix well to combine.

Arrange the koftas on warmed plates and drizzle over the yoghurt dressing. Add the pitta halves and garnish with lemon wedges to serve.

QUICK LAMB COBBLER

The scone topping is the perfect foil to the lamb in this dish, as it is as light as a feather.

Serves 2

350g (12oz) lamb neck fillet, cut into 1cm (½ in) cubes

2 tbsp plain flour, seasoned with salt and pepper

3 tbsp olive oil

1 onion, finely chopped

1 large carrot, diced

1 small swede, diced

100g (4oz) plain flour, plus extra for dusting

1 tsp baking powder

1 tbsp chopped fresh sage

1 egg

2 tbsp milk

1 tsp paprika

300ml (½ pint) lamb stock

salt and freshly ground black pepper

Preheat the oven to 190°C/375°F/gas 5. Coat the lamb pieces in the seasoned flour. Fry the lamb for 2–3 minutes until well sealed in 2 tablespoons of oil in a heavy-based pan. Keep warm.

Fry the onion for 2–3 minutes in the remaining oil until just softened. Add the carrot and swede and fry for 4–5 minutes.

Sift the flour and baking powder into a bowl and season generously, then stir in the sage. Make a well in the centre and break in the egg, then add the milk and mix well until you have a soft dough – if the mixture is too sticky, add a little more flour.

Return the lamb to the pan with the paprika and stock. Season and combine. Bring to the boil, then simmer for a few minutes until the liquid has slightly thickened. Move to an ovenproof dish.

Tip the dough out onto a lightly floured work surface and gently roll out a 13cm (5in) circle. Divide the dough into 4 triangles and arrange on top of the lamb. Bake for 15–20 minutes or until the scones are well risen and lightly golden.

LAMB WITH APRICOT RICE AND TARRAGON CREAM SAUCE

There's a lovely range of complementary flavours here.

Serves 2

1 onion, chopped

1 tbsp sunflower oil

15g (½ oz) butter

100g (4oz) long-grain rice

300ml (10fl oz) chicken stock

50g (2oz) ready-to-eat dried apricots, finely chopped

150g (5oz) runner beans, cut into 2cm (¾ in lengths)

5 tbsp white wine

150ml (¼ pint) double cream

2 tbsp chopped fresh tarragon

2 x 100g (4oz) boneless lamb leg steaks

1 tbsp olive oil

a few drops of Tabasco sauce

salt and freshly ground black pepper

chopped fresh mint and flat-leaf parsley sprigs, to garnish

Cook half the onion for 2 minutes in a large pan in the sunflower oil and butter. Stir in the rice and cook for 1 minute. Add the stock, apricots and a little seasoning and cook for 10–12 minutes until the liquid is absorbed and the rice is tender.

Cook the runner beans in a large pan of boiling salted water for 3 minutes until tender but firm. Drain and cool under cold water.

Place the wine and remaining onion in a separate pan, bring to the boil and simmer for 3 minutes. Stir in the cream and tarragon and cook for another 3 minutes. Stir in the drained runner beans and cook for 2 minutes; season to taste.

Brush the steaks with olive oil and season well. Cook in a hot griddle pan or heavy-based frying pan for 4 minutes, turning once. Sprinkle over the Tabasco sauce and cook for a further 1–2 minutes until well browned but still a little pink in the centre.

To serve, spoon the apricot rice into 2 ramekins, pressing down well, then turn out onto serving plates and sprinkle over the chopped mint. Place the lamb steaks and creamy beans next to the rice and garnish with the parsley sprigs.

BANANA AND CHOCOLATE TRIFLE

Bananas and chocolate are a classic combination, and with a measure
of Irish Cream this is a dessert to die for.

Serves 2

100g (4oz) ready-made chocolate slab cake

1 large banana

1 miniature Irish Cream (about 50ml/2fl oz in total)

120ml (4fl oz) double cream

cocoa powder, to dust

FOR THE PECAN BRITTLE

sunflower oil, for greasing

50g (2oz) caster sugar

25g (1oz) toasted pecan nuts, roughly chopped

To make the pecan brittle, lightly oil a baking sheet, then place the sugar in a very clean, heavy-based pan and heat gently until it has dissolved. Bring to the boil and boil fast for a few minutes until the resulting syrup begins to turn pale brown, gently swirling the pan to ensure even cooking. When the caramel is a rich golden-brown, dip the base of the pan into a sink of cold water to prevent further cooking. Add the toasted pecan nuts, shaking the pan to coat evenly. Pour onto the oiled baking sheet and leave to set.

Meanwhile, cut the chocolate cake into small pieces and use about half to line 2 individual glass dishes. Slice the banana and divide between the dishes. Sprinkle over half of the Irish Cream, then arrange the remaining cake on top in an even layer. Whip the cream and the remaining Irish Cream in a bowl until soft peaks have formed. Swirl over the chocolate cake layer to cover completely. Break the pecan brittle into small pieces with a rolling pin and scatter on top. Add a light dusting of cocoa powder and serve at once.

PAIN PERDU WITH CARAMELIZED PEACH SAUCE

This dish is called a 'perdu' (lost) because the stale bread would otherwise
be thrown away.

Serves 2

2 eggs

2 tbsp milk

2 tbsp double cream

1 tbsp caster sugar

4 slices brioche (1 day old is best)

25g (1oz) butter

FOR THE CARAMELIZED PEACH SAUCE

75g (3oz) caster sugar

1 x 200g (7oz) tin of peach slices in natural juice

Heat a large sauté pan. Break the eggs into a shallow dish with the milk, cream and sugar. Whisk until well combined. Using a cookie cutter, stamp out circles from the slices of brioche and soak each one in the egg mixture. Melt the butter in the heated sauté pan. Once it starts foaming, add the soaked brioche and cook for 3–4 minutes until golden brown, turning once.

Meanwhile, make the peach sauce. Melt the sugar over a gentle heat in a heavy-based pan, swirling the pan occasionally so it cooks evenly. Increase the heat under the melted sugar and bring to the boil, then boil fast until the sugar syrup begins to caramelize. Stir 4 tablespoons of the juice from the peaches into the caramel to prevent it cooking any further. Pour the caramel into a food-processor and add the peach slices. Blend to a smooth sauce, adding a little more peach juice if necessary.

Arrange the pain perdu on warmed plates and spoon over the sauce to serve.

Pancake Day recipe

CHOCOLATE DROP SCONES WITH PECAN TOFFEE SAUCE

CHOCOLATE DROP SCONES WITH PECAN TOFFEE SAUCE

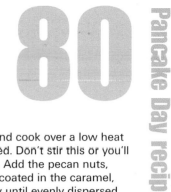

The secret is in the batter, which should be the consistency of thick cream and must be mixed as quickly and as lightly as possible.

Serves 4

115g (4oz) self-raising flour

¼ tsp baking powder

2 eggs

120ml (4fl oz) milk

1 tbsp clear honey

50g (2oz) plain chocolate, finely chopped (at least 70 per cent cocoa solids)

FOR THE SAUCE

50g (2oz) caster sugar

50g (2oz) pecan nuts, chopped

150ml (¼ pint) double cream

vanilla ice cream, to serve (optional)

Place the sugar in a heavy-based pan and cook over a low heat until dissolved and a caramel has formed. Don't stir this or you'll end up with a pan of crystallized sugar. Add the pecan nuts, shaking the pan until the nuts are well coated in the caramel, then pour in the cream and cook gently until evenly dispersed and slightly thickened, swirling the pan occasionally. Keep warm.

Heat a non-stick frying pan. Sift the flour into a bowl with the baking powder. Lightly whisk together the eggs and milk to combine. Make a well in the centre of the flour and gradually add in enough of the egg mixture to make a smooth batter, the consistency of thick cream. Fold in the honey and chocolate.

Ladle spoonfuls of the batter onto the heated pan, allowing them to spread to about 7½ cm (3in) in diameter. Reduce the heat and cook for about 1½ minutes until small bubbles appear on the surface. Flip and cook for another 1–2 minutes until lightly golden. Stack on a plate and keep warm. Repeat until you have 12 drop scones. Arrange on warmed serving plates, spoon over the pecan toffee sauce and add a scoop of ice cream, if liked.

FRENCH PANCAKES WITH FLAMBÉED FRUIT AND CARAMEL-UGLI

Whether sweet or savoury, pancakes are just great and children always love them.

Serves 4

100g (4oz) granulated sugar

4 tbsp water

1 ugli fruit, segmented

25g (1oz) butter

2 bananas, sliced

2 Cox's apples, peeled and sliced

grated rind and juice of 1 lime

juice of 1 orange

2 tbsp orange liqueur, such as Cointreau or Grand Marnier

1 tbsp icing sugar

100g (4oz) plain flour

1 tbsp caster sugar

175ml (6fl oz) milk

2 eggs, beaten

1–2 tbsp vegetable oil

150ml (¼ pint) single cream, to serve

Place the sugar and water in a small pan and heat gently, stirring until the sugar dissolves. Bring to the boil and boil rapidly, without stirring, for 3–5 minutes until the mixture turns golden. Add the ugli fruit segments and coat them in the caramel, then transfer to a tray lined with greaseproof paper and leave to set.

Heat the butter in a heavy-based frying pan and when it begins to foam, add the sliced fruit and the lime rind. Cook for 1 minute, add the orange and lime juice and cook on a high heat for 2–3 minutes until starting to brown. Pour over the orange liqueur and ignite. When the flames have died down, stir in the icing sugar.

Beat together the flour, caster sugar, milk and eggs to make a smooth batter. Heat a little of the oil in a small, heavy-based frying pan and add 2 tablespoons of batter, swirling it round to coat the base. Cook for 1–2 minutes on each side, then repeat.

To serve, divide the flambéed fruit between the pancakes and fold over into quarters to enclose the filling. Arrange the caramel-ugli fruit on top, pour over the cream and serve immediately.

KIWI CHARLOTTES

The charlottes are best if made one or two hours in advance and chilled in the fridge until ready to serve.

Serves 4

225ml (8fl oz) double cream

150ml (¼ pint) milk

1 vanilla pod, halved lengthways

100g (4oz) granulated sugar

300ml (½ pint) water

rind of 1 orange, cut into needleshreds

rind of 2 limes, cut into needleshreds

2 kiwi fruit, 1 sliced, 1 diced

225g (8oz) clear honey

4 tbsp white wine

75g (3oz) sponge fingers

4 tbsp mascarpone

3 egg yolks

75g (3oz) caster sugar

25g (1oz) butter

75g (3oz) ready-to-eat stoned prunes

25g (1oz) toasted almonds, roughly chopped

Pour half the cream into a small pan with the milk and vanilla pod and heat without boiling. Heat the granulated sugar and water in a separate pan, stirring until the sugar dissolves. Add the orange and lime needleshreds, reserving a few for the garnish. Simmer gently for 8 minutes.

Line 4 ramekins with cling film. Place a slice of kiwi in the base of each dish. Place the honey and wine in a heatproof bowl over a pan of simmering water. Stir occasionally until blended. Cut the sponge fingers to the depth of the ramekin dishes. Dip them in the honey mixture and use to line the insides of the ramekins.

Whip the remaining cream to soft peaks and fold with the mascarpone and diced kiwi. Spoon into the ramekins and fold over the cling film. Chill for 15 minutes.

Place the egg yolks and 50g (2oz) of caster sugar in a heatproof bowl over a pan of simmering water. Whisk until pale and thickened, then strain in the hot milk mixture and whisk for 2–3 minutes until thickened. Remove the citrus needleshreds and stir the syrup into the custard; keep warm.

Heat the butter and remaining caster sugar in a separate pan. Stir in the prunes and cook for 5 minutes, stirring occasionally.

Turn out the charlottes onto a plate with the prunes and pour around the citrus custard. Top with the toasted almonds and garnish with the reserved needleshreds.

LEMON CURD CHEESECAKE

This dessert is perfect if you're short on time but searching for the wow factor. (See illustration, page 2.)

Serves 4–6

2 tbsp lemon curd

1 tbsp caster sugar

finely grated rind and juice of 1 lemon

250g (9oz) flan sponge case

75g (3oz) redcurrants

50g (2oz) white chocolate

FOR THE FILLING

100g (4oz) mascarpone

1 tbsp icing sugar, plus extra for dusting

finely grated rind and juice ½ lemon

120ml (4fl oz) double cream

2 tbsp lemon curd

To make a lemon glaze, heat the lemon curd and caster sugar with the lemon rind and juice in a small pan for 2–3 minutes until the sugar has dissolved, stirring occasionally.

Place the flan case on a flat plate and drizzle over the lemon glaze in an even layer. Set aside to allow the lemon to penetrate the sponge.

Meanwhile, prepare the filling. Place the mascarpone in a bowl with the icing sugar, lemon rind and juice and double cream. Whisk until you have achieved soft peaks, then fold in the lemon curd for a ripple effect.

Pile the filling into the flan case. Using a palette knife, smooth the top. Scatter over the redcurrants and pare shavings of the white chocolate on top. Finally add a light dusting of icing sugar and chill until ready to serve.

VALENTINE'S HEARTS

These Madeira-cake hearts with crunchy toffee almonds and vanilla chocolate sauce are the perfect recipe for Valentine's Day.

Serves 2

100ml (4fl oz) water

100g (4oz) caster sugar

juice of 1 orange

1 x 200g (7oz) rectangular Madeira cake

50g (2oz) butter

2 tbsp milk

50g (2oz) flaked almonds

100g (4oz) plain chocolate

3 tbsp water

a few drops of vanilla extract

150ml (¼ pint) double cream

200g (7oz) strawberries, sliced

1 orange, cut into segments

fresh mint leaves, to decorate

icing sugar, for dusting

Slowly bring the water and half the sugar to boil in a small pan, stirring until the sugar dissolves. Boil rapidly, without stirring, until the mixture becomes syrupy but doesn't colour. Stir in the orange juice and remove from the heat.

Cut the Madeira cake in half lengthways. Cut out 4 heart shapes, place on a plate and brush liberally with the orange syrup. Cook the butter, remaining sugar, milk and almonds in a heavy-based frying-pan for 4–5 minutes, stirring occasionally, and spoon over the hearts.

While making the almond topping, at the stage where the almonds begin to brown, the mixture may start to separate. To correct this, add 2 tablespoons of cold water to the pan (taking care because the mixture will bubble up), then whisk vigorously to achieve a smooth toffee sauce.

Meanwhile, break the chocolate into a small pan with the water, vanilla extract and 3 tablespoons of cream. Heat gently, stirring until the chocolate melts, then pour around the Madeira hearts. Whip the remaining cream to soft peaks and spoon swirls on top of each heart. Decorate with the sliced fruit and mint leaves. Dust with icing sugar and serve immediately.

SCENTED GRAPEFRUIT JUICE

A refreshing drink that would be a perfect start to the day. It's a light breakfast-in-a-glass, and much tastier than anything you can buy.

Serves 2

1 ripe grapefruit

1 lime

6 fresh mint leaves

a handful of ice cubes

1–2 tbsp clear honey

Cut the grapefruit and lime in half and squeeze the juice into a liquidizer. Add the mint, ice and 1 tablespoon of the honey. Whizz until well combined, then taste and add a little more honey if you think it needs it.

Pour the scented grapefruit juice into glasses to serve.

VIRGIN MARY

The secret of a good Virgin Mary is in the balance of the seasonings – experiment until you find the right combination for you.

Serves 2

1 x 400g (14oz) tin of tomato juice

1 tbsp Worcester-shire sauce

½ tsp Tabasco sauce

½ tsp salt

a good pinch of black pepper

juice of 1 lime

1 tbsp chopped fresh coriander (optional)

175g (6oz) crushed ice

6 anchovy-stuffed green olives

Place the tomato juice in a large cocktail shaker with the Worcestershire sauce, Tabasco, salt, pepper and lime juice, and the coriander if liked. Fill up with ice and shake until very well chilled. Taste and adjust the seasoning as necessary.

Strain the Virgin Mary into tall, sturdy glasses, top with fresh ice and garnish each one with the olives. Add swizzle sticks to serve.

BANANA AND VANILLA BEAN SMOOTHIE

This is a favourite for adults and children alike. It's ideal for using up an overripe banana, and because of their natural sweetness you need only a little honey.

Serves 2

1 ripe banana

225ml (8fl oz) milk, well-chilled

100g (4oz) Greek yoghurt

1 vanilla pod, split in half and seeds scraped out

1–2 tbsp clear honey

75g (3oz) ice cubes

Peel the banana and place in a liquidizer with the milk, yoghurt, vanilla seeds and 1 tablespoon of honey. Chuck in a handful of the ice cubes and blend until smooth. Taste and add a little more honey if necessary.

Fill tall glasses half full with ice and then top up with the banana and vanilla bean smoothie. Serve at once.

BAILEYS AND BANANA DREAMBOAT

Baileys Irish Cream is a unique blend of cream and whisky
with a touch of chocolate and vanilla.

Serves 2

50g (2oz) plain
chocolate

2 ripe miniature
bananas

100ml (3½ fl oz)
Baileys Irish Cream

2 tbsp maple syrup

100g (4oz) Greek
yoghurt

100ml (3½ fl oz) milk

a good handful of ice
cubes

Break the chocolate into squares and melt in a heatproof bowl
set over a pan of simmering water for 3 minutes or on high in
the microwave for 2 minutes. Leave to cool a little and then swirl
around 2 tall glasses and set aside for 5 minutes to set.

Peel and slice the bananas and add to a liquidizer. Add the
Baileys, maple syrup, yoghurt, milk and ice and blend until
smooth. Pour the dreamboat into the chocolate-decorated
glasses and serve.

WHITE WINE SPRITZER

This is a refreshing twist on an old favourite. You could use a mixture
of orange and lemon, but I prefer the sharpness of the lemon.

Serves 2

1 lemon

4 fresh basil leaves

2 tbsp caster sugar

6 ice cubes

200ml (7fl oz) dry
white wine

200ml (7fl oz) soda or
sparkling water

Cut the lemon into small pieces, discarding any pips, and place
in a mini food-processor or liquidizer with the basil, sugar and ice
cubes. Blend to a pulp.

Divide the lemon pulp between tall glasses and pour in the white
wine. Top up with the soda or sparkling water and stir to
combine. Serve at once.

BUCK'S FIZZ

Named after London's Buck's Club, where it was first served in 1921, this is
the English version of the French Mimosa. It is usually served at brunch but
seems to go down well at any time.

Serves 2

2 oranges

a splash of grenadine

200ml (7fl oz)
champagne or cava
(ice cold)

Cut the oranges in half and squeeze out the juice into a bowl,
then pass through a fine strainer into a jug. Divide between
2 champagne glasses and add a dash of grenadine to each one.

Top up with the champagne or cava and serve at once.

SUMMER

CREAM OF WATERCRESS SOUP

When watercress is in season and at its best, this is an excellent, almost instant soup. Just don't be tempted to overcook the watercress or it will lose its beautiful, vibrant colour.

Serves 2

4 tbsp double cream

a knob of unsalted butter

1 garlic clove, finely chopped

300ml (½ pint) hot vegetable stock (from a cube is fine)

120ml (4fl oz) milk

200g (7oz) bunch of watercress

a good handful of fresh flat-leaf parsley leaves

salt and freshly ground black pepper

fresh chives, to garnish

Lightly whip the cream in a small bowl, then cover with cling film and chill until needed.

Melt the butter in a pan and add the garlic. Cook for 1–2 minutes until softened but not coloured, stirring constantly. Pour the stock into the pan with the milk. Season to taste and cook for a further 2 minutes until the liquid is just beginning to simmer. Trim the bunch of watercress, remove any thick stalks and discoloured leaves, then chop up the remainder.

Add the chopped watercress to the pan with the parsley. Simmer for 1 minute – any longer and the watercress will start to lose its colour. Purée the soup in a food-processor or liquidizer and ladle into warmed bowls. Add swirls of the lightly whipped cream and garnish with the chives to serve.

CANNELLINI BEAN SOUP WITH CHORIZO

This recipe requires little preparation and is quick to cook. The sizzling chorizo makes a delicious topping.

Serves 2

2 tbsp olive oil

a knob of butter

1 small onion, finely chopped

2 celery sticks, peeled and finely chopped

2 garlic cloves, finely chopped

½ tsp chopped fresh thyme

450ml (¾ pint) hot chicken stock (from a cube is fine)

1 x 400g (14oz) tin of cannellini beans, drained and rinsed

100g (4oz) raw chorizo, peeled and diced

salt and freshly ground white pepper

Heat half the oil and the butter in a large pan and add the onion, celery and garlic. Cook gently for 2–3 minutes until softened but not coloured.

Stir the thyme into the pan and cook for another 30 seconds and then pour in the stock. Tip in the beans and bring to the boil, then reduce the heat and simmer for another 4–5 minutes until the flavours have combined and the liquid has slightly reduced. Season to taste.

Meanwhile, heat a seperate frying pan and add the remaining oil to the heated frying pan. Add the chorizo and sauté for 3–4 minutes until sizzling and the chorizo has begun to bleed its colour into the oil.

Blitz the cannellini bean soup with a hand blender until smooth and ladle into warmed bowls. Spoon over the sizzling chorizo and any oil left in the pan to serve.

PEA AND MINT SOUP

This soup is as instant as you are ever going to get and is brilliant if you've got almost nothing in the house. (See illustration, page 64.)

Serves 4

50g (2oz) unsalted butter

1 onion, finely chopped

2 garlic cloves, crushed

1 green chilli, seeded and finely chopped

450g (1lb) frozen peas

a pinch of sugar

900ml (1½ pints) vegetable or chicken stock

2 tbsp chopped fresh mint, plus extra leaves to garnish

salt and freshly ground black pepper

softly whipped cream, to serve

Melt the butter in a large pan and add the onion, garlic and chilli. Sauté for 3–4 minutes until softened but not coloured. Add the peas and sugar, then pour in the stock and season generously. Bring to the boil, then reduce the heat and simmer for about 5 minutes or until the peas are completely tender.

Add the mint to the soup and blend to a purée in a food-processor, or with a hand-held blender. Reheat gently in the pan and season to taste. Ladle into bowls and add swirls of cream and mint leaves to garnish. Serve immediately.

CHILLED MELON SOUP

This delicate soup makes a wonderful first course in the summer. Choose melons that are heavy for their size. They should be slightly soft at the stalk end and perfumed. Try making this with a sweet white wine such as Muscat or Sauternes and omit the sugar.

Serves 2

50g (2oz) caster sugar

1 ripe melon (such as charentais)

50ml (2fl oz) dry white wine

a small handful of fresh basil leaves, plus extra tiny sprigs to garnish

a good handful of ice cubes

a squeeze of lemon juice

Place the caster sugar in a small pan with 120ml (4fl oz) of water and heat gently until the sugar has dissolved. Remove from the heat and pour into a jug.

Cut the melon in half and discard the pips, then scoop the flesh into a food-processor or liquidizer.

Add the sugar syrup to the food-processor with the wine and basil, and then tip in the ice. Blend to a purée and taste, adding a squeeze of the lemon juice if you think it needs it.

Divide the soup between glass bowls and garnish each one with a basil sprig to serve.

CHINESE-STYLE CRAB AND SWEETCORN SOUP

95

This is a super-quick version of an old favourite. If you can't get hold of fresh corn on the cob, use 100g (4oz) of frozen sweetcorn kernels instead.

Serves 2

1 corn on the cob

2 tbsp sunflower oil

4 spring onions, finely chopped

2 garlic cloves, finely chopped

300ml (½ pint) hot chicken stock (from a cube is fine)

50g (2oz) fresh white crabmeat, thawed if frozen

a little sesame oil

salt and freshly ground black pepper

Heat a griddle pan until hot and cook the corn on the cob for 3–4 minutes until the kernels are lightly toasted, turning regularly. Using a sharp knife, cut the toasted sweetcorn kernels off the cob.

Meanwhile, heat the oil in a pan and sauté the spring onions and garlic for 2 minutes until softened but not coloured. Pour the stock into the pan and bring to the boil, then add the toasted corn and simmer for 4–5 minutes until the sweetcorn is tender.

Stir the crabmeat into the soup until just warmed through and season to taste. Ladle into warmed bowls and drizzle with a little sesame oil to serve.

PRAWN AND COCONUT BROTH

96

Very contemporary, easy to make, fragrant and delicious: the perfect soup. It's Thailand in a bowl.

Serves 2

1 tbsp sunflower oil

1 shallot, finely diced

1 mild red chilli, seeded and finely chopped

1 lemongrass stalk, outer leaves removed and core finely chopped

300ml (½ pint) hot chicken stock (from a cube is fine)

120ml (4fl oz) coconut milk

100g (4oz) raw, peeled tiger prawns, cleaned

1 baby pak choi, finely shredded

juice of ½ a lime

a small handful of torn fresh coriander leaves

wafer-thin lime slices, to garnish

Heat the oil in a large pan and gently fry the shallot, chilli and lemongrass for 1–2 minutes until fragrant.

Pour the stock and coconut milk into the pan and simmer for 2–3 minutes to allow the flavours to combine.

Add the prawns and pak choi to the coconut mixture and allow to just warm through. Add the lime juice and coriander leaves, stirring to combine.

Ladle the broth into warmed bowls and garnish with the lime slices to serve.

SWEET AND SOUR PEPPERS WITH GRILLED GOATS' CHEESE

97

The flavour of the goats' cheese determines the success of this dish. (See illustration, page 64.)

Serves 2

2 tbsp olive oil

1 small red onion, thinly sliced

1 red pepper, seeded and cut into batons

50g (2oz) raw chorizo sausage, skinned and diced

2 x 100g (4oz) individual soft-rinded goats' cheese

4 tbsp seasoned flour

1 tbsp caster sugar

1 tbsp balsamic vinegar

1 tbsp extra-virgin olive oil

2 tbsp chopped fresh flat-leaf parsley

salt and freshly ground black pepper

Heat 1 tablespoon of the olive oil in a pan. Add the onion, pepper and chorizo and sauté for 3–4 minutes until tender but without colouring. Season to taste.

Meanwhile, heat a frying pan with the remaining tablespoon of olive oil. Cut each goats' cheese in half horizontally and coat in the flour, shaking off any excess. Add to the heated pan and cook for 2–3 minutes on each side until heated through and lightly golden.

Sprinkle the sugar into the pepper mixture, add the balsamic vinegar, then allow to reduce for another 2–3 minutes.

Remove the sweet and sour peppers from the heat, divide between plates and drizzle over the extra-virgin olive oil. When the goats' cheese is ready, arrange alongside or on top, scatter over the parsley and serve.

CRAB BITES WITH MANGO SALSA

98

For a healthier option you could bake these crab bites in a preheated oven at 200°C/400°F/gas 6, for 10–12 minutes, turning half-way through, until crisp golden brown.

Serves 4

2 thick slices white bread, crusts removed (about 100g/4oz in total)

1 x 175g (6oz) tin of white crabmeat, drained

1 egg yolk

2 tbsp chopped mixed fresh coriander and flat-leaf parsley

4 spring onions, finely shredded

1 large mild red chilli, seeded and finely chopped

1 small ripe mango, peeled, stoned and diced

juice of 1 large lime

sunflower oil, for shallow-frying

salt and freshly ground black pepper

lightly dressed spinach, rocket and watercress salad, to serve

Place the bread in a shallow dish, cover with water and leave to soak for about 10 seconds, then squeeze out the excess water. Place in a food-processor and add the crabmeat, egg yolk, coriander and parsley, and half of the spring onions and chilli. Season to taste and pulse until just blended.

To make the mango salsa, place the mango in a bowl and add the remaining spring onions and chilli. Stir in the lime juice and season to taste. Set aside at room temperature to allow the flavours to develop.

Heat a frying pan with about 5mm (¼ in) of oil. Shallow-fry 12 equal-sized spoonfuls of the crab mixture for 2–3 minutes on each side until puffed up and golden brown – you may have to do this in batches depending on the size of your pan. Drain on kitchen paper. Arrange the crab cakes on serving plates with the mango salsa. Add a small mound of the spinach, rocket and watercress salad and serve at once.

TOMATO TART WITH BASIL OIL

A very simple tart, eaten with a fresh-tasting basil oil. Try to use mozzarella made from buffalo milk. It's creamier and much richer than the cow's milk version, which can be rubbery and bland.

Serves 2

175g (6oz) sheet of ready-rolled puff pastry, thawed if frozen

1 egg yolk, lightly beaten

6 mini mozzarella balls, sliced (buffalo, if possible)

a handful of small fresh basil leaves

8 small cherry tomatoes, halved

a little olive oil

FOR THE BASIL OIL

juice of 1 lemon

4 tbsp extra-virgin olive oil

1 garlic clove, roughly chopped

a good handful of fresh basil leaves

salt and freshly ground black pepper

Preheat the oven to 220°C/425°F/gas 7. Cut the pastry into two 10cm (4in) circles and place on a large baking sheet. Brush with the egg yolk and prick all over with a fork.

Scatter the mozzarella balls, basil leaves and cherry tomatoes on top. Season to taste and add a drizzle of olive oil to the basil leaves to prevent them from burning. Bake for 8–9 minutes until the pastry is crisp and golden.

To make the basil oil, place the lemon juice, olive oil, garlic and basil in a mini food-processor and blend until smooth. Season to taste.

When the tarts are cooked, transfer to warmed plates and drizzle over the basil oil to serve.

GRIDDLED TOMATOES, ARTICHOKES AND PARMESAN CRISPS

This simple starter is a masterpiece – everyone will be blown away, as long as you use good-quality ingredients.

Serves 2

100g (4oz) piece of Parmesan

3 small ripe plum tomatoes

a good pinch of caster sugar

a pinch of chilli powder

olive oil, for cooking

100g (4oz) artichoke hearts preserved in olive oil, drained and halved

2 tbsp chopped fresh flat-leaf parsley

salt and freshly ground black pepper

Preheat the oven to 220°C/425°F/gas 7 and heat a griddle pan until very hot. Finely grate the Parmesan and arrange six small piles on a non-stick baking sheet, well spaced apart. Bake for 5–6 minutes until crisp and golden. Remove from the oven and leave to cool.

Meanwhile, cut the plum tomatoes in half and sprinkle over the sugar and chilli powder. Drizzle the heated griddle pan with a little oil and add the tomatoes, cut-side down. Cook for 2–3 minutes until nicely marked, then turn over and cook for another 1–2 minutes until well heated through.

Arrange the griddled tomatoes on plates with the artichoke hearts and season to taste. Scatter over the parsley and then pile up the Parmesan crisps to the side to serve.

RED PEPPER AND COURGETTE TORTILLA

For a more substantial meal, scatter curds of creamy goats' cheese into the tortilla and serve with a tumble of Parma ham on top of each tortilla wedge and dressed salad leaves to the side.

Serves 2–4

1 tbsp olive oil

4 spring onions, finely chopped

1 romero red pepper, seeded and thinly sliced

1 small courgette, thinly sliced on the diagonal

1 x 400g (14oz) tin cooked baby new potatoes, drained and sliced

½ tsp fresh thyme leaves

2 tbsp shredded fresh basil

6 eggs

2 tbsp freshly grated Parmesan

salt and freshly ground black pepper

Preheat the grill to high and heat the oil in a non-stick frying pan. Add the spring onions, red pepper, courgette and potatoes and sauté for 2–3 minutes until the pepper has softened and the potatoes are heated through. Stir in the thyme and basil, then season to taste and cook for another minute.

Meanwhile, lightly beat the eggs in a bowl with a good pinch of seasoning. Add to the pepper mixture and cook for another few minutes, stirring very gently until the eggs begin to set. Spread the mixture out evenly over the pan and press down very gently with a fish slice until the bottom of the tortilla is set.

Sprinkle over the Parmesan and place the tortilla directly under the grill for 1–2 minutes until glazed and slightly puffed. Turn out onto a warm plate and cut into wedges to serve.

HUMMUS WITH GRIDDLED APRICOT FLATBREAD

These flatbreads take no time at all to prepare and are just as good as any you will have ever tasted.

Serves 2

1 tbsp sesame seeds

1 x 400g (14oz) tin of chickpeas, drained and rinsed

1 small garlic clove, crushed

2 tbsp freshly squeezed lemon juice

1 tbsp chopped fresh coriander

100–120ml (3½– 4fl oz) olive oil, plus extra to serve

FOR THE GRIDDLED APRICOT FLATBREAD

4 spring onions, finely chopped

½ tsp medium curry powder

100g (4oz) plain flour

1 tsp baking powder

finely grated rind of 1 lemon

4 ready-to-eat dried apricots, finely chopped

olive oil, for drizzling

salt and freshly ground black pepper

To make the flatbread, heat a large, flat griddle pan. Mix together the spring onions, curry powder, flour, baking powder, lemon rind and apricots in a large bowl. Season to taste. Make a well in the centre and gradually add about 4 tablespoons of water to make a soft dough.

Turn the dough out onto a lightly floured surface and knead gently until rounded and smooth. Cut into 2 pieces and roll each one out into an oval shape, then drizzle with a little olive oil. Add to the heated griddle pan and cook for 2–3 minutes on each side until cooked through and lightly golden, drizzling the other side with a little more olive oil if necessary.

Meanwhile, to make the hummus, toast the sesame seeds in a small frying pan, then tip into a food-processor. Add the chickpeas, garlic, lemon juice and coriander and whizz until smooth. With the machine still running, gradually add enough olive oil to make a smooth creamy dip. Season to taste and spoon into a bowl. Drizzle with a little more olive oil and set on a large plate. When the flatbreads are cooked, cut them into fingers and pile up alongside the hummus to serve.

FLATBREAD PIZZA

If you think making a pizza from scratch takes loads of time and effort
kneading and tossing, then have a go at this super-quick version.

Serves 1–2

150g (5oz) self-raising flour, plus extra for dusting

a pinch of salt

2 tbsp olive oil, plus extra for drizzling

1 small green pepper, seeded and thinly sliced

50g (2oz) tiny cherry tomatoes, halved

1 x 100g (4oz) ball of buffalo mozzarella, roughly torn into pieces

a handful of small basil leaves

Preheat the oven to 220°C/425°F/gas 7 and heat a large ovenproof frying pan. Place the flour in a bowl with a pinch of salt. Make a well in the centre and whisk in about 4 tablespoons of water until the mixture just binds together. Drizzle in the olive oil and work the ingredients together with your hands to make a soft dough.

On a lightly floured work surface, roll out the dough into a circle that will fit the bottom of the frying pan comfortably. Add to the heated frying pan and, while the underneath is cooking, use a blowtorch to cook the top for 2 minutes until puffed up.

Then flip the base over and continue to cook for another 1–2 minutes, while you scatter the green pepper and cherry tomatoes on top. Interweave with the mozzarella and finish with a drizzle of olive oil. Transfer to the oven and bake for 5 minutes or so until the mozzarella has melted and the base is cooked through.

Remove the pizza from the oven. Transfer to a large, flat plate, scatter over the basil leaves and cut into slices to serve.

PANZANELLA

This is a variation on a very old recipe that has its origins in Tuscany, where it was traditional to soak the bread in pure seawater to give a distinctive taste of the sea.

Serves 2

¼ loaf rustic white bread (about 100g/4oz in total)

1–2 tbsp olive oil

75g (3oz) pitted black olives

75g (3oz) cherry tomatoes, halved

25g (1oz) fresh flat-leaf parsley leaves

a handful of pecorino shavings

FOR THE DRESSING

25g (1oz) cherry tomatoes

1 tsp tomato purée

1 tbsp red wine vinegar

3 tbsp extra-virgin olive oil

salt and freshly ground black pepper

Preheat the oven to 200°C/400°F/gas 6. Cut the bread into pieces roughly 1cm (½ in) across. Place in a baking tin and drizzle with enough of the olive oil to barely coat. Bake for about 8 minutes until crisp and golden brown, tossing occasionally for even cooking.

To make the dressing, place the cherry tomatoes in a mini food-processor with the tomato purée, vinegar and olive oil. Blitz to a purée and season to taste. Pour into a small jug and set aside.

Place the olives, cherry tomatoes and parsley in a large bowl. Add the croûtons, tossing to combine, then drizzle in enough dressing to coat the salad evenly. Divide between plates and scatter over the pecorino shavings to serve.

PESTO SPAGHETTI WITH ANCHOVIES AND SUN-DRIED TOMATOES

This quick and delicious pasta dish is a great store-cupboard standby. Basil is the only fresh ingredient you need.

Serves 2

225g (8oz) spaghetti

1 x 50g (2oz) tin of anchovies in olive oil, drained

2 garlic cloves, peeled

a good handful of fresh basil leaves

2 tsp sesame oil

4 tbsp olive oil

100g (4oz) sun-dried tomatoes preserved in oil, drained

100g (4oz) black olives

salt and freshly ground black pepper

freshly grated Parmesan, to serve

Plunge the spaghetti into a large pan of boiling salted water and cook for 8 minutes or according to the packet instructions.

Meanwhile, make the pesto. Place 2 anchovies in a mini food-processor with the garlic, basil and sesame and olive oils. Blend until smooth and season with black pepper.

Finely chop the remaining anchovies and place in a large bowl. Cut the sun-dried tomatoes into thin strips and add to the bowl, along with the olives. Stir in the pesto.

Drain the spaghetti and then add to the bowl with the anchovy mixture, stirring to combine. Divide between warmed bowls and sprinkle Parmesan on top to serve.

GRIDDLED LIME AND CHILLI PRAWNS

Tiger prawns are full of flavour, even if frozen. They cook in no time on a griddle pan and are perfect with a mango salsa, bursting with freshness.

Serves 2

10 large, raw tiger prawns, peeled but tails intact, thawed if frozen

juice of 1 lime

a pinch of dried crushed chillies

a little olive oil

FOR THE MANGO SALSA

3 small yellow peppers

1 small mango

4 spring onions, finely chopped

2 tbsp chopped mixed fresh herbs (such as flat-leaf parsley, mint and coriander)

finely grated rind and juice of 1 lime

1 tbsp olive oil

sea salt

To make the salsa, scorch the skins of the peppers with a blowtorch and, when cool enough to handle, peel off the skins, cut the peppers in half, remove the seeds and dice the flesh. Place in a bowl. Peel the mango and dice the flesh, discarding the stone. Add to the peppers with the spring onions, herbs, lime rind and juice, olive oil and a pinch of salt. Stir to combine and set aside to allow the flavours to develop.

Heat a griddle pan until searing hot. Butterfly the prawns by splitting each one down the centre, keeping the tails intact. Place in a bowl and add the lime juice and dried chillies, tossing to coat. Drizzle a thin film of olive oil onto the griddle pan and add the prawns. Cook for 20–30 seconds on each side until lightly charred but still tender. Arrange on plates with the mango salsa alongside to serve.

CHICKEN AND PRAWN STIR FRY

Flavours of ginger, lemongrass, soy and coriander are all the rage, and are a wonderful combination for this oriental-style dish of stir-fried chicken and prawns with noodles.

Serves 4

4 garlic cloves, peeled

2 tsp ginger purée

1 tsp dried lemongrass

4 tbsp olive oil

1 courgette, thinly sliced

1 red pepper, seeded and chopped

5 spring onions, sliced on the diagonal

100g (4oz) skinless chicken breasts, cut into 1cm (½ in) strips

3 eggs

25g (1oz) butter

200g (7oz) rice noodles

600ml (1 pint) boiling water

1 tbsp sunflower oil

250g (9oz) raw, peeled tiger prawns, cleaned

4 tsp fish sauce

1 tbsp soy sauce

2 tbsp chopped fresh coriander and chives

salt and freshly ground black pepper

fresh coriander leaves, to garnish

Pound the garlic in a pestle and mortar to form a paste. Stir in the ginger purée and lemongrass.

Heat 3 tablespoons of the olive oil in a wok or large frying pan and stir-fry the courgette, red pepper and spring onions for 2 minutes. Add the chicken strips and cook for 4–5 minutes until cooked through. Remove from the heat and set aside.

Beat the eggs with a little seasoning. Melt half the butter in a large frying pan, pour in half the beaten eggs, swirl around the pan and cook for 2–3 minutes on each side. Repeat to make a second omelette, roll and cut into 5mm (¼ in) thick slices.

Cover the noodles with boiling water. Rest for for 4–5 minutes.

Heat the sunflower oil in the pan used for the omelettes and cook the prawns for 30 seconds until pink. Add 2 teaspoons of the fish sauce and cook for 20 seconds or so until just cooked.

Heat the remaining olive oil in a clean wok and stir-fry the garlic paste mixture for 1 minute. Drain the noodles and add to the wok with the remaining fish sauce and the soy sauce. Stir in the prawns, chicken and vegetables, the omelette slices, chopped coriander and chives and stir-fry for 1–2 minutes until piping hot. Serve in a large bowl garnished with the coriander leaves.

CHORIZO AND ARTICHOKE PILAFF

For cooking, raw chorizo is best and it just needs to be sautéed to bring out the wonderful smoky flavours. This dish would be really good with a grilled cod fillet or some pan-fried monkfish.

Serves 4

1 tbsp olive oil

a knob of unsalted butter

1 small onion, finely chopped

100g (4oz) raw chorizo sausage, thinly sliced

225g (8oz) long-grain rice

100ml (3½ fl oz) dry white wine

400ml (14fl oz) chicken stock

100g (4oz) artichoke hearts preserved in olive oil, drained and roughly chopped

4 tbsp chopped fresh flat-leaf parsley

salt and freshly ground black pepper

Heat the oil and butter in a heavy-based pan with a tight-fitting lid. Add the onion and sauté for about 2 minutes until softened, stirring occasionally. Add the chorizo and rice and cook for 2 minutes, stirring to ensure the chorizo has begun to release its oil and all the rice grains are well coated.

Pour the wine into the pan and bring to a simmer, then allow it to bubble down for 1 minute. Pour in the stock, season generously and bring to the boil, then reduce the heat, cover and simmer for 10–12 minutes or until the rice is cooked through and completely tender. Fold in the artichoke hearts and allow to warm through. Season to taste and carefully stir in the parsley. Tip into a warmed serving dish and serve at once.

SPICY PINTO BEAN CAKE WITH WARM ROASTED PEPPER SALSA

These tasty bean burgers are miles ahead of any of the shop-bought ones that are now so readily available.

Serves 2

¼ tsp each cumin seeds, dried oregano and dried chilli flakes

1 x 400g (14oz) tin of pinto beans, drained and rinsed

50g (2oz) plain flour, plus extra for dusting

1 egg white

2 tbsp olive oil

crème fraîche or thick Greek yoghurt, to serve

FOR THE SALSA

1 tbsp olive oil

1 red pepper, seeded and finely diced

4 spring onions, thinly sliced

2 ripe tomatoes, seeded and chopped

a squeeze of fresh lemon juice

2 tbsp chopped fresh coriander, plus extra sprigs to garnish

salt and freshly ground black pepper

Heat a small frying pan over a low heat and dry-fry the cumin seeds, oregano and chilli flakes for 30 seconds, tossing occasionally, until aromatic.

Place the beans in a food-processor with the flour and egg white, then pulse until roughly blended. Add the toasted spices and blend briefly to combine – the mixture should still have some texture left and not be completely smooth.

Heat 2 small frying pans. Season the bean mixture generously, tip onto a lightly floured board and shape into 2 patties about 2½ cm (1in) thick. Add 1 tablespoon of oil to each pan and fry the cakes for 2–3 minutes on each side, until cooked through.

Meanwhile, make the salsa. Heat the olive oil in a small pan. Add the pepper and sauté for about 2–3 minutes until just beginning to soften. Add the spring onions and cook for another 2 minutes, stirring, then add the tomatoes, lemon juice and fresh coriander, and continue to cook for 1 minute to warm through. Season.

Arrange the pinto bean cakes on warmed serving plates and spoon over the salsa. Using 2 dessertspoons that have been briefly dipped in boiling water, make quenelles of crème fraîche or Greek yoghurt and arrange on top. Garnish with coriander sprigs and serve immediately.

RICOTTA AND SPINACH STUFFED MUSHROOMS

118

Spinach and ricotta complement each other very well, and they make a delicious filling for these giant mushrooms.

Serves 2

4 large open-cap mushrooms

40g (1½ oz) butter

3 garlic cloves, chopped

1 onion, finely chopped

2 bay leaves

½ tsp dried oregano

½ tsp dried thyme

1 tsp chopped fresh rosemary

3 tbsp dry white wine

1 x 400g (14oz) tin of chopped tomatoes

1 tbsp chopped fresh parsley

1 tbsp chopped fresh basil

150g (5oz) freshly grated Cheshire cheese

225g (8oz) young spinach leaves

225g (8oz) ricotta cheese

salt and freshly ground black pepper

a few basil leaves, to garnish

Preheat the oven to 200°C/400°F/gas 6.

Peel the mushrooms and remove the stalks. Place the caps in a roasting tin; chop the stalks finely and set aside. Divide 25g (1oz) of the butter between the mushroom caps, season with salt and pepper and put in the oven for 5 minutes.

Heat the remaining butter in a frying pan, add the garlic, onion, bay leaves, dried herbs and rosemary and cook gently for about 5 minutes, until the onion is softened. Remove half this mixture from the pan and set aside. Add the chopped mushroom stalks, white wine and tinned tomatoes to the pan and simmer for about 10 minutes, until slightly thickened. Stir in the parsley and basil and cook for a further 3–4 minutes, then add half the grated cheese and season with pepper to taste.

Wash the spinach, discarding any large stalks, then place it in a pan with only the water clinging to the leaves and cook for about 2 minutes, until just wilted. Leave until cool enough to handle and then squeeze out as much liquid as you can. Blend the spinach, ricotta and reserved onion mixture in a food-processor until smooth, then season to taste. Spoon onto the mushroom caps and return them to the oven for 5–10 minutes to heat through.

Sprinkle with the remaining cheese and place under a hot grill until golden and bubbling.

To serve, pour the tomato and herb sauce onto 2 warmed serving plates, place the mushrooms on top and garnish with the basil leaves.

TOMATO SALAD WITH ROASTED RED PEPPERS

This great-looking salad would be perfect as a meal on its own with a chunk of crusty bread, or as part of a barbecue spread.

Serves 2

2 ripe beef tomatoes, thinly sliced

100g (4oz) roasted red peppers from a jar, drained with 2 tbsp of the oil reserved

50g (2oz) pitted black olives

a handful of fresh basil leaves, shredded

½ tsp balsamic vinegar

salt and freshly ground black pepper

Arrange the beef tomatoes in a single layer on the base of a large plate.

Mix together the roasted red peppers, olives and basil in a bowl and then scatter on top of the tomatoes. Drizzle the roasted red pepper oil on top with the balsamic vinegar. Add a good grinding of pepper and a sprinkling of salt. Serve at once.

GRIDDLED POLENTA WITH ROASTED PEPPER AND BASIL DRESSING

As with all simple dishes the quality of ingredients is of paramount importance, so try to get Italian ready-made polenta – it's by far the best. Serve with a chargrilled chicken fillet or piece of fish.

Serves 2

1 x 225g (8oz) roll of ready-made polenta

1 tbsp olive oil

1 roasted red pepper, drained (from a jar)

2 tbsp extra-virgin olive oil

finely grated rind of 1 lemon

a small handful of fresh basil leaves, shredded

1 garlic clove, crushed

salt and freshly ground black pepper

Heat a large griddle pan until very hot. Cut the polenta into 1cm (½ in) slices – you'll need about 6 in total. Brush on both sides with the olive oil and arrange on the heated griddle pan. Cook for 2–3 minutes on each side until nicely marked and heated through.

Meanwhile, make the roasted pepper and basil dressing. Cut the pepper into strips, discarding any seeds, then finely dice. Place in a bowl with the extra-virgin olive oil, lemon rind, basil and garlic. Season to taste and stir until well combined.

Divide the griddled polenta between warmed plates and spoon over the dressing to serve.

GREEK SALAD WITH BAKED FETA CHEESE

The baked feta topping gives this refreshing and healthy Greek salad a twist. It's delicious served on its own with plenty of crusty bread to mop up all the fantastic juices. Alternatively, try the salad piled on to some charred bread, or serve as part of an antipasto platter.

Serves 2

150g (5oz) feta cheese, halved

2 garlic cloves, finely chopped

2 tsp fresh thyme leaves

5 tbsp extra-virgin olive oil

juice of ½ lemon

1 tbsp chopped fresh flat-leaf parsley

2 ripe tomatoes, seeded and chopped

1 small red onion, chopped

100g (4oz) pitted black olives

1 mini cucumber, roughly chopped

salt and freshly ground black pepper

Preheat the oven to 220°C/425°F/gas 7. Place the 2 pieces of feta side by side in a shallow ovenproof dish. Sprinkle over the garlic and thyme, then season with black pepper. Drizzle over 2 tablespoons of the oil and bake for 6–8 minutes until heated through and slightly bubbling.

To make the dressing, place the remaining oil in a bowl and whisk in the lemon juice and parsley. Season to taste. Place the tomatoes, onion, olives and cucumber in the bowl and gently turn in the dressing. Arrange on serving plates and spoon over the baked feta cheese. Serve at once.

BABA GANOUSH

Baba Ganoush is a Middle-Eastern accompaniment that's delicious served with pitta bread, hummus and olives.

Serves 2

3 tbsp olive oil, plus extra for shallow-frying

1 large aubergine, halved and flesh scored in a criss-cross pattern

1 small garlic clove, crushed

a good squeeze of lemon juice

6 fresh mint leaves

1 tbsp light tahini paste

5 walnut halves

salt and freshly ground black pepper

Heat 1cm (½ in) of olive oil in a large frying pan. Add the aubergine halves to the pan and cook, flesh-side down, for 5 minutes, then turn them over and cook for 2 minutes until softened and tender. Remove from the pan and leave to cool.

Peel and discard the aubergine skin. Roughly chop the aubergine flesh and place in a food-processor with the garlic, lemon juice, mint, tahini and walnuts. Season and add 3 tablespoons of oil, then whizz for about 20 seconds to make a rough purée.

Divide between small dishes to serve.

LEMON COUSCOUS

Perfect as an accompaniment to fish or as part of a barbecue spread. It's great hot or cold and can be made 24 hours in advance. (See illustration, page 6.)

Serves 2

120ml (4fl oz) hot chicken stock

100g (4oz) couscous

finely grated rind and juice of ½ lemon

2 tbsp extra-virgin olive oil

1 baby yellow pepper

1 baby fennel

1 shallot

2 tbsp chopped mixed fresh flat-leaf parsley and coriander

salt and freshly ground black pepper

2 lemon wedges, to garnish

Heat the stock in a small pan until boiling. Place the couscous in a large heatproof bowl with the lemon juice and olive oil, stirring to combine.

Pour over the stock, then stir well, cover and leave to stand for 5 minutes.

Meanwhile, cut the yellow pepper in half, remove the seeds and finely dice. Finely dice the baby fennel and the shallot and set aside until needed.

Separate the couscous grains with a fork. Season and place in a pan to reheat, stirring continuously with a fork. Remove from the heat and fold in the lemon rind, herbs, yellow pepper, fennel and shallot, then season to taste. Spoon onto a platter and garnish with lemon wedges to serve.

EGG-FRIED RICE

To prevent leftover rice from sticking together in one solid mass, stir in a little sunflower oil before refrigerating it.

Serves 2

2 tsp sunflower oil

1 x 250g (9oz) packet of cooked white rice (or use leftover rice)

4 spring onions, finely chopped

1 mild green chilli, seeded and finely chopped

1 tbsp chopped fresh coriander

1 egg, beaten

salt and freshly ground black pepper

1 tsp snipped fresh chives, to garnish

dark soy sauce, to serve

Heat a wok until very hot. Add the oil, swirling it up the sides, then tip the rice into the wok and stir-fry for 2–3 minutes until piping hot. Add the spring onions, chilli and coriander, then season to taste, tossing to combine all the ingredients.

Make a small well in the middle of the rice, quickly pour in the beaten egg, then continue to stir for 30 seconds until the egg is lightly scrambled. Gently fold the egg into the rice and divide among warmed bowls or plates. Garnish with the chives and serve at once, with dark soy sauce to hand around.

PEA AND ONION BHAJIS

Onion bhajis are made using gram (chickpea) flour but this recipe uses regular self-raising flour coloured with turmeric and paprika. These are delicious served on their own with a squeeze of lime.

Serves 4

sunflower oil, for deep-frying

¼ tsp each cumin seeds, dried chilli flakes and cracked black pepper

100g (4oz) self-raising flour

1 tsp ground turmeric

½ tsp each ground paprika and salt

1 bunch of spring onions, shredded (about 6 in total)

100g (4oz) frozen peas, thawed

1 lime, cut into wedges, to garnish

selection of chutneys and pickles, to serve (optional)

Preheat a deep-fat fryer or fill a deep-sided pan one-third full with sunflower oil and heat to 190°C/375°F. Heat a small frying pan and dry-fry the cumin seeds, chilli flakes and pepper for 30 seconds until aromatic.

Place the flour in a bowl with the turmeric, paprika and salt, then tip in the toasted spices. Stir to combine, then mix in about 150ml (¼ pint) of cold water to make a smooth, thick batter. Stir in the spring onions and peas until well coated.

Carefully drop the mixture into the hot oil using 2 tablespoons – one to scoop up the batter and the other to push it into the oil; you may have to do this in batches. Deep-fry for 4–5 minutes until crisp and golden brown, turning occasionally with tongs. Drain on kitchen paper, then pile onto a warmed serving platter. Serve immediately with the lime wedges and selection of chutneys and pickles, if liked.

PAD THAI

Who could ever tire of Pad Thai? – It is one of the world's great dishes. Use whatever ingredients you have to hand, but the basic ingredients are always the same.

Serves 2

100g (4oz) soba noodles

2 tsp sesame seeds

2 tbsp sunflower oil

4 spring onions, finely chopped

2 garlic cloves, finely chopped

2½ cm (1in) piece of fresh root ginger, peeled and finely chopped

2 tbsp dark soy sauce

juice of ½ lime

1 baby pak choi, shredded

1 egg, beaten

Bring a large pan of water to the boil. Add the noodles, stir until the water boils and cook for 4 minutes, or until tender but firm to the bite. Drain, rinse with boiling water and drain again.

Heat a wok until very hot. Toast the sesame seeds in a seperate dry frying pan, tossing occasionally; tip onto a plate to cool. Add the oil to the heated wok and swirl up the sides, then add the spring onions, garlic and ginger and stir-fry for 20 seconds. Tip in the drained soba noodles and drizzle over the soy sauce and lime juice, then stir-fry for 1–2 minutes until heated through.

Add the pak choi and stir-fry for a minute or so until wilted. Make a small well in the middle of the noodle mixture, pour in the beaten egg, then stir for 1 minute until the egg is lightly scrambled. Fold into the noodles and serve in warmed dishes.

SUMMER VEGETABLE STACK WITH CHUNKY CHUTNEY

This is a lovely summery dish that you can make with a variety of seasonal vegetables such as courgettes and asparagus.

Serves 2

1 aubergine, cut lengthways into 5mm (½ in) thick slices

6 tbsp olive oil

1 bunch of spring onions, thinly sliced (green and white parts separated)

3 yellow tomatoes, diced

1½ tbsp clear honey

grated rind and juice of ½ lime

2 tbsp snipped fresh chives

6 tbsp sunflower oil

1 red pepper

1 yellow pepper

1 tsp ground coriander

juice of 1 lime

1 tbsp chopped fresh coriander

2 courgettes, cut lengthways into 5mm (¼ in) thick slices

a good squeeze of lemon juice

salt and freshly ground black pepper

Sprinkle the aubergine with salt, set aside for 10 minutes, then rinse and pat dry. Heat 1 tablespoon of the oil in a small pan and cook the white part of the spring onions for 1 minute. Add the lime rind and juice, tomatoes, 1 tablespoon of honey and cook for 5–6 minutes until soft. Season. Add 1 tablespoon of chives.

Preheat the grill. Heat 5 tablespoons of sunflower oil in a large frying pan and cook the aubergine slices for 2–3 minutes on each side until tender and golden brown.

Grill the peppers for 8–10 minutes, turning frequently until the skin is blistered. Cover with a clean tea towel and leave to cool for 2 minutes. Skin, seed and quarter the peppers. Finely dice 1 red and 1 yellow pepper quarter; set the whole pieces aside.

Heat the remaining olive oil in a small pan and add the reserved green part of the spring onions, the ground coriander, lime juice, fresh coriander and diced peppers. Cook gently for 5 minutes, then stir in the remaining honey and chives and season to taste.

Heat the remaining sunflower oil in a large frying pan and cook the courgette slices for 1 minute on each side until golden. Squeeze in the lemon juice and season to taste. To serve, fold the aubergine and courgette slices in half widthways and layer up with the peppers, placing a teaspoon of chutney between each layer. Pour around the sauce.

CHARGRILLED SALMON WITH COUSCOUS SALAD AND SAUCE VIERGE

This dish is a great dinner-party staple. Most of the work can be done well in advance and it looks and tastes fantastic.

Serves 2

1 red and 1 yellow pepper, seeded and cut into eighths

1 courgette, cut into slices on the diagonal

85ml (3fl oz) extra-virgin olive oil, plus extra for brushing

2 spring onions, finely chopped

1 garlic clove, lightly crushed

150ml (¼ pint) vegetable stock

100g (4oz) couscous

4 tbsp roughly chopped fresh basil

juice of 1 lemon

2 x 150g (5oz) salmon fillets

2 ripe plum tomatoes, seeded and chopped

sea salt and freshly ground black pepper

2 lemon wedges, to serve

Brush the pepper and courgette with olive oil and chargrill in a searing hot griddle pan for 5 minutes on each side. Place in a shallow dish, season generously and set aside.

In a small pan over a gentle heat, warm through the spring onions and garlic for 5 minutes in 4 tablespoons of olive oil until the sauce is hot, but not boiling – soften, but don't colour them. Heat the stock and pour over the couscous in a heatproof bowl. Cover with cling film and set aside for 5 minutes, then remove the cling film and fluff up the grains with a fork. Dice the chargrilled vegetables, stir into the couscous with half the basil, the remaining olive oil and half the lemon juice. Season to taste.

Season the salmon fillets and chargrill for 2–3 minutes on each side. To finish the sauce, lift out the garlic and discard, then stir in the remaining basil and lemon juice with the tomatoes. Warm through. Serve on warm plates, with lemon wedges on the side.

CAJUN-STYLE SALMON WITH HOT RELISH AND COURGETTE CHIPS

On the barbecue this dish would taste wonderful, slightly blackened but still moist and tender in the centre – delicious.

Serves 2

sunflower oil, for deep-frying

1 tsp each ground cumin, coriander, mixed spice and dried oregano

2 x 100g (4oz) salmon fillets, scaled and boned

2 tbsp olive oil

1 red onion, finely diced

10 cherry tomatoes, finely diced

1 tsp dried chilli flakes

1 tbsp dry white wine

juice of 1 lime

2 tsp caster sugar

2 tbsp chopped fresh coriander

2 large courgettes, trimmed, halved and cut into sticks

50g (2oz) seasoned flour

2 eggs

salt and freshly ground black pepper

thick soured cream, to garnish

Preheat a deep-fat fryer or a deep-sided pan one-third full of sunflower oil to 190°C/375°F. Preheat a non-stick, heavy-based frying pan. Mix the spices and oregano in a shallow dish. Season and use to coat the flesh-side of each salmon fillet. Add 1 tablespoon of the oil to the heated frying pan and then add the salmon fillets, skin-side down. Cook for 3–4 minutes until the skin is crisp and golden, then turn over and cook for another couple of minutes until lightly seared.

Heat the remaining olive oil in a frying pan. Sauté the onions for 2–3 minutes until soft but not coloured, stirring occasionally. Add the tomatoes and chilli flakes and simmer for 2 minutes. Sprinkle over the wine, lime juice and sugar, combine and allow the sugar to melt. Tip in the coriander, season and keep warm.

To prepare the courgette chips, first place the flour in one bowl and beat the eggs with a little seasoning in another. Dip the courgette sticks into the egg and then toss in the flour to coat, shaking off any excess. Deep-fry for 2–3 minutes or until crisp and golden brown – you may have to do this in batches. Drain well on kitchen paper and arrange in the middle of warmed serving plates. Top each one with a salmon fillet, garnish with a spoonful of soured cream and spoon around the hot relish.

BACON, SAGE AND CHICKEN KEBABS WITH AVOCADO SALSA

You'll need 4 x 15cm (6in) metal or bamboo skewers that have been soaked in water for at least 30 minutes because the kebabs get finished in the oven. They would also work on the barbecue.

Serves 2

2 x 200g (7oz) boneless, skinless chicken breasts, cut into 24 even-sized cubes

8 fresh sage leaves

4 rindless streaky bacon rashers, each cut into 3 pieces

1 tbsp olive oil

4 soft flour tortillas

shredded Little Gem lettuce and soured cream, to serve

FOR THE SALSA

1 firm, ripe avocado, peeled, stoned and finely diced

4 spring onions, finely chopped

2 tbsp chopped mixed fresh flat-leaf parsley and mint

2 tbsp olive oil

juice of 1 lime

a pinch of chilli powder

salt and freshly ground black pepper

Preheat the oven to 220°C/425°F/gas 7 and heat a griddle pan over a medium heat until smoking hot. Thread the chicken cubes onto four 15cm (6in) metal or soaked bamboo skewers, alternating them with sage leaves and pieces of bacon.

Drizzle each kebab with a little oil, then place on the griddle pan and chargrill for 1–2 minutes on each side until nicely marked. Transfer to a small baking sheet and bake for 10–12 minutes or until the chicken is just tender and cooked through.

Place all the salsa ingredients in a bowl and combine. Season to taste, cover with cling film and set aside at room temperature to allow the flavours to develop – just don't try to make this too far in advance or the avocado is in danger of going black.

Reheat the griddle pan. Add a tortilla and heat for 30 seconds, turning once, until soft and pliable. Repeat with the remaining tortillas and stack them up on a warmed plate. Arrange the skewers on a warmed platter and hand around the avocado salsa, warmed tortillas, shredded lettuce and soured cream.

TANDOORI CHICKEN SKEWERS WITH CUCUMBER SALAD

The tandoori chicken skewers contrast beautifully in both flavour and texture with the fresh, crispy cucumber salad.

Serves 2

2 garlic cloves, crushed

½ tsp minced ginger from a jar

2 tsp medium tandoori paste

3 tbsp Greek yoghurt

1 lemon

225g (8oz) skinless, boneless chicken breast fillet, cut into 2½ cm (1in) cubes

½ cucumber, halved, seeded and thinly sliced

1 red chilli, seeded and finely chopped

a handful of fresh basil, roughly torn

a pinch of paprika

a pinch of salt

2 tbsp mango chutney, to glaze

lemon wedges and chapatis or naan bread, to serve (optional)

Mix together the garlic, ginger, tandoori paste and yoghurt in a non-metallic bowl. Add a good squeeze of lemon juice, then stir in the chicken and marinate for at least 5 minutes or up to 24 hours, covered, in the fridge.

To make the cucumber salad, place the cucumber, chilli and basil in a bowl. Squeeze over the remaining lemon juice and stir in the paprika and a little salt, to taste. Toss well to combine.

Preheat the grill to high. Arrange the chicken on four 15cm (6in) bamboo skewers, soaked in water for at least 30 minutes to prevent them burning, and grill for 2–3 minutes on each side until just tender. Brush with a little mango chutney and serve hot with the cucumber salad, lemon wedges, and chapatis or naan bread, if liked.

THAI CHICKEN SALAD WITH GLASS NOODLES

This salad is beautifully fragrant and perfect for a light supper.
Try adding a couple of handfuls of small, crisp salad leaves as a variation.

Serves 2

100g (4oz) rice vermicelli

1 small red onion, thinly sliced

1 large cooked chicken breast

a small bunch of fresh coriander

a handful of fresh mint leaves

½ small red pepper, seeded and cut into fine strips

4 tbsp roughly chopped peanuts

FOR THE DRESSING

1 tsp caster sugar

2 tbsp dark soy sauce

1 tbsp sweet chilli sauce

juice of 1 lime

4 tbsp sunflower oil

Place the rice vermicelli in a large bowl and cover with boiling water. Leave for about 5 minutes until softened, or follow packet instructions. Place the red onion in a bowl of iced water for 2–3 minutes; this will make the onion crisp and mellow out the flavour. Remove the skin from the chicken breast and strip the flesh from the bones before chopping finely. Set aside.

Dissolve the sugar in the soy sauce in a small bowl and then whisk in the sweet chilli sauce, lime juice and sunflower oil.

Drain both the vermicelli and red onion well and place in a large bowl. Tear the coriander and mint leaves away from the stalks and add to the bowl along with the red pepper.

Toss the dressing, chicken and salad gently with your hands to combine. Divide between plates, scatter over the peanuts and serve at once.

CRISPY CHICKEN TROPICANA

A superb, exotic-flavoured dish adding real interest to chicken.
It's worth making a double quantity of the pineapple salsa as any
leftovers will add zest to sandwiches, sausages and cold-cuts.

Serves 2

vegetable oil, for deep-frying

4 chicken thighs

400ml (14fl oz) water

1 chicken stock cube

225g (8oz) easy-cook rice

grated rind and juice of 1 orange

1 bunch of spring onions, finely chopped

1 red chilli, seeded and finely chopped

1 green pepper, seeded and chopped

1 x 220g (8oz) tin of pineapple chunks in natural juice, drained and roughly chopped

juice of 1 lime

2 tbsp cornflour

1 tsp ground mixed spice

2 fresh thyme sprigs

2 fresh basil leaves

salt and freshly ground black pepper

Preheat a deep-fat fryer or fill a deep-sided pan one-third full with vegetable oil and heat to 190°C/375°F. Discard the skin from the and cut the flesh away from the bone; reserve the bones and cut the flesh into 1cm (½ in) wide strips and set aside.

Bring the water, stock cube, chicken bones and rice to the boil in a large pan. Stir in the rind and half of the orange juice, the spring onions, chilli and green pepper. Cook for 10 minutes or according to the packet instructions, until tender. Season.

Stir together the pineapple and lime juice with the remaining spring onions, chilli, green pepper and orange juice. Season with salt and pepper, then transfer to a serving bowl.

In a small bowl, mix together the cornflour and mixed spice. Coat the chicken strips in the spiced flour, shaking off any excess. Deep-fry in batches for 4–5 minutes until cooked through and golden brown. Drain on kitchen paper. Deep-fry the thyme sprigs and basil leaves for 30 seconds. Drain on kitchen paper.

Remove the chicken bones from the rice and discard. To serve, spoon the rice onto plates and arrange the fried chicken on top. Garnish with the deep-fried herbs and serve with the salsa.

CHARGRILLED CHICKEN WITH COUSCOUS AND HERB SALAD

This dish brings all the flavours of the Middle East right onto your plate.

Serves 2

2 skinless chicken breast fillets, thinly sliced

1 garlic clove, crushed

1 small hot red chilli, seeded and finely chopped

5 tbsp olive oil

1 lemon

175ml (6fl oz) hot chicken stock (from a cube is fine)

150g (5oz) couscous

1 small red onion, finely diced

1 small red pepper, seeded and very finely diced

a good handful of mixed fresh herbs, such as chives, flat-leaf parsley and basil leaves

a little balsamic vinegar

1 tbsp extra-virgin olive oil

salt and freshly ground black pepper

Place the chicken in a bowl with the garlic, chilli, 2 tablespoons of the olive oil and seasoning. Pare in the lemon rind and mix well to combine, then set aside to marinate.

Bring the stock to the boil in a small pan and then pour in the couscous in a thin, steady stream, mixing well until all the stock is absorbed. Season to taste and fold in the red onion and pepper. Cover, remove from the heat and leave for 3 minutes.

Heat a heavy-based frying pan until searing hot. Flash-fry the marinated chicken pieces for a few minutes until cooked through and lightly browned. Squeeze over the juice from half the lemon. Drain on kitchen paper. Remove the lid from the couscous, stir in the remaining olive oil and juice from the rest of the lemon.

Spoon the couscous into the centre of warmed plates and scatter the chicken over. Place all the herbs in a bowl and dress with a little balsamic vinegar and a dash of the extra-virgin olive oil. Finish with a pile of the herb salad on top, and drizzle the rest of the extra-virgin olive oil around the plates to serve.

CHICKEN CHIMICHANGAS

These chimichangas are simply deep-fried Mexican tortillas. They would be delicious served with guacamole and a hot tomato salsa.

Serves 2

sunflower oil, for deep-frying

2 tbsp olive oil

100g (4oz) skinless chicken breast fillets, thinly sliced

2 garlic cloves, finely chopped

½ tsp dried crushed chillies

6 pepperdew peppers, drained and sliced (from a jar)

4 baby courgettes, thinly sliced on the diagonal

2 tbsp roughly chopped fresh coriander

juice of 1 lime

2 large soft flour tortillas

1 Little Gem lettuce, shredded

4 tbsp soured cream

paprika, for dusting

salt and freshly ground black pepper

lime wedges, to serve

Preheat a deep-fat fryer or fill a deep-sided pan one-third full with oil and heat to 190°F/375°F. If you don't have a thermometer, the oil should be hot enough so that when a bread cube is added, it browns in 40 seconds.

Heat the olive oil in a frying pan and sauté the chicken, garlic and chillies for a few minutes over a high heat until lightly golden. Season to taste. Add the peppers and courgettes and continue to sauté for 2–3 minutes until tender. Stir in the coriander and lime juice, then remove from the heat.

Meanwhile, warm the tortillas in a hot, dry frying pan until soft and flexible. Spoon half of the chicken mixture into the centre of each tortilla and fold over the edges to form a neat parcel, then fix in place with wooden cocktail sticks.

Deep-fry the chimichangas for 2 minutes until golden brown, then drain well on kitchen paper and slice on the diagonal. Pile the shredded lettuce onto plates and arrange the chimichangas on top. Add a good dollop of soured cream to the side and dust with paprika. Garnish with lime wedges to serve.

TURKEY SALTIMBOCCA WITH HERB MASH AND BROAD BEANS

Turkey is not only extremely cheap to buy but also very low in fat, but it can lack in the flavour department, which is why this recipe works so well. For a perfect match, they're served with a garlic-infused, olive-oil mash and some marinated broad beans.

Serves 2

350g (12oz) potatoes, roughly chopped

100g (4oz) frozen broad beans

120ml (4fl oz) extra-virgin olive oil

2 tbsp roughly chopped fresh flat-leaf parsley, plus extra sprigs to garnish

3 tbsp torn fresh basil

2 tbsp balsamic vinegar

2 turkey fillets, about 225g (8oz) in total

2 tbsp roughly chopped fresh sage

4 Parma ham slices

2 garlic cloves, finely chopped

salt and freshly ground black pepper

Place the potatoes in a pan of boiling salted water, cover and simmer for about 15 minutes or until tender. Cook the broad beans in a pan of boiling salted water for 1–2 minutes until tender. Drain well and cool under cold running water, then pop the beans out of their skins and place in a bowl.

Add 2 tablespoons of the olive oil to the broad beans with 1 tablespoon each of the parsley and basil and all the balsamic vinegar. Place in a small pan, season and set aside to marinate for 10–15 minutes, but no longer as the beans will lose their brilliant colour.

Heat a large frying pan over a medium heat. Cut each turkey fillet horizontally in half into 2 even-sized thin slices, then sprinkle over the sage and season with pepper and a little salt, remembering that Parma ham is quite salty. Wrap a slice of Parma ham around each slice of turkey and secure with a wooden cocktail stick. Add a thin film of oil to the pan and cook the wrapped turkey for 2–3 minutes on each side, until cooked through and lightly golden.

Meanwhile, finish making the mash. Gently simmer the remaining olive oil in a pan with the garlic for 5 minutes to infuse the flavours, but be careful not to allow the garlic to colour (or pop in the microwave on high for 2 minutes). Stir in the remaining parsley with the basil, then remove from the heat. When the potatoes are cooked, drain and return to their pan for a couple of minutes to dry out. Mash until smooth, then beat in the infused oil mixture and season to taste.

Reheat the broad beans to warm through. Pile the mash into the centre of 2 warmed serving plates and arrange the turkey saltimbocca on top. Spoon over the broad beans and garnish with parsley sprigs to serve.

PERFECT PROSCIUTTO-STUFFED PORK

This is a delicious juicy meal with the flavour of the ham and pork balancing perfectly with the crisp, courgette salad.

Serves 2

350g (12oz) pork fillet, cut into bite-size pieces

3 prosciutto or Parma ham slices, cut into strips

grated rind and juice of ½ lemon

5 tbsp olive oil

2 garlic cloves, crushed

5 tbsp white wine

½ tsp red wine vinegar

3 tbsp chopped fresh herbs, e.g. parsley, basil, coriander

4 tomatoes, roughly chopped

1 courgette, sliced into ribbons with a vegetable peeler

3 fresh basil leaves, roughly torn

salt and freshly ground black pepper

Make a hole in the centre of each pork cube and stuff each with a strip of ham and a little grated lemon rind.

Heat 3 tablespoons of the olive oil in a large frying pan and cook the pork cubes and any remaining Parma ham for 5–8 minutes, turning occasionally, until browned and almost cooked through. Add the garlic and cook for 1 minute, then pour in the wine and cook for a further 1–2 minutes until the pork is cooked through. Season with salt and pepper.

To make the vinaigrette, whisk together the remaining 2 tablespoons of olive oil, the lemon juice, vinegar and herbs. Add salt and pepper to taste.

Stir together the chopped tomatoes, courgette ribbons and vinaigrette. Transfer to a serving bowl and sprinkle over the torn basil leaves. Serve with the pork cubes.

SIZZLING SPAGHETTI CARBONARA

The secret to this dish lies in getting the pasta dough just right – too much flour and it will be dry and crack when you roll it out; too little and the dough will be soft and stick to itself.

Serves 2

1 tbsp olive oil

6 thin slices pancetta (Italian streaky bacon)

4 tbsp double cream

4 tbsp freshly grated Parmesan, plus extra to garnish

2 egg yolks

a handful of fresh basil leaves, roughly torn

FOR THE PASTA DOUGH

200g (7oz) Italian '00' flour

2 eggs

salt and freshly ground black pepper

Bring a large pan of salted water to a rolling boil. Place the flour in a food-processor and start it whizzing round. Add the eggs and keep whizzing until the mixture resembles fine breadcrumbs (it shouldn't be dusty, nor should it be a big gooey ball). Knead briskly into a ball shape and cut into 2 pieces.

Pass one piece of the pasta dough through a pasta machine set at its widest setting. Repeat this process, decreasing the roller setting grade by grade with each pass, taking it down to the second-lowest setting. Finally, pass through the cutting rollers to make spaghetti. Repeat with the remaining piece of dough.

Meanwhile, heat the olive oil in a frying pan. Add the pancetta and cook for about 2 minutes on each side until crisp and golden brown. Drain well on kitchen paper.

Plunge the pasta into the boiling salted water and cook for 2–3 minutes until al dente. Place the cream in a bowl with the Parmesan and egg yolks and stir to combine. Season to taste. Drain the spaghetti in a colander and return to the pan off the heat. Add the cream mixture and stir until thickened.

Divide between warmed bowls and arrange the crispy pancetta slices on top. Scatter with basil and garnish with Parmesan.

CHILLI BEEF SALAD WITH SHOESTRING POTATOES

This colourful salad is bursting with flavours. For the potatoes you need a mandolin cutter or a food-processor with the correct attachment because it is difficult to get them right by hand.

Serves 2

sunflower oil, for deep-frying, plus 4 tbsp

3 tsp sesame oil

3½ tbsp dark soy sauce

2 tsp clear honey

1 sirloin steak, about 4cm (1½ in) thick (about 300g/11oz in total)

1 large potato

100g (4oz) button chestnut mushrooms, halved

1 red chilli, seeded and thinly sliced

juice of 1 large lime (about 3 tbsp in total)

1 tsp caster sugar

a few drops of Tabasco sauce

50g (2oz) baby salad leaves

a handful each of fresh chervil, flat-leaf parsley and dill

salt and freshly ground black pepper

Preheat a deep-fat fryer or a deep-sided pan one-third full of sunflower oil to 160°C/325°F. Place 2 teaspoons of the sesame oil in a shallow dish with 2 teaspoons of the soy sauce and the honey and season with pepper. Whisk to combine and add the steak, turning to coat. Set aside for at least 5 minutes to allow the flavours to penetrate (or up to 24 hours if time allows).

Preheat a griddle pan over a medium-high heat until it is smoking hot. Remove the steak from the sesame mixture, shaking off any excess, and add to the pan. Chargrill for 2–3 minutes on each side, a little longer if you prefer your steak more well done. Transfer to a plate and season with salt.

Peel the potato and then, using a mandolin or a food-processor with an attachment blade, cut it into long, thin strips so they resemble shoestrings (fine julienne). Deep-fry the potato shoestrings for 3–4 minutes until golden brown. Meanwhile, heat a frying pan. Drain the potato on plenty of kitchen paper and season to taste. Add a tablespoon of the sunflower oil to the heated frying pan, then add the mushrooms and chilli. Season and sauté for 2–3 minutes, adding a tablespoon of the lime juice and a teaspoon of the soy sauce and tossing to coat.

To prepare the dressing, place the remaining 2 tablespoons of lime juice in a small bowl with the sugar and whisk until dissolved. Add the remaining 2 tablespoons of soy sauce, teaspoon of sesame oil and 3 tablespoons of sunflower oil with the Tabasco, then season with pepper and whisk until emulsified.

Place the salad leaves in a serving bowl and coat with the salad dressing. Season generously and toss until lightly dressed. Spoon the mushroom and chilli mixture on top and scatter over the shoestring potatoes. Slice the rested steak on the diagonal, cutting away and discarding any fat, then scatter on top. Finish with a little pile of herbs and serve immediately.

TANGY LAMB KEBABS WITH SATAY SAUCE

Lamb and satay sauce are such a tasty match.

Serves 2

2 x 150g (5oz) lamb chump chops, cubed

1 onion, cut into 2½ cm (1 in) pieces

½ green pepper, seeded and cut into 2½ cm (1in) pieces

juice of 2 limes

3 tbsp soy sauce

1 tbsp chopped fresh coriander

2 tbsp olive oil

200g (7oz) beansprouts

5 spring onions, sliced on the diagonal

1 garlic clove, crushed

1 tsp dried lemongrass

FOR THE SATAY SAUCE

2 tbsp crunchy peanut butter

120ml (4fl oz) white wine

3 tbsp soy sauce

3 tbsp olive oil

a pinch of lemongrass

salt and freshly ground black pepper

radish flowers, spring onion tassels and parsley, to garnish

Preheat the grill. Thread the lamb, onion and pepper onto 4 skewers and place in a shallow dish. Mix together the lime juice, soy sauce and coriander and pour over the kebabs, turning to coat them in the mixture.

Heat 1 tablespoon of the olive oil in a heavy-based frying pan and cook the kebabs for 1 minute on each side until well browned. Remove from the pan and cook under a hot grill for 5 minutes, turning once, until tender but still a little pink in the centre.

Meanwhile, heat the remaining olive oil in a wok or large frying pan and cook the beansprouts, spring onions, garlic and lemongrass for 2–3 minutes until tender but still firm.

To make the satay sauce, whisk together the peanut butter, wine, soy sauce, olive oil, lemongrass and salt and pepper to taste. Spoon into a serving bowl and garnish with a parsley sprig.

To serve, spoon the stir-fried beansprouts onto a plate and place the kebabs on top. Garnish with the radishes and spring onions and serve with the bowl of satay sauce.

GLAM LAMB BURGERS

Minced lamb is very good value for money and often has more flavour than minced beef. Make up a double batch of these burgers and freeze some for another day.

Serves 4

50g (2oz) fresh white breadcrumbs

450g (1lb) minced lamb

1 onion, finely chopped

1 garlic clove, crushed

grated rind of 1 lemon

1 tbsp chopped fresh rosemary

1 egg, beaten

3 tbsp olive oil

1 red pepper, seeded and cut into 1cm (½ in) pieces

5 baby courgettes, diced

3 tbsp white wine

75g (3oz) pine nuts

salt and freshly ground black pepper

In a large bowl, mix together the breadcrumbs, minced lamb, half the chopped onion, the garlic, lemon rind, rosemary and plenty of salt and pepper. Stir in the beaten egg, then shape the mixture into 4 even-sized burgers.

Heat 2 tablespoons of the olive oil in a frying pan and cook the burgers for 5–6 minutes on each side until golden brown.

Heat the remaining oil in a pan and cook the reserved onion, the red pepper and courgettes for 5 minutes until softened. Stir in the wine, cover and cook for 3–4 minutes, then season to taste.

Heat a small, non-stick pan and cook the pine nuts for 1–2 minutes, shaking the pan continuously, until golden brown.

To serve, spoon the ratatouille onto plates, place the burgers on top and sprinkle over the pine nuts. Serve immediately.

Independence Day recipe

BARBECUED LAMB WITH FRENCH BEAN SALAD

This dish captures all that is lovely about 'sunshine' summer ingredients.

Serves 2

7 tbsp extra-virgin olive oil

3 garlic cloves, finely sliced

1 tsp roughly chopped fresh rosemary

1 tsp roughly chopped fresh thyme

juice of 1 lemon

2 lamb neck fillets, well-trimmed

1 tbsp baby capers, drained and well rinsed

1 tbsp balsamic vinegar

1 tbsp chopped fresh flat-leaf parsley

225g (8oz) French beans, trimmed

5cm (2in) slice of bread (from a large farmhouse loaf), quartered and crusts removed

120ml (4fl oz) red wine

175ml (6fl oz) lamb or vegetable stock

salt and freshly ground black pepper

Preheat the barbecue, if using. In a shallow, non-metallic dish, mix together 4 tablespoons of olive oil, half the garlic and the rosemary, thyme and lemon juice. Season with pepper. Add the lamb and coat well. Cover and marinate for at least 5 minutes.

Place the capers, balsamic vinegar, parsley, remaining garlic clove and the rest of the olive oil in a bowl. Season and mix well.

Blanch the beans in boiling salted water for 3–4 minutes or until just tender. Drain, refresh under cold running water and toss in the caper dressing while they are still warm.

Heat a griddle pan, if using, until smoking hot. Drain the lamb fillets, reserving the marinade, and cook on the barbecue or in the pan for 8–10 minutes, turning occasionally, until tender. Rest under foil for a few minutes. Hollow out the 4 bread cubes and grill on all sides until crisp and lightly charred. Place the reserved marinade in a small pan with the red wine and reduce to 1 tablespoon. Add the stock and reduce again until the sauce is thickened and bubbling.

Place 2 grilled bread boxes on each plate and fill with the beans. Arrange the lamb on the side and pour over the red wine sauce.

PORK PATTIES WITH SPICED COCONUT CREAM

These would be fantastic on the barbecue. You could also make them with minced lamb or beef.

Serves 2

2 tbsp sunflower oil

1 small red onion, finely chopped

1 garlic clove, crushed

1 small bunch of fresh coriander (roots intact)

¼ tsp ground coriander

¼ tsp ground cumin

1 tsp tomato purée

½ tsp medium curry powder

1 x 250ml (9 fl oz) carton of coconut cream

175g (6oz) lean minced pork

1 x 275g (10oz) packet of cooked basmati rice

salt and freshly ground black pepper

Heat a heavy-based frying pan. Put half the oil in a separate pan, add the onion and garlic and sauté for 2–3 minutes until softened but not coloured.

Blitz the coriander, ground coriander, cumin, tomato purée and curry powder to a fine paste in a blender. Stir the paste into the sautéed onion mixture, gradually add the coconut cream, then simmer for 4–5 minutes until slightly reduced and thickened.

Season the pork and shape into 10 even-sized patties. Add the remaining oil to the heated, heavy-based frying pan and cook for 6–8 minutes until cooked through and golden brown. Heat the rice in the microwave according to the packet instructions.

Divide the rice and pork patties between warmed plates, pour over the coconut cream to cover completely. Serve at once.

ITALIAN MERINGUE BAKED ALASKA WITH SUMMER BERRIES

The sharpness of the soft summer berries makes a wonderful contrast to the sweet crunch and chewiness of the meringue.

Serves 4

225g (8oz) caster sugar

50g (2oz) unsalted butter

175g (6oz) digestive biscuits

1 x 500ml (18fl oz) tub of vanilla ice cream, softened slightly at room temperature

225g (8oz) raspberries

2 tbsp icing sugar, plus extra for dusting

4 egg whites

mixed summer berries and fresh mint sprigs, to decorate

To make the meringue, dissolve the sugar with 6 tablespoons of water in a heavy-based pan and bring slowly to the boil, without stirring. If sugar crystals get stuck to the side of the pan, brush them down into the syrup with a pastry brush dipped in cold water. Now increase the temperature so that the syrup cooks rapidly. Insert the sugar thermometer, if one is available, to check the temperature with later.

Meanwhile, prepare the base. Melt the butter in a small pan, and crush the biscuits in a food-processor or a polythene bag with a rolling pin. Stir the crushed biscuits into the melted butter, then spoon the crumbs into a pile in the centre of a large serving dish. Press the crumbs into a 15cm (6in) disc that is at least 5mm (¼ in) thick. Place the softened ice cream on top of the base and carefully mould with a palette knife briefly dipped in boiling water – do not press too hard or the base will break. Place in the freezer until ready to use.

To make the raspberry coulis, tip most of the raspberries into a food-processor (reserving a few to decorate) along with 2 tablespoons of water and the icing sugar. Blend to a purée, then pass through a sieve into a serving jug. Set aside.

When the sugar syrup reaches 110°C/220°F, beat the egg whites in the bowl of a food mixer until stiff. Check the sugar syrup and when it reaches 120°C/240°F, remove the pan from the heat. (If you haven't got a sugar thermometer, drop 1 teaspoon of syrup into cold water. It is ready when it forms a firm but soft ball that can be squeezed between your fingers.) Switch the food mixer back onto whisk, then pour the hot syrup onto the egg white in a steady stream. Continue to whisk until the mixture is stiff and shiny. When the whisk is lifted, the meringue should have no movement. Spoon into a large piping bag fitted with a 2½ cm (1in) plain nozzle and pile around the ice cream until completely smothered.

Use a blowtorch to finish off the meringue and give it an even, golden colour. Decorate with the reserved raspberries, summer berries and mint sprigs. Add a light dusting of icing sugar and serve immediately, handing around the raspberry coulis separately.

FRUITY TIRAMISU

Tiramisu is a household Italian dessert that has many regional variations. It is quite rich and is purported to give lots of energy, hence its name that translates as 'pick-me-up'. This tiramisu does not use the classic coffee and chocolate combination; however, the resulting dessert is just as good as the original.

Serves 4

5 plums

5 eggs, separated

250g (9oz) mascarpone

4 tbsp caster sugar

100g (4oz) dark chocolate, at least 70 per cent cocoa solids

100g (4oz) clotted cream

8 sponge fingers (about 50g/2oz)

1 banana, sliced

Poach the plums in a small pan of boiling water for 5 minutes until tender. Drain well, remove the skins and stones then mash the flesh.

Beat together the egg yolks, mascarpone and sugar.

In a separate bowl, whisk the egg whites until stiff, then fold into the mascarpone mixture with a metal spoon.

Break the chocolate in half and, using a rolling pin, smash one half into small pieces. Stir into the mascarpone mixture.

Grate the remaining chocolate and stir all but 1 tablespoonful into the clotted cream.

Dip the sponge fingers into the plum mixture to soften them, then divide between 2 plates. Spoon over the poached plum mixture followed by half of the mascarpone mixture. Top with the banana slices followed by the remaining mascarpone mixture. Top with clotted cream and sprinkle with grated chocolate. Chill until ready to serve.

PAVLOVA NESTS WITH PEACHES AND STRAWBERRIES

Use any fruit you fancy for this dessert, but this combination works well with the sweetness of the pavlova.

Serves 2

2 egg whites

a pinch of cornflour

2 drops of white wine vinegar

100g (4oz) icing sugar, sifted

225ml (8fl oz) dry white wine

1 vanilla pod, split

1 tbsp clear honey

1 firm ripe peach, peeled and sliced

100g (4oz) strawberries, hulled, halved if large

4 tsp thick Greek yoghurt

Preheat the oven to 160°C/325°F/gas 3. Line a baking sheet with non-stick baking paper. Whisk the egg whites to stiff peaks. Whisk in the cornflour, vinegar and icing sugar, a spoonful at a time, until the mixture is thick and glossy. Spoon it into a piping bag fitted with a 2½ cm (1in) fluted nozzle, and pipe 2 meringue nests, a little apart, onto the lined baking sheet. Bake for 15–20 minutes until firm. Allow to cool.

Meanwhile, heat the wine in a pan with the vanilla pod and honey. Add the peach slices and poach for 1–2 minutes until just tender. Tip in the strawberries, stirring to combine, then remove from the heat and set aside to allow the flavours to mingle.

Place the meringue nests on serving plates and use a slotted spoonto fill with the poached fruits. Add a dollop of yoghurt on top and drizzle around a little of the syrup to serve.

RASPBERRY FRANGIPANE

This is an incredibly easy pudding, best made in the summer when British raspberries are at their best. Or use blackberries, blueberries or stoned cherries instead – whatever's in season.

Serves 2

100g (4oz) macadamia nuts

50g (2oz) butter, plus extra for greasing

2 tbsp caster sugar

2 tbsp self-raising flour

1 egg

25g (1oz) raspberries

icing sugar, to dust

crème fraîche, to serve

Preheat the oven to 200°C/400°F/gas 6. Place the macadamia nuts in a mini food-processor and grind down.

Place the butter and sugar in a food-processor and whizz until well creamed together. Add the ground macadamias, flour and egg. Continue to blend until you have a smooth batter.

Divide the raspberries between 2 buttered blini pans and pour over the batter. Place on the top shelf in the oven and bake for 8 minutes or until well risen and golden brown.

Turn the raspberry frangipanes out onto plates, add a light dusting of icing sugar and serve at once with a quenelle of crème fraîche on the side.

POACHED PEACHES WITH SABAYON

Choose the ripest peaches for this exquisite dessert and they will poach in no time at all. If you like, reduce the poaching liquid and drizzle around the peaches before adding the sabayon.

Serves 2

25g (1oz) caster sugar

300ml (½ pint) Muscat wine

2 ripe peaches

FOR THE SABAYON

3 egg yolks

25g (1oz) caster sugar

2 tbsp muscat wine

½ vanilla pod, split in half and seeds scraped out

Heat the sugar and muscat wine in a small pan until the sugar has dissolved. Cut the peaches in half and remove the stone, then add to the pan, ensuring they are completely covered in the liquid. Poach for 6–8 minutes until tender, basting occasionally as the liquid reduces.

Meanwhile, make the sabayon. Place the egg yolks, sugar, wine and vanilla seeds in a heatproof bowl set over a pan of simmering water. Using a large balloon whisk, beat for 6–8 minutes until the sabayon becomes pale and thickened and leaves a trail when you lift the whisk.

Transfer the peaches to warmed wide-rimmed bowls with a slotted spoon and ladle over the sabayon to serve.

PEACH MELBA KNICKERBOCKER GLORY

A glorious finale to any meal, and the real beauty of these is that they are assembled in minutes.

Serves 2

1 tbsp flaked almonds

2 ready-made meringue nests

1 ripe peach or nectarine, halved, stone removed and sliced

100g (4oz) raspberries

4 scoops vanilla ice cream

4 biscuit curls or 'cigars'

FOR THE FUDGE SAUCE

4 tbsp double cream

50g (2oz) butter

50g (2oz) light muscovado sugar

juice of ½ orange

First make the fudge sauce. Place the cream in a small pan with the butter, sugar and orange juice. Heat gently until the sugar dissolves, then simmer for 4–5 minutes until slightly reduced and fudge-like. Remove from the heat and allow to cool a little.

Toast the almond flakes in a dry frying pan, tossing occasionally to ensure they cook evenly. Tip out onto a plate to cool.

Lightly crush the meringue nests and arrange in the base of 2 tall glasses. Scatter over the peach or nectarine with half of the raspberries, and top each one with 2 scoops of the ice cream. Top with the remaining raspberries.

Drizzle the fudge sauce generously into each glass. Sprinkle over the toasted nuts and decorate with the biscuits to serve.

Wimbledon recipe

**LEMON STRAWBERRY WAFER STACKS
WITH RASPBERRY COULIS**

LEMON STRAWBERRY WAFER STACKS WITH RASPBERRY COULIS

This is a mouthwatering way to spice up those traditional Wimbledon favourites – strawberries and cream.

Serves 2

75g (3oz) caster sugar

4 tbsp mascarpone

100ml (3½ fl oz) double cream

1 tsp sifted icing sugar, plus extra for dusting

1 tbsp lemon curd

6 round, thin shortbread biscuits (each about 5–7½ cm/2–3in in diameter)

12 evenly sized small strawberries (about 150g/5oz in weight)

FOR THE RASPBERRY COULIS

100g (4oz) raspberries

juice of 1 lime

2 tsp sifted icing sugar

Place the sugar in a very clean, heavy-based pan and heat gently until dissolved, then boil fast for a few minutes until the syrup begins to turn brown, swirling the pan to ensure even cooking.

Mix the mascarpone in a bowl with the cream, icing sugar and lemon curd until combined. Place 1 shortbread biscuit on each plate and divide half the mascarpone mixture between them. Cut the strawberries in half. Stand 6 of the halves on each shortbread in the mascarpone mixture, cut-side facing out. Top with another biscuit and repeat the mascarpone and strawberry layer. Finish each stack with the 2 remaining biscuits and dust with icing sugar. Heat a flat metal skewer on an open flame and mark the tops of the stacks, reheating the skewer as necessary.

Place the raspberries, lime juice and icing sugar in a mini food-processor and blend until smooth. Pass through a sieve into a bowl and pour into a jug. Drizzle around each strawberry stack.

When the caramel is a rich golden-brown colour, dip the base of the pan into a sink of cold water to stop it cooking. Take a clean, small metal spoon and a knife-sharpening steel, and dip the spoon into the caramel. Move the spoon up and down the steel, pulling the sugar with your fingers until a candy-floss texture is achieved. Pile some of the spun sugar on top and serve at once.

STRAWBERRY TORTE WITH BRANDY AND CHOCOLATE SAUCE

It is important that the cream and mascarpone cheese are well chilled if you want to be able to serve the tortes immediately.

Serves 2

200ml (7fl oz) double cream, well chilled

50g (2oz) caster sugar

100g (4oz) mascarpone, well chilled

finely grated rind of 1 lime

10 large strawberries, hulled and halved lengthways

6 fresh mint leaves

2 tsp brandy

FOR THE CHOCOLATE SAUCE

50g (2oz) cocoa powder

2 tbsp caster sugar

1 tbsp boiling water

Lightly whip the cream and caster sugar in a large bowl until you have soft peaks. Fold in the mascarpone and lime rind.

Place a 10cm (4in) cooking ring on each of 2 serving plates and line with the strawberry halves, cut side against the ring. Spoon in the cream mixture and gently press to the edges, keeping the strawberries in place. Level off the tops of the tortes with a palette knife briefly dipped in boiling water. Chill for at least 5 minutes to set (up to 8 hours is fine if time allows).

Place the cocoa powder and caster sugar in a small pan with the boiling water, simmer gently to combine, stirring occasionally. Remove from the heat and allow to cool. Remove the cooking rings by carefully warming the edges with a blowtorch or warm cloth and lifting them off. Arrange the mint leaves on top of each torte and drizzle over the brandy. Drizzle the chocolate sauce around the edges of the plates and serve at once.

SPEEDY SUMMER PUDDING

This fab dessert can be rustled up in no time. It was traditionally made wth raspberries and redcurrants, but adding a few blackcurrants will take away some of the sweetness and give it a little kick.

Serves 4

50g (2oz) sugar

100ml (3½ fl oz) water

500g (1lb 2oz) frozen summer fruits, such as raspberries, redcurrants and blackcurrants, thawed

butter, for greasing

2 tbsp icing sugar

12 slices white bread, crusts removed

150ml (¼ pint) single cream, to serve

Place the sugar and water in a small pan and heat gently, stirring until the sugar has dissolved. Bring to the boil and simmer rapidly for 2 minutes. Whizz half the summer fruits with the icing sugar and syrup in a food-processor to form a purée.

Line a buttered 1.2 litre (2 pint) pudding basin with the bread, setting aside a slice for the top. Spoon in the whole fruit and place the slice of bread on top, pressing down to seal. Pour over the fruit syrup, then place a small plate on top. Place the pudding in the fridge and leave to cool completely.

To serve, invert the pudding onto a plate, slice into wedges and serve with cream.

ORANGE SOUFFLÉ OMELETTE AND FLAMING BLUEBERRIES

Dried fruits such as blueberries, cherries and cranberries add a much-needed lift to soufflés.

Serves 2

50g (2oz) dried blueberries

100ml (3½fl oz) boiling water

50g (2oz) unsalted butter

3 tbsp plain flour

1 x 284ml (½ pint) carton of buttermilk

6 eggs, separated

50g (2oz) caster sugar plus 1 tbsp

a pinch of salt

fresh mint sprigs, to garnish

FOR THE ORANGES

2 mineola oranges, segmented

4 tbsp caster sugar

1 tbsp water

juice and grated rind of 1 orange

juice of ½ lemon

grated rind of 1 lemon

100g (4oz) fresh blueberries

2 tbsp whisky

Preheat the oven to 190°C/375°F/gas 5. Place the blueberries in a bowl, pour over the boiling water and soak for 3–5 minutes. Melt the butter in a pan, stir in the flour and cook for 1 minute. Remove from the heat and gradually beat in the buttermilk. Return to the heat, bring to the boil, stirring continuously, until smooth and thickened, then remove from the heat and allow to cool for 2–3 minutes. Stir in the egg yolks. Drain the blueberries, chop finely, then stir into the buttermilk sauce with the tablespoon of caster sugar.

In a large, clean bowl, whisk the egg whites with a pinch of salt until they form soft peaks, then gradually add the 50g (2oz) caster sugar to make a stiff, shiny meringue. Gradually fold the meringue into the buttermilk sauce. Divide the mixture between 2 skillets or ovenproof frying pans and bake for 10–12 minutes until puffed up and golden brown.

Meanwhile, heat through the orange segments for a few minutes on a baking sheet in the oven. Heat the caster sugar and water gently in a small pan, stirring until the sugar dissolves. Raise the heat and cook the mixture, without stirring, for 3–4 minutes until golden. Stir in the juice and grated rind of the orange and lemon and the fresh blueberries and heat through gently. Pour over the whisky and ignite. Arrange the warm orange segments on a serving dish and pour over the blueberry sauce.

To serve, remove the soufflés from the oven and garnish with the mint sprigs. Serve immediately with the flambéed blueberries.

FRUITY CLAFOUTI AND BANANA MOUSSE

169

This double dessert of classic French cherry clafouti with a banana mousse demands that you rest for at least three hours after consumption – very sturdy and not for the faint-hearted.

Serves 4

FOR THE CLAFOUTI

1 x 400g (14oz) tin of stoned black cherries in syrup

50g (2oz) self-raising flour

2 eggs

300ml (½ pint) milk

50g (2oz) caster sugar

grated rind of ½ lemon

grated rind of ½ orange

100g (4oz) plain chocolate

2 tbsp cornflour

FOR THE BANANA SURPRISE

150g (5oz) marshmallows

6 coconut macaroons

2 tbsp Tia Maria

2 bananas

juice of ½ lemon

300ml (½ pint) double cream

1 orange, segmented, and 1 lime, peeled and sliced, to decorate

icing sugar, to dust

Preheat the oven to 200°C/400°F/gas 6. Lightly butter a 23cm (9in) pie dish. Strain the cherries, reserving the juice, and arrange them in a single layer in the base of the dish.

Whisk together the flour, eggs, milk and sugar until smooth. Stir in the grated citrus rind and carefully pour the batter into the pie dish. Bake for 15–20 minutes until well-risen and browned.

Meanwhile, make the banana mousse. Place the marshmallows in a small pan and heat very gently, stirring occasionally, until melted. Place the macaroons and Tia Maria in a food-processor and whizz to form a crumb mixture. Mash together the bananas and lemon juice. In a separate bowl, whip the cream until it forms soft peaks, then stir in the mashed bananas and melted marshmallows. Spoon the crumb mixture into a buttered ring mould, pressing down well. Spoon the banana mixture on top, cover and chill for 15 minutes or until firm.

Break the chocolate into a heatproof bowl and place over a pan of simmering water to melt, stirring occasionally, until smooth. Mix the cornflour with a little water to form a smooth paste. Place the cherry syrup in a small pan and stir in the cornflour mixture. Bring to the boil, stirring continuously, to make a smooth sauce. To serve, turn out the banana mousse and decorate with fruit slices. Remove the clafouti from the oven, dust with icing sugar, drizzle with melted chocolate and pour the cherry syrup around.

UPSIDE-DOWN APRICOT PANCAKES

170

This dessert makes great use of the store cupboard. It's perfect for when you fancy something sweet but don't have much in the house. Use canned pears, peaches or cherries with excellent results.

Serves 2

100g (4oz) caster sugar

50g (2oz) plain flour

50g (2oz) butter

1 egg

1 vanilla pod, split in half and seeds scraped out

1 x 400g (14oz) tin of apricot halves in syrup, drained

vanilla ice cream, to serve

Preheat the oven to 200°C/400°F/gas 6. Heat 50g (2oz) of the sugar in an ovenproof sauté pan until it begins to dissolve and caramelize. Swirl the pan occasionally to ensure it cooks evenly.

Place the flour in a food-processor with the remaining sugar, butter, egg and vanilla seeds. Blend to a smooth batter.

Arrange the apricot halves, cut-side up, in the caramel in the bottom of the pan. Take the pan off the heat, pour over the batter, transfer to the oven and bake for about 8 minutes until well risen and golden brown.

Invert the pancake onto a flat plate and rearrange the apricots. Slice and serve on warmed plates with a scoop of ice cream.

PEACH MELBA MERINGUES

Meringues are really very simple to make and in this recipe they offer a nice change in texture to the peaches they are served with. If fresh raspberries are in season, use them.

Serves 2

FOR THE MERINGUES

2 egg whites

100g (4oz) caster sugar

2 tsp ground cinnamon

FOR THE CHOCOLATE NUTS

50g (2oz) plain chocolate (at least 70 per cent cocoa solids)

75g (3oz) whole brazil nuts, toasted

FOR THE POACHED PEACHES

150g (5oz) caster sugar

3 tbsp white wine

4 tbsp water

juice of 1 orange

4 cloves

2 peaches, halved and stoned

FOR THE RASPBERRY SAUCE

100g (4oz) frozen raspberries

1 tbsp icing sugar

2 fresh mint sprigs, to decorate

100g (4oz) crème fraîche, to serve

Preheat the oven to 190°C/375°F/gas 5. Whisk the egg whites until they form soft peaks, then gradually whisk in the caster sugar until the mixture is stiff and glossy. Fold in the cinnamon. Using two tablespoons, shape the mixture into 9 quenelles (egg shapes). Place on a lined baking sheet and bake for 6–7 minutes until golden and set but still soft in the centre.

Break the chocolate into a heatproof bowl and place over a pan of simmering water for 3–4 minutes, stirring occasionally, until melted. Dip the nuts into the chocolate so that one half is covered. Leave to set on baking parchment. Drizzle the remaining chocolate over the meringues.

To make the syrup for poaching the peaches, place the sugar, wine and water in a small pan and heat gently, stirring until the sugar dissolves. Stir in the orange juice and cloves; add the peach halves, flesh-side down, and simmer gently for 8–10 minutes until tender but still firm.

Meanwhile, place the frozen raspberries in a food-processor with the icing sugar and blend to make a sauce.

To serve, flood 2 plates with the raspberry sauce and place 2 peach halves in the centre of each. Arrange the meringues and chocolate nuts around the edge and decorate with the sprigs of mint. Serve with the crème fraîche.

CRÈME BRÛLÉE

It's always nice to be able to produce a quick and simple version of a classic. Use a blowtorch at home to caramelize the top of puddings. Easy-to-use models are available in kitchen shops.

Serves 2

150ml (¼ pint) condensed milk (from a tin)

50ml (2fl oz) milk

2 egg yolks

icing sugar, to dust

Preheat the oven to 220°C/425°F/gas 7. Place the condensed milk in a small pan with the milk and egg yolks. Cook over a gentle heat for 2–3 minutes until the mixture coats the back of a wooden spoon, stirring constantly.

Divide the mixture between two 100ml (3½ fl oz) ramekins and place on a baking sheet. Put on the top shelf of the oven for 5–6 minutes until just set.

Sit each ramekin in a bowl of ice cubes so that it cools down as quickly as possible. Dust the top liberally with icing sugar and then flash each one with a blowtorch until the tops are caramelized. Set on plates and serve at once.

MANGO MOUSSE IN BRANDY SNAPS

This clever little dessert requires no cooking at all. For those with a sweeter tooth, drizzle a little of the syrup of the stem ginger over the mango mousse to serve.

Serves 2

1 small ripe mango

juice of 1 lime

4 tbsp double cream

1 knob of crystallized stem ginger, finely chopped, plus 1 tbsp ginger syrup

4 fresh mint leaves, shredded, plus fresh mint sprigs, to decorate

2 brandy-snap baskets

Peel the mango and cut away the flesh, discarding the stone. Place in a mini blender with the lime juice and blitz to a smooth purée.

Whip the cream in a bowl until soft peaks have formed. Fold in 4 tablespoons of the mango purée with the stem ginger, ginger syrup and shredded mint until well combined.

Spoon the mango mousse into the brandy-snap baskets set on plates and decorate with the mint sprigs. Drizzle the remaining mango purée around the edges of the plates, thinning it with a little water if necessary. Serve at once.

SPICED MANGO WITH LIME-SCENTED CREAM

This dessert would also be delicious cooked in foil parcels over gentle coals at the end of a barbecue.

Serves 2

1 large ripe mango

1 tbsp clear honey

juice of 1 lime

a good pinch of dried crushed chilli flakes

1 tbsp light muscovado sugar

FOR THE LIME-SCENTED CREAM

100ml (3½ fl oz) double cream

4 fresh mint leaves, shredded

finely grated rind of 1 lime

1 tbsp sifted icing sugar

Preheat the oven to 200°C/400°F/gas 6. Peel the mango and cut the flesh away from the stone, then cut into chunks. Spread out on a non-stick baking sheet and drizzle over the honey and lime juice. Scatter the crushed chillies and muscovado sugar on top and bake for 5 minutes until the sugar has melted and begun to caramelize.

Meanwhile, make the lime-scented cream. Whip the cream until soft peaks have formed. Shred the mint and fold into the cream with the lime rind and enough icing sugar to sweeten.

Divide the spiced mango between plates and add a good dollop of the lime cream to serve.

CHOCOLATE ROULADE AND CHERRY SAUCE

Chocolate and cherries are one of those classic combinations and with a good measure of double cream you're guaranteed a dessert to die for.

Serves 6–8

3 eggs

100g (4oz) caster sugar

50g (2oz) plain flour

25g (1oz) cocoa powder

300ml (½ pint) double cream

4 tbsp kirsch

100g (4oz) plain chocolate, at least 70 per cent cocoa solids, melted

1 x 425g (14oz) tin of stoned black cherries, drained and juice reserved

fresh mint sprigs, to decorate

Preheat the oven to 200°C/400°F/gas 6. Whisk together the eggs and sugar until pale and fluffy. Sift the flour and cocoa together; then very carefully fold in to the eggs and sugar using a metal tablespoon. Pour the mixture into a lined Swiss roll tin and bake for 8–10 minutes until risen and just firm to the touch. Cool in the tin for a few minutes, then turn out onto a wire rack.

Whisk the cream until thick enough to form soft peaks, then stir in half the kirsch.

Spoon a tablespoon of the melted chocolate into a greaseproof paper piping bag and pipe 6–8 swirls of chocolate onto a sheet of greaseproof paper. Place in the fridge to set.

Stir the remaining kirsch into the remaining melted chocolate with 2 tablespoons of the cherry juice. Pour into a jug and keep warm.

Spread the sponge with the whipped cream mixture. Spoon the cherries over the cream then roll up the sponge lengthways, peeling away the paper as you go. Slice into individual portions and transfer to serving plates, decorate with sugar, mint leaves and chocolate shapes and serve with the warm sauce.

MANGO AND COCONUT SPLASH

For a variation, try replacing the mango with a chopped banana
or some chopped pawpaw with twice the lime juice.

Serves 2

1 ripe firm mango

2 tbsp clear honey

100ml (3½ fl oz)
Greek yoghurt

200ml (7fl oz)
coconut milk

juice of 1 lime

a handful of ice cubes

Peel the mango, cut away all the flesh from the stone and place
in a liquidizer. Add the honey with the yoghurt, coconut milk and
lime juice. Tip in the ice cubes with 100ml (3½ fl oz) of water
and blend to a purée.

Pour the drink into tall glasses and serve at once.

MELON AND ORANGE SMOOTHIE

Smoothies are now big business, but they are very simple to make
yourself when you're at home.

Serves 2

1 small ripe melon

4 oranges

2 limes

6 fresh basil leaves

1 x 200g (7oz) carton
of Greek yoghurt

1–2 tbsp clear honey

a good handful of ice
cubes

Cut the melon in half and scoop out the seeds. Using a spoon,
scoop the flesh into a liquidizer. Cut the oranges and limes in
half and squeeze in the juice. Add the basil with the yoghurt,
1 tablespoon of the honey and the ice cubes. Blend until smooth,
then taste and add more honey if you think it needs it.

Pour into tall glasses and serve at once.

LYCHEE AND RASPBERRY LASSI

This would be a fantastic finale to any meal. Use a drained tin of
lychees in syrup if you have difficulty finding fresh ones.

Serves 2

20 ripe lychees

2 tbsp clear honey

1 vanilla pod, split in
half and seeds
scraped out

4 tbsp Greek yoghurt

a good handful of ice
cubes

50g (2oz) raspberries

juice of 1 lime

Peel the lychees and remove the stones, then place in a liquidizer
with the honey, vanilla seeds, Greek yoghurt and ice. Blend until
smooth and pour into 2 tall glasses.

Place the raspberries and lime juice in a small bowl and mash
together with a fork. Divide between the 2 glasses and stir once
or twice to create a ripple effect. Serve at once.

PINK PANTHER

Hold the redcurrant stalk and run it through the prongs of
a fork to release the berries. (See illustration, page 2.)

Serves 2

50g (2oz) redcurrants

100g (4oz)
raspberries

a squeeze of lime
juice

1 tbsp sifted icing
sugar

50g (2oz)
strawberries, hulled,
halved if large

2 tbsp Greek yoghurt

4 tbsp milk

a good handful of ice
cubes

Hold the redcurrant stalks and run the prongs of a fork through
them to release the berries.

To make a raspberry coulis, blend 50g (2oz) of the raspberries
with the lime juice and icing sugar in a mini food-processor and
then pass through a sieve.

Place the remaining raspberries, the strawberries, redcurrants,
Greek yoghurt, milk and ice cubes in a liquidizer and blend until
smooth.

Pour the berry mixture into tall glasses and then drizzle in the
raspberry coulis to serve.

FRESH COCONUT AND PEACH MILKSHAKE

This is a brilliant summertime drink, but you need good-quality vanilla
ice cream made with real vanilla seeds for a truly spectacular result.

Serves 2

1 small coconut

2 firm, ripe peaches

4 scoops vanilla ice
cream

4 tbsp Greek yoghurt

1 tsp caster sugar

Break open the coconut, reserving the milk. Break the coconut
flesh into pieces and place in a liquidizer with the reserved
coconut milk.

Drop the peaches into a pan of boiling water for 30 seconds,
then slip off their skins and chop the flesh, discarding the stones.
Add to the food-processor with the ice cream, yoghurt and sugar.
Blend until thick and smooth and then pour into tall glasses. Add
straws to serve.

FRAPPACCINO

To add a caffeine hit to this, freeze your leftover
coffee in ice cubes and use those.

Serves 2

2 tbsp cocoa powder

1 tbsp clear honey

4 tbsp double cream

4 tbsp vanilla ice
cream

300ml (½ pint) milk

175g (6oz) ice cubes

Place the cocoa powder in a small pan with the honey and
cream. Heat gently for a couple of minutes until a smooth
chocolate sauce has formed, stirring occasionally.

Place the ice cream in a liquidizer with the milk and ice cubes.
Blend until smooth, then pour in the chocolate sauce and blend
again.

Pour the frappaccino into tall glasses and add a straw to each
one to serve.

MINT AND GINGER-INFUSED TEA

This tea has incredible natural healing properties and is just the thing if you are feeling under the weather with a cold or flu.

Serves 2

600ml (1 pint) boiling water

5cm (2in) piece of fresh root ginger

a good handful of fresh mint leaves

2 tbsp clear honey

Pour a little of the boiling water into a teapot and set aside for a couple of minutes to warm through.

Thinly slice the ginger. Pour out the water from the teapot and add the ginger, mint and honey with the rest of the boiling water, stirring with a long spoon until the honey has dissolved. Set aside for 3–4 minutes to allow all the ingredients to infuse, then pour into cups while still hot to serve.

LIME AND MINT VODKA

This is a refreshing drink, but beware – although it goes down easily it is very alcoholic. (See illustration, page 64.)

Serves 2

a small bunch of fresh mint, plus extra sprigs to decorate

1 lime, cut into slices

2 tbsp caster sugar

1 miniature bottle of vodka (about 50ml/2fl oz in total)

150g (5oz) ice cubes

600ml (1 pint) soda water

Strip the mint leaves into a cocktail shaker or tall, sturdy jug. Add the lime slices and sugar, then, using the end of a rolling pin, press together to form a lumpy pulp. Pour in the vodka and fill up with ice, then shake or stir until very well chilled.

Half-fill tall glasses with fresh ice cubes and strain over the chilled lime vodka, then top up with soda water.

Decorate with mint sprigs to serve.

PINA COLADA

This is a *Ready Steady Cook* version of a truly decadent cocktail.

Serves 2

1 miniature pineapple

1 miniature bottle of Malibu (about 50ml/2fl oz in total)

2 scoops coconut ice cream

2 natural glacé cherries, to decorate

Cut off the leaf crown and bottom of the pineapple so that it sits flat. Using a sharp knife, remove the skin by cutting down the length of the fruit. Cut the flesh into slices and remove the woody core. Reserve 2 slices for decoration and dice the remainder, then place in a liquidizer. Add the Malibu to the liquidizer with the coconut ice cream and blitz until smooth.

Pour into large-bowled glasses and decorate with a slice of pineapple and a glacé cherry before serving immediately.

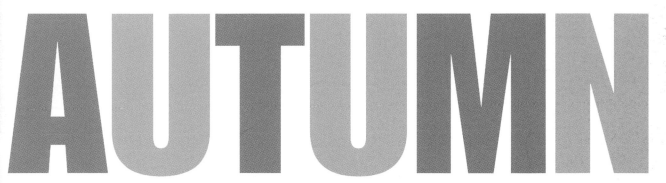

AUTUMN

BROCCOLI AND CHEDDAR SOUP

This soup is inspired by America, where there is quite a tradition of putting cheese in soup.

Serves 4–6

40g (1½oz) unsalted butter

1 large onion, finely chopped

225g (8oz) potato, finely diced

900ml (1½ pints) vegetable stock

675g (1½ lb) broccoli head, trimmed and finely chopped

150g (5oz) finely grated mature Cheddar

salt and freshly ground black pepper

4 tbsp double cream, to serve

Melt the butter in a large pan, add the onion and cook for a few minutes until softened. Stir in the potato and season generously, then cover and cook gently for 10 minutes, shaking the pan occasionally, until the potatoes are just tender.

Pour the stock into the pan and bring to the boil, then reduce the heat, add the broccoli and simmer for 5 minutes or so until the broccoli is just tender. Season to taste.

Purée the soup in batches in a food-processor and return to the pan, or use a hand-held blender. Stir in the Cheddar and reheat gently for a minute or so until just warmed through. Season to taste and ladle into bowls. Add a swirl of cream to each one and serve at once.

WILD MUSHROOM AND STILTON SOUP

Soup made from wild mushrooms has the most extraordinarily intense flavour. It also works well with wild mushrooms that are a few days old and have darkened a bit. If you are watching what you eat, omit the cream and use milk instead.

Serves 2

1 stale slice country-style bread

600ml (1 pint) vegetable or chicken stock

1 garlic clove, crushed

4 spring onions, thinly sliced

150g (5oz) mixed wild mushrooms, wiped clean and finely chopped (such as chanterelle, shiitake and blewit)

50ml (2fl oz) double cream or milk

85g (3½ oz) Stilton, diced

1 tbsp each roughly chopped fresh chervil, flat-leaf parsley and tarragon

salt and freshly ground black pepper

Moisten the bread with a little water and leave to soak for a few minutes. Place the stock in a pan with the garlic and spring onions and bring to a simmer. Squeeze out the excess moisture from the bread, tear into pieces and add to the simmering stock with the mushrooms. Season with pepper, reduce the heat slightly and simmer gently for 5–6 minutes or until the mushrooms are tender.

Ladle the soup into a food-processor, blend to a purée and return to the pan, or use a hand-held blender. Season to taste and reheat gently. Stir in the cream or milk, and whisk in the Stilton. Cook for another minute until the Stilton is completely melted, stirring, then add the herbs. Ladle the soup into warmed bowls to serve.

BEETROOT SOUP

This soup is similar to a Russian borscht, which is traditionally made with beetroot, cabbage and potatoes simmered in beef stock. However, this version has surprising depth of flavour and a wonderful rich colour.

Serves 2

1 tbsp olive oil

1 bunch of spring onions, finely chopped

1 x 300ml (½ pint) carton of fresh beef stock

a dash of Worcestershire sauce

1 x 400g (14oz) jar of baby beetroot, drained and roughly chopped

2 tbsp soured cream

½ tsp snipped fresh chives

salt and freshly ground black pepper

Heat the olive oil in a pan and sauté the spring onions for 2–3 minutes until softened but not coloured.

Pour the beef stock and Worcestershire sauce into the pan and bring to a simmer, then transfer to a food-processor or liquidizer. Add the beetroot and blend until smooth. Season to taste.

Return the soup to a clean pan and allow to just warm through, adding a little water if you think it's too thick.

Divide the soup between warmed bowls and add a spoonful of soured cream to each one. Sprinkle over the chives and serve at once.

CARROT AND CORIANDER SOUP

This is cheap and easy to make and has a fantastic colour. Try a tablespoon of freshly grated root ginger instead of the coriander. (See illustration, page 122.)

Serves 2

1 tbsp olive oil

4 spring onions, finely chopped

2 large carrots (about 350g/12oz in total)

1 tsp clear honey

a squeeze of fresh lemon juice

450ml (¾ pint) hot vegetable or chicken stock (from a cube is fine)

a small handful of fresh coriander leaves

salt and freshly ground black pepper

a drizzle of extra-virgin olive oil, to garnish

warmed focaccia, to serve

Heat the olive oil in a large pan and sauté the spring onions for a minute or so until softened but not coloured.

Meanwhile, using the grater attachment of a food-processor, finely grate the carrots. Add to the pan with the honey and lemon juice, stirring to combine.

Pour the hot stock into the pan and bring to the boil, then boil fast for 5 minutes or until the carrots are tender. Stir in the coriander and blitz with a hand-held blender until smooth. Season to taste.

Ladle the soup into warmed bowls and add a swirl of the extra-virgin olive oil to garnish. Serve at once with warmed focaccia.

SMOKY BACON AND TOMATO SOUP WITH GARLIC TOASTS

Soda bread is a traditional Irish quick-leavened white bread that is cooked on a flat griddle pan. You could also use slices of focaccia.

Serves 2

2 tbsp olive oil

1 onion, finely chopped

1 celery stick, finely chopped

100g (4oz) rindless smoked bacon rashers, diced

1 x 400g (14oz) can of chopped tomatoes

300ml (½ pint) hot chicken stock (from a cube is fine)

1 tbsp tomato purée

FOR THE GARLIC TOASTS

50g (2oz) unsalted butter, softened

1 garlic clove, crushed

1 tbsp chopped fresh flat-leaf parsley, plus extra to garnish

1 soda farl, cut into 8 slices

salt and freshly ground black pepper

Preheat the grill and heat the oil in a large pan. Add the onion, celery and bacon and cook over a high heat for about 2–3 minutes or until the onion has softened and the bacon is cooked through and lightly golden, stirring occasionally.

Add the chopped tomatoes, chicken stock and tomato purée to the pan, stirring to combine. Bring to a simmer and cook for another minute or so until all the flavours are well combined, stirring occasionally.

Meanwhile, make the garlic toasts. Mix the butter in a bowl with the garlic, parsley and a good pinch of salt, then spread over the soda farl slices. Arrange on a baking sheet, buttered-side up and grill for a few minutes until bubbling.

Season the soup and then whizz with a hand-held blender until smooth. Ladle into warmed bowls and set on plates. Garnish with a sprinkling of parsley and a good grinding of black pepper. Arrange the garlic toasts to the side to serve.

BROCCOLI SOUP WITH BRIE CROSTINI

Impressive enough to grace any sophisticated table, and it can be made in the time it takes your guest to have a drink.

Serves 2

1 tbsp olive oil

1 small onion, finely chopped

450ml (¾ pint) hot vegetable stock (from a cube is fine)

275g (10oz) broccoli florets

1 small French baguette

2 tbsp olive oil

1 garlic clove, halved

100g (4oz) ripe Brie, cut into slices

2 tbsp double cream (optional)

1 tbsp chopped fresh flat-leaf parsley

salt and freshly ground black pepper

Preheat the grill. Heat the oil in a pan and pan-fry the onion for 2–3 minutes until softened but not coloured. Pour the stock into the pan and then tip in the broccoli florets. Bring to the boil, then reduce the heat and simmer for 4–6 minutes until the broccoli is tender but still retains its vibrant colour.

Meanwhile, make the Brie crostini. Cut the baguette into ½ cm (¼ in) diagonal slices and arrange on the grill rack. Drizzle over the olive oil and season generously. Toast on both sides until lightly golden, then remove from the heat. Rub each piece with garlic, arrange the Brie on top and season with pepper. Flash under the grill until the Brie is bubbling.

Carefully transfer the broccoli and stock mixture to a food-processor and season to taste, then whizz to a purée, adding cream if desired. Ladle into warmed bowls set on plates and scatter the parsley on top. Arrange the Brie crostini to the side to serve.

RED ONION SOUP WITH GOATS' CHEESE CROÛTES

If you haven't got any goats' cheese, use any Swiss cheese or try an equal mixture of Gruyère and Parmesan.

Serves 2

1 tbsp olive oil

a knob of unsalted butter

2 red onions, finely diced

1 tsp plain flour

2 tbsp red wine

2 tsp tomato purée

500ml (18fl oz) beef stock

salt and freshly ground black pepper

FOR THE CROÛTES

2 thick slices of French baguette, cut on the diagonal

1 tbsp olive oil

50g (2oz) goats' cheese log

Heat the oil in a pan and add the butter. Once it stops sizzling, tip in the onions and cook for 8–10 minutes until softened and lightly browned, stirring occasionally. Season with plenty of black pepper.

Stir the flour into the onions and cook for 1 minute, then pour in the wine and cook for another minute, stirring. Mix the tomato purée with the stock and then pour into the pan, stirring to combine. Bring to the boil, then reduce the heat to a simmer for 8–10 minutes or until thickened and slightly reduced.

Meanwhile, make the goats' cheese croûtes. Preheat the grill and a griddle pan. Drizzle the bread with the oil and griddle for 2 minutes on each side or until lightly charred. Cut the goats' cheese into 2 even-sized slices and place one on top of each piece of bread.

Season the soup to taste and ladle into flameproof soup tureens. Float a goats' cheese croûte on each one and place under the grill for a minute or so until the cheese is bubbling and melted. Serve at once.

SWEETCORN SOUP WITH TOMATO SALSA

This soup is wonderfully sweet, rich and full of flavour. Fresh, frozen or tinned sweetcorn kernels all work well. In summer, when sweetcorn is at its best, this also makes a delicious chilled soup.

Serves 2–4

500ml (18fl oz) chicken stock

350g (12oz) sweetcorn kernels

100ml (3½fl oz) double cream

FOR THE SALSA

1 ripe plum tomato, peeled, seeded and finely diced

4 spring onions, finely chopped

1 green chilli, seeded and finely chopped

2 tbsp chopped fresh coriander

salt and freshly ground black pepper

Place the stock in a small pan with the sweetcorn and bring to a simmer, then reduce the heat and simmer gently for 4–5 minutes until tender. Transfer to a food-processor and blend to a purée, or use a hand-held blender. The mixture will not be completely smooth, but this improves the texture. Return the soup to the pan and stir in the cream. Season to taste, and heat through.

Meanwhile, prepare the salsa. Place the tomato in a bowl with the spring onions, chilli and coriander. Stir to combine and season to taste. Ladle the soup into warmed serving bowls and place a spoonful of salsa on top. Serve immediately.

GRIDDLED RICOTTA-STUFFED FIGS WRAPPED IN PARMA HAM WITH ROCKET

The combination of warm figs and salty, crisp Parma ham is sublime and needs nothing more than the dressed rocket leaves to serve.

Serves 2

2 tbsp ricotta cheese

1 tbsp shredded fresh basil

6 ripe figs

6 thin Parma ham slices

50g (2oz) wild rocket

1 tsp balsamic vinegar

2 tbsp extra-virgin olive oil

salt and freshly ground black pepper

Heat a griddle pan until very hot. Place the ricotta in a bowl with the basil and season to taste. Cut a cross into the top of each fig and then, using a teaspoon, stuff with the ricotta mixture.

Wrap each stuffed fig in a slice of Parma ham and add to the heated griddle pan. Cook for 4–5 minutes until the Parma ham is crispy and the figs are heated through, turning occasionally.

Place the rocket in a bowl and add the balsamic vinegar and olive oil. Season generously and then toss until the leaves are evenly coated. Divide between plates and arrange the griddled figs on top to serve.

MARINATED SHIITAKE PARCELS

Shiitake mushrooms have a distinctive, almost meaty scent and flavour. Washing will make them waterlogged, so use as they are or give them a quick wipe with a piece of damp kitchen paper.

Serves 2

225g (8oz) shiitake mushrooms, stalks trimmed

juice of 1 lime

2 tsp white wine

2 tsp balsamic vinegar

1 tbsp olive oil

a dash of sesame oil

1 tbsp chopped fresh coriander

salt and freshly ground black pepper

Preheat the oven to 220°C/425°F/gas 7. Cut two 20cm (8in) squares of foil and divide the shiitake mushrooms between them. Scrunch up the sides so you have containers and sprinkle over the lime juice, white wine and balsamic vinegar. Season generously, then drizzle over the olive oil and add a few drops of sesame oil to each parcel. Finally scatter over the coriander and scrunch up the sides of the foil squares to form parcels.

Place the foil parcels on a baking sheet and bake for 8 minutes until the mushrooms are tender. Remove the parcels from the oven and transfer to warmed serving plates. Serve immediately, allowing guests to open their own parcels at the table.

DRESSED CRAB WITH HOMEMADE MAYONNAISE

195

It's well worth making homemade mayonnaise to serve with a fresh crab – simple but delicious.

Serves 4

2 slices of white bread, crusts removed

1 cooked crab, shell-on, weighing 700g (1½lb)

3 tsp white wine vinegar

2 eggs, plus 1 egg yolk

1 tsp Dijon mustard

65ml (2½fl oz) sunflower oil

65ml (2½fl oz) olive oil

salt and freshly ground black pepper

½ lettuce, shredded, to serve

TO GARNISH

parsley sprigs

1 lemon, quartered

Make the bread into breadcrumbs. Twist off the claws and legs of the crab. Press down on the mouth end to split the body apart. Remove and discard the 'dead man's fingers' (part of the stomach, located under the shell). Spoon the brown flesh into a bowl, add salt and pepper, a teaspoon of vinegar and the breadcrumbs. Wash the crab shell, pat it dry, and reserve it. Crack open the claws and legs with a rolling pin and remove the white flesh. Put it in a separate bowl and set it to one side.

Hard-boil the eggs; shell and chop. Whisk together the egg yolk, mustard and the remaining vinegar. Combine the oil in a jug and add to the egg yolk mixture very slowly, whisking vigorously and continuously, until thick. Spoon a little of the mayonnaise over the white crab meat and mash together.

To serve, put the brown flesh into the crab shell and spoon the white meat on top. On a plate, make a bed of lettuce and arrange the dressed crab on top. Garnish with the chopped egg, parsley and lemon. Serve the rest of the mayonnaise separately.

CHILLI CRAB CAKES WITH DIPPING SAUCE

196

A lovely easy starter for an intimate dinner for two. They will whet the appetite and set the tone for the rest of the meal.

Serves 2

50g (2oz) fresh white breadcrumbs

175g (6oz) white crabmeat, thawed if frozen

1 mild red chilli, seeded and finely chopped

3 tbsp chopped fresh coriander

1 egg, beaten

a good dash of dark soy sauce

2 tbsp seasoned flour

sunflower oil, for shallow-frying

salt and freshly ground black pepper

FOR THE DIPPING SAUCE

2 tbsp sesame seeds

4 tsp dark soy sauce

2 tsp sesame oil

1 tsp Tabasco sauce

2 tbsp chopped fresh coriander

2 lime wedges, to serve

Place the breadcrumbs in a food-processor with the crabmeat, chilli, coriander, egg, soy sauce and seasoning. Pulse together until just combined.

Divide the mixture into 8 and, using slightly dampened hands, shape into patties. Lightly dust in the seasoned flour, shaking off the excess.

Heat 2½ cm (1in) of oil in a large frying pan and gently fry the chilli crab cakes for 2–3 minutes on each side until cooked through and golden brown.

Meanwhile, make the dipping sauce. Place the sesame seeds in a bowl with the soy sauce, sesame oil, Tabasco and coriander. Stir to combine and then pour into individual dipping bowls.

Arrange the chilli crab cakes on warmed plates and add a bowl of the dipping sauce to each one. Garnish with lime wedges and serve at once.

PARMA HAM WITH CARAMELIZED BALSAMIC ONION AND BEETROOT

The saltiness of the Parma ham in this dish really sets off the sweetness of the beetroot. To do the Parma ham justice make sure you take it out of the fridge and allow it to come back up to room temperature before serving it.

Serves 2

2 tbsp olive oil, for frying

1 small red onion, thinly sliced

2 tsp light muscovado sugar

1 tbsp balsamic vinegar

4 cooked whole baby beetroot, halved

½ tsp Dijon mustard

1 tsp white wine vinegar

85ml (3fl oz) extra-virgin olive oil

50g (2oz) rocket, watercress and baby spinach salad (from a bag)

6 Parma ham slices, torn

salt and freshly ground black pepper

Heat a small frying pan over a low heat and add the 2 tablespoons of oil. Tip in the onion and cook for 2–3 minutes until softened but not coloured, stirring occasionally. Sprinkle over the sugar and cook for a minute or so to melt, stirring. Pour in the balsamic vinegar and allow to bubble down, then tip in the beetroot and cook for a couple of minutes until heated through and caramelized, tossing the pan occasionally.

To make the vinaigrette, place the mustard in a screw-topped jar with the white wine vinegar and seasoning. Shake to dissolve, then add the extra-virgin olive oil and shake again until emulsified. Place the salad leaves in a bowl and pour over enough dressing to coat. Arrange the Parma ham with the lightly dressed salad leaves on 2 serving plates. Scatter around the caramelized beetroot and onion and serve.

STUFFED FIELD MUSHROOMS

Flat (field) mushrooms are full of flavour and perfect for roasting. It's important not to wash them – just wipe them with a damp cloth or gently brush off any dirt. (See illustration, back cover.)

Serves 2

6 large flat mushrooms, stalks removed (each about 7½ cm/3in in diameter)

olive oil, for drizzling

25g (1oz) butter

2 garlic cloves, crushed

2 tbsp chopped fresh mixed herbs (such as flat-leaf parsley, basil and chives)

50g (2oz) fresh white breadcrumbs

6 small discs of fresh goats' cheese

50g (2oz) wild rocket

a little extra-virgin olive oil

a dash of balsamic vinegar

salt and freshly ground black pepper

Preheat the oven to 220°C/425°F/gas 7 and place the mushrooms in a non-stick baking tin. Season lightly and drizzle a little olive oil over each one. Bake in the oven for 3–4 minutes.

Meanwhile, melt the butter in a frying pan over a low heat. Sauté the garlic, herbs, breadcrumbs and seasoning for a few minutes until lightly golden.

Take the mushrooms from the oven and divide the breadcrumbs between them. Place a disc of goats' cheese on each and return to the oven for 5 minutes, until the breadcrumbs are golden and the cheese has melted.

Place the rocket leaves in a bowl and barely coat them with extra-virgin olive oil and balsamic vinegar. Season to taste. Arrange the mushrooms on plates and serve the rocket salad to the side.

CREAMY GARLIC MUSHROOMS ON TOAST

All manner of mushrooms respond well to being quickly fried and finished with a splash of cream.

Serves 2

1 tbsp olive oil

a knob of butter

1 garlic clove, finely chopped

2 large flat mushrooms, sliced

2 thick slices of sourdough bread

a good splash of Madeira

85ml (3fl oz) double cream

salt and freshly ground black pepper

1 tbsp shredded fresh basil

Preheat the grill to high and heat a large frying pan. Add the oil and butter to the pan and once the butter stops foaming, tip in the garlic and sauté for 20 seconds without colouring. Add the mushrooms and continue to sauté for 3–4 minutes until tender and all the liquid has evaporated. Season to taste.

Meanwhile, toast the sourdough slices on both sides under the hot grill.

Pour the Madeira over the mushrooms. As soon as it has evaporated, drizzle in the cream, then allow to bubble down and reduce a little.

Place the toasted sourdough on warmed plates and spoon the creamy mushrooms on top. Scatter over the basil and serve at once.

WILD MUSHROOM OMELETTE

Omelettes are so quick to make that it's just not worth cooking a large one for two. Don't be tempted to over-beat the eggs – that will spoil the texture.

Serves 1

2 tsp sunflower oil

a knob of butter

100g (4oz) mixed wild mushrooms, sliced

4 tbsp double cream

3 eggs

1 tbsp chopped mixed fresh herbs (such as flat-leaf parsley, chives and basil)

salt and freshly ground black pepper

crusty bread, to serve

Heat a 20cm (8in) non-stick frying pan. Heat half of the oil and butter in a separate frying pan and once the butter is foaming, tip in the wild mushrooms. Season to taste and then sauté for 2–3 minutes until tender. Stir in the cream and cook gently for 1–2 minutes.

Meanwhile, break the eggs into a bowl and add the herbs, then season and lightly beat. When the frying pan is hot, add the remaining oil and butter, swirling it round the base and sides.

While the butter is still foaming, pour in the eggs, tilting the pan from side to side. Stir gently with a wooden spatula, drawing the mixture from the sides to the centre as it sets. When almost set, carefully turn the omelette and cook for another minute. Tilt the pan away from you slightly and use a palette knife to fold over a third of the omelette to the centre, then fold over the opposite third. Slide onto a warmed plate. Spoon over the wild mushroom cream and serve at once with crusty bread.

POTATO AND CARROT LATKES WITH SPICY VINAIGRETTE

These are great served with sausages or grilled chicken, or with bacon and eggs for a brunch-style breakfast.

Serves 2–4

1 large potato, grated

1 large carrot, grated

50g (2oz) plain flour

1 egg, beaten

5 tbsp milk

5 tbsp olive oil

1 tbsp balsamic vinegar

1 tbsp wholegrain mustard

salt and freshly ground black pepper

fresh whole chives, to garnish (optional)

Dry the grated potato and carrot in a tea towel to remove excess moisture. Put the flour in a large bowl, make a well in the centre and gradually add the egg and milk to form a smooth batter. Season generously and stir in the grated vegetables to combine.

Heat 1 tablespoon of olive oil in a large, non-stick frying pan. Spoon 4 heaps of the potato and carrot mixture into the pan and press down to form 4 rough, flat rounds. Fry over a medium heat for 4–5 minutes until golden, then flip over and cook for a further 4–5 minutes until cooked through and lightly golden. Keep warm. Repeat with another tablespoon of olive oil and the rest of the potato and carrot mixture to make another 4 latkes.

Place the remaining 3 tablespoons of olive oil in a small bowl, add the balsamic vinegar and mustard, season, then whisk until an emulsion has formed. Pile the latkes on a warmed dish. Drizzle over the dressing and garnish with the chives.

MUSSEL DUET

Fresh mussels are marvellous. They're easy to cook, cheap, really good for you and they taste great!

Serves 2

900g (2lb) live mussels

300ml (½ pint) dry white wine

a pinch of saffron strands

3 tbsp double cream

75g (3oz) butter, softened

3 tbsp chopped fresh herbs, such as parsley, coriander and basil

2 garlic cloves, crushed

freshly ground black pepper

Preheat the grill. Scrub the mussels, removing the gritty beards and discarding any that are damaged or do not close when tapped. Cook the mussels with the wine over a high heat in a large pan with the lid on for 4–5 minutes until the mussels have opened. Remove them with a large slotted spoon, discarding any that have not opened. Stir the saffron and cream into the liquor in the pan and simmer rapidly until reduced by half. Remove from the heat. Add all but 12 of the mussels to the pan, replacing the lid.

Stir together the butter, herbs, garlic and plenty of pepper. Snap the top shells off each of the reserved mussels and dot with the herby butter. Cook under a hot grill for 2–3 minutes until the butter is bubbling, then transfer to a serving dish. Turn the saffron mussels into a large bowl and serve.

SQUID-INK RISOTTO

This squid-ink risotto is a fabulous dish – it's about time supermarkets started selling squid ink sachets.

Serves 2

50g (2oz) butter

225g (8oz) risotto rice, such as Arborio

1 packet of squid ink

600ml (1 pint) hot vegetable stock

2 slices of country-style bread, cut into 2cm (¾ in) cubes

4 tbsp olive oil

225g (8oz) clean fresh squid, halved lengthways

1 cos lettuce, roughly torn into bite-sized pieces

2 tomatoes, skinned, seeded and quartered

FOR THE SALAD DRESSING

2 garlic cloves

1 tsp Worcestershire sauce

1 egg yolk

40g (1½ oz) freshly grated Parmesan

juice of 1 lemon

2 tbsp olive oil

1 tsp wholegrain mustard

salt and freshly ground black pepper

snipped fresh chives, to garnish

Preheat the oven to 200°C/400°F/gas 6. Melt the butter in a large pan, stir in the rice and cook for 1 minute. Stir in the squid ink and, keeping the heat fairly high, gradually add the hot stock a ladle at a time, stirring until the liquid is absorbed and the rice is tender and creamy. This will take about 20 minutes.

Toss the bread cubes with the olive oil in a large bowl. Scatter onto a non-stick baking sheet and cook in the oven for about 8 minutes, turning occasionally until crisp and golden brown.

Meanwhile, make the salad dressing. Place the garlic, Worcestershire sauce, egg yolk, Parmesan and lemon juice in a food-processor and whizz until smooth. Add the olive oil and mustard and blend again. Season to taste and set aside.

Preheat a griddle pan or heavy-based frying pan. Score the inside of the squid flesh in a lattice pattern. Brush the squid with a little oil and cook for 30 seconds on each side. Season with salt and pepper.

To serve, spoon the risotto into a large serving bowl, top with the griddled squid and sprinkle over the snipped chives. Toss together the lettuce, tomatoes, salad dressing and croûtons and transfer to a serving bowl.

WARM CHORIZO AND CHICKPEA SALAD WITH ROASTED RED PEPPERS

This Middle Eastern-inspired salad is a meal on its own. (See illustration, front cover.)

Serves 2

4 mini white pitta breads

olive oil, for cooking

3 small raw chorizo sausages, thinly sliced on the diagonal

1 x 400g (14oz) tin of chickpeas, drained and rinsed

2 roasted peppers, drained and sliced into strips (from a jar, preserved in oil)

a squeeze of lemon juice

2 tbsp roughly chopped fresh coriander

2 tbsp roughly chopped fresh flat-leaf parsley

2–3 tbsp extra-virgin olive oil

salt and freshly ground black pepper

Heat a griddle pan until very hot and heat a frying pan. Brush both sides of the pitta breads with a little oil and chargrill for a minute or so on each side. Cut into strips on the diagonal and place in a large bowl.

Add the chorizo to the heated frying pan and cook for 3–4 minutes until its oil begins to ooze out, turning occasionally. Add the contents of the pan to the pitta bread with the chickpeas and roasted peppers.

Add the lemon juice to the bowl and then fold in the herbs with a good glug of extra-virgin olive oil. Season to taste. Tip onto a warmed platter and serve immediately.

SMASHING HASH AND SWEETCORN FRITTERS

Hash is great because it's tasty, satisfying, and can be made from ingredients you have sitting in your store cupboard.

Serves 2

½ onion, finely chopped

1 garlic clove, crushed

2 tbsp vegetable oil

1 x 340g (12oz) tin of corned beef, roughly chopped

grated rind and juice of ½ orange

1 tbsp brown sauce

2 tsp Worcestershire sauce

1 x 400g (14oz) tin of chopped tomatoes

2 tbsp chopped fresh basil

2 eggs

100g (4oz) self-raising flour

6 tbsp milk

1 x 200g (7oz) tin of sweetcorn with peppers, drained

175g (6oz) dried instant mashed potato

750ml (1¼ pints) boiling water

a knob of butter

salt and freshly ground black pepper

fresh dill sprigs, to garnish

Fry the onion and garlic in 1 tablespoon of the oil for 5 minutes until soft. In a large bowl, mix together the corned beef, orange rind and juice. Add to the pan of onions with the brown sauce and half the Worcestershire sauce and cook for 3–4 minutes, stirring until warmed through. Season, cover and keep warm.

Heat the chopped tomatoes in a small pan. Stir in the basil and the remaining Worcestershire sauce; season. Using a blender, whizz the mixture until smooth; keep warm. In a bowl, whisk together the eggs and flour and gradually beat in half the milk to make a smooth, thick batter. Add the sweetcorn; season.

Heat the remaining tablespoon of oil in a large, heavy-based frying pan and sit four 4cm (1½ in) rings in the pan. Ladle the batter into the rings to a 2½ cm (1in) thickness. Cook for 2 minutes, turn over the fritters and cook for a further 2 minutes.

Place the instant mashed potato in a large bowl and pour over the boiling water, stirring continuously. Beat in the remaining 3 tablespoons of milk and the butter; season. Spoon the mixture into a piping bag. Spoon the hash onto plates and pipe the potato over the top. Arrange the fritters on the potato and garnish with the dill. Spoon around the tomato sauce to serve.

BROCCOLI TEMPURA WITH GINGER DIPPING SAUCE

Perfect tempura should have a thin, almost transparent coating of lightly browned, crisp batter. Long thin florets of broccoli work best.

Serves 2

sunflower oil, for deep-frying

5 tbsp dark soy sauce

1 tbsp dry sherry or sake (optional)

2 tsp freshly grated root ginger

100g (4oz) plain flour, plus extra for dusting

1 egg yolk

120ml (4fl oz) ice-cold water

225g (8oz) broccoli florets (long-stemmed, if possible)

salt and freshly ground black pepper

Preheat a deep-fat fryer or a deep-sided pan one-third full of sunflower oil to 190°C/375°F. Mix together the soy sauce, dry sherry or sake, if using, and ginger in a bowl and dilute with a little cold water to taste. Pour into individual dipping bowls.

Tip the flour into a bowl and make a well in the centre. Add the egg yolk and gradually whisk in the ice-cold water until the batter reaches the consistency of single cream, then season it.

Drop pieces of the broccoli into the batter, lift them out with tongs or your fingers, shaking off any excess, then quickly lower them gently into the hot oil – you'll have to do this in batches.

Cook the tempura for 2 minutes, separating and turning the pieces when necessary, until the coating is crisp. Remove with a slotted spoon onto a plate lined with kitchen paper. Arrange on warmed plates and serve at once with the bowls of ginger dipping sauce on the side.

ONION RINGS WITH SWEET AND SOUR DIP

There's nothing nicer than a tender steak served with a huge pile of these crispy onion rings and a tangy dipping sauce.

Serves 2

sunflower oil, for deep-frying

1 red onion

100g (4oz) self-raising flour

200ml (7fl oz) sparkling water

FOR THE SWEET AND SOUR DIP

100g (4oz) ricotta cheese

2 tbsp tomato ketchup

1 tbsp snipped fresh chives

½ tsp Tabasco sauce

½ tsp Worcestershire sauce

salt and freshly ground black pepper

Preheat a deep-fat fryer or fill a deep-sided pan one-third full with oil and heat to 190°C/375°F. If you don't have a thermometer, the oil should be hot enough so that when a bread cube is added, it browns in 40 seconds.

Peel the onion and slice into 1cm (½ in) slices, then separate into rings. Place the flour in a bowl and make a well in the centre. Pour in the sparkling water and quickly whisk into the flour until you have achieved a smooth batter. Season to taste.

Dip the onion rings into the batter, gently shaking off any excess, then deep-fry for 2–3 minutes until crisp and golden brown. Drain on kitchen paper.

Meanwhile, make the sweet and sour dip. Place the ricotta cheese in a bowl with the tomato ketchup, chives, Tabasco and Worcestershire sauce. Season to taste and mix until well combined. Transfer to a small bowl set on a warmed plate. Pile up the hot onion rings around the sweet and sour dip and serve immediately.

DEEP-FRIED SPICY POTATO SLICES

208

These are excellent served with an aromatic curry or tagine, or they'd make a nice change from poppadoms with bowls of chutneys and a raita for dipping. Just don't forget the glasses of ice-cold beer as they are thirsty work.

Serves 2

sunflower oil, for deep-frying

50g (2oz) plain flour

2 tsp medium curry powder

2 potatoes, cut into 1cm (½ in) slices (such as Desirée or King Edward)

salt and freshly ground black pepper

FOR THE BATTER

100g (4oz) plain flour

175ml (6fl oz) ice-cold water

Preheat a deep-fat fryer or a deep-sided pan one-third full of sunflower oil to 190°C/375°F. Place the flour in a bowl and stir in the curry powder, then season generously. To make the batter, place the flour in a separate bowl with a pinch of salt and then whisk in enough of the water to make a smooth batter with the consistency of single cream. Coat the potato slices in the seasoned flour, shaking off any excess, then quickly dip into the batter.

Carefully drop the coated potato slices into the heated oil and deep-fry for 6–8 minutes until crisp and golden brown – you may have to do this in batches depending on the size of your pan. Remove with a slotted spoon and drain on kitchen paper. Pile onto a warmed serving dish and season with salt to serve.

BOMBAY CURRIED POTATOES WITH PEAS

209

This simple dish is prepared with traditional curry spices and shows how a few humble ingredients can be transformed into a quick and delicious supper.

Serves 2

2 large baking potatoes, cut into cubes

2 tbsp sunflower oil

1 onion, halved and sliced

1 red or yellow pepper, seeded and diced

2–3 tsp medium curry powder

2 tsp coriander seeds, crushed to a powder

2 garlic cloves, finely chopped

juice of ½ lemon

85ml (3fl oz) hot water

75g (3oz) frozen peas

2 tbsp Greek yoghurt (optional)

2 tbsp roughly chopped fresh coriander, to garnish

salt and freshly ground black pepper

naan bread, to serve (optional)

Place the potatoes in a pan of boiling salted water, bring back to the boil and simmer for 5 minutes, then drain well.

Meanwhile, heat a wok or large frying pan and add the oil. Tip in the onion and pepper and cook gently for 5 minutes or until softened. Add the curry powder, coriander seeds and garlic and stir-fry for 20 seconds. Add the blanched potatoes and toss until well coated in the spices.

Stir the lemon juice and ½ teaspoon of salt into the hot water and mix well to combine. Pour into the wok or frying pan, cover and simmer, stirring occasionally, for 8–10 minutes, or until most of the liquid has evaporated and the potatoes are tender when pierced with a knife.

Add the peas, stir in and cook for 2–3 minutes until they are tender but still bright green. Season to taste.

Spoon the potatoes onto each serving plate and add a dollop of yoghurt, if using. Scatter over the coriander and serve with naan bread, if liked.

SESAME PRAWN TOASTS WITH CUCUMBER DIPPING SAUCE

Try to use bread that's a day or two old for this recipe so that it has dried out slightly.

Serves 2

sunflower oil, for deep-frying

150g (5oz) raw, peeled tiger prawns, cleaned

1 spring onion, chopped

1 tsp freshly grated root ginger

½ mild red chilli, seeded and finely chopped

1 tbsp chopped fresh coriander

½ tsp cornflour

1 small egg white

3 slices white bread

1 tbsp sesame seeds

FOR THE CUCUMBER DIPPING SAUCE

2 tbsp rice wine vinegar

1 tbsp caster sugar

½ small cucumber, peeled, halved, seeded and finely chopped

½ mild red chilli, seeded and thinly sliced

salt and freshly ground black pepper

Preheat a deep-fat fryer or fill a deep-sided pan one-third full with oil and heat to 180°F/350°F. If you don't have a thermometer, the oil should be hot enough so that when a bread cube is added, it browns in 60 seconds.

To make the cucumber dipping sauce, place the vinegar in a bowl and stir in the sugar and a pinch of salt to dissolve. Add the cucumber and chilli and toss to coat. Cover with cling film and set aside for at least 5 minutes.

Place the prawns in a food-processor with the spring onion, ginger, chilli, coriander, cornflour, egg white and seasoning. Blitz until well combined and then spread over the slices of bread. Sprinkle each slice of bread with a teaspoon of sesame seeds and then cut off the crusts.

Deep-fry the toasts for 1–1½ minutes on each side until golden brown. Drain well on kitchen paper and cut each slice into four triangles. Arrange the prawn toasts on warmed plates with individual bowls of the cucumber dipping sauce to serve.

BLACK BEAN SALSA

This salsa is almost a salad in its own right, particularly if you were to add some cooked sweetcorn or podded broad beans. Try it with chargrilled pork or lamb chops.

Serves 2–4

1 roasted red pepper, drained (from a jar)

400g (14oz) tin of black beans, drained and rinsed

½ small red onion, finely chopped

2 tbsp chopped fresh flat-leaf parsley

a pinch of dried crushed chillies

1 tbsp extra-virgin olive oil

2 tsp freshly squeezed lemon juice

salt and freshly ground black pepper

Cut the roasted red pepper in half and remove any remaining seeds, then finely dice the flesh and place in a bowl.

Add the black beans to the bowl with the red onion, parsley, crushed chillies, olive oil and lemon juice. Season to taste and leave the flavours to combine for as long as time allows. To serve, use as required.

WARM COUSCOUS SALAD

This dish is full of contemporary flavours and textures. It is just as good cold and would make wonderful picnic food, or serve it warm alongside grilled fish fillets marinated in chilli oil.

Serves 2

100g (4oz) couscous

4 tbsp extra-virgin olive oil

juice of ½ lemon

2 shallots, finely chopped

100g (4oz) wild mushrooms, chopped

1 ripe red tomato, halved, seeded and diced

1 ripe yellow tomato, halved, seeded and diced

75g (3oz) artichoke hearts preserved in olive oil, drained and chopped

2 tbsp roughly chopped mixed fresh herbs (such as basil, flat-leaf parsley and chives)

salt and freshly ground black pepper

Place the couscous in a large bowl and drizzle over 2 tablespoons of the olive oil with the lemon juice, stirring gently. Pour over 120ml (4fl oz) of boiling water, then stir well, cover and leave to stand for 5 minutes.

Meanwhile, heat the remaining olive oil in a frying pan. Add the shallots and sauté for 1–2 minutes until softened. Add the wild mushrooms and cook for 2–3 minutes, until tender. Add the tomatoes and artichokes and cook for another minute or so until heated through but the tomatoes still hold their shape. Remove from the heat and season to taste.

Gently separate the couscous grains with a fork. Season to taste and place in a pan to reheat gently. Fold in the vegetable mixture with the herbs and divide between warmed plates to serve.

GLAZED CARROTS

The sharp crunchiness of these carrots is a perfect foil for the creamy richness of the goats' cheese. Serve with a roast leg of lamb or some pan-fried hake or cod.

Serves 2

25g (1oz) butter

1 tbsp olive oil

275g (10oz) small carrots, cut on the diagonal

a few whole coriander seeds

a good pinch of fresh thyme leaves

a splash of red wine vinegar

120ml (4fl oz) dry white wine

1 disc of fresh soft goats' cheese

1 tsp chopped fresh flat-leaf parsley

salt and freshly ground black pepper

Heat half the butter and the olive oil in a pan. Add the carrots and sweat for a couple of minutes to soften without colouring.

Place the coriander seeds in a pestle and mortar and lightly crush, then tip into the pan with the thyme and vinegar, and season to taste. Pour in enough wine to barely cover the carrots and boil fast for 6–8 minutes until tender and all the liquid has evaporated.

Melt the remaining butter in a small frying pan and fry the goats' cheese disc for 1–2 minutes on each side until golden. Transfer the carrots to a warmed dish and scatter over the parsley. Arrange the goats' cheese disc on top to serve.

WILD MUSHROOM AND LEEK CANNELLONI

214

Once you've mastered the technique, making your own pasta is really easy. Alternatively, start with six shop-bought fresh lasagne sheets and you are halfway there.

Serves 2

3 egg yolks

100g (4oz) plain flour, plus extra for dusting

2 tbsp olive oil

1 small onion, finely chopped

2 leeks, sliced on the diagonal

350g (12oz) mixed wild mushrooms, sliced (such as chanterelle, cep, shiitake, oyster and chestnut)

120ml (4fl oz) dry white wine

225ml (8fl oz) double cream

1 tsp Dijon mustard

butter, for greasing

50g (2oz) freshly grated Parmesan

salt and freshly ground black pepper

lightly dressed mixed leaf salad, to serve (optional)

Preheat the oven to 200°C/400°F/gas 6 and preheat the grill to medium. To make the pasta, place 2 of the egg yolks and a pinch of salt in a food-processor, then with the motor running add the flour, tablespoon by tablespoon, through the feeder tube until the mixture resembles fine breadcrumbs. Tip out onto a lightly floured work surface and squeeze the mixture together to form a ball, then divide into 6 balls. Wrap in cling film and chill for at least 5 minutes (or up to 2 hours if time allows).

Roll out the dough a piece at a time using a pasta machine, dusting with flour as you go. Pass through the widest setting three times, then gradually narrow the setting as you roll out until you have a thin, pliable pasta sheet, finally passing through the thinnest setting three times. Trim down to a square of about 10 x 5cm (4 x 6in). Repeat, covering the pasta with a damp cloth, until you have 6 in total.

Meanwhile, heat the oil in a frying pan and fry the onion and leeks for 1–2 minutes until just beginning to soften. Stir in the mushrooms, season and cook for another 3–4 minutes until the mushrooms are tender, stirring occasionally. Pour in the wine and allow it to bubble down, then pour in 150ml (¼ pint) of the cream and add the mustard. Cook for 1–2 minutes until slightly reduced and thickened, stirring. Season to taste, then transfer to a bowl to cool down slightly.

Blanch the pasta sheets briefly in a pan of boiling salted water, then plunge into a bowl of ice-cold water and drain. Pat dry with kitchen paper. Lightly butter an ovenproof dish. Spoon some of the mushroom and leek mixture into each lasagne sheet and carefully roll up to enclose. Arrange in the buttered dish.

Mix the rest of the cream in a small bowl with the remaining egg yolk and half of the Parmesan. Spoon over the cannelloni and scatter the rest of the Parmesan on top. Bake for 5–10 minutes until heated through, then flash under the hot grill until lightly golden. Serve straight from the dish with a bowl of the salad, if liked.

PERFECT PUMPKIN RAVIOLI WITH SAGE BUTTER

Cappellacci or pumpkin ravioli are a speciality of Bologna and although time-consuming are a most impressive dish for a special occasion.

Serves 2

225g (8oz) plain flour

2 eggs

FOR THE FILLING

¼ pumpkin, seeded and chopped

1 tbsp mixed candied peel

50g (2oz) flaked almonds

250g (9oz) ricotta cheese

1 egg yolk

1 egg, lightly beaten

FOR THE SAUCE

100g (4oz) butter

2 tbsp chopped fresh sage

a pinch of freshly grated nutmeg

1 tbsp freshly grated Parmesan, to serve

salt and freshly ground black pepper

fresh sage leaves, to garnish

Blend the flour, eggs and a pinch of salt in a food-processor until the mixture resembles fine breadcrumbs. Turn the mixture out onto a floured surface and bring together to form a firm dough. Knead lightly, cover with cling film and set aside to rest, ideally for an hour. This makes rolling the pasta much easier.

Chop the pumpkin into 2½ cm (1in) pieces and simmer for about 8 minutes. Meanwhile, in a clean food-processor, whizz together the mixed peel and almonds until finely chopped. Add the ricotta, pumpkin and egg yolk and blend until smooth; season. Divide the pasta dough into 4 and, using a pasta machine or rolling pin, roll each piece out thinly to a rectangle measuring roughly 25 x 8cm (10 x 3in).

Lay the pasta on a work surface and put 2 teaspoons of the pumpkin mixture in even rows on 2 of the sheets. Brush around the filling with beaten egg. Place the other 2 sheets on top and press around each mound of filling to seal well. Using a 5cm (2in) pastry cutter, cut around each mound. This mixture makes about 20 ravioli. Bring a pan of salted water to the boil and cook the pasta for 3 minutes.

Melt the butter in a small pan. When foaming, stir in the sage and nutmeg. Drain the ravioli and toss in the butter. Transfer to a plate and dust, pour over the sage sauce, sprinkle with Parmesan and garnish with the fresh sage.

BROCCOLI AND FETA PANCAKES WITH TOMATO SAUCE

Tinned tomatoes make surprisingly fresh-tasting sauces, especially if you add a handful of fresh herbs and some garlic.

Serves 4

150g (5oz) plain flour

2 eggs

300ml (½ pint) milk

2 tbsp snipped fresh chives

2 tbsp of olive oil

50g (2oz) unsalted butter, plus extra for greasing

1 small red onion

1 garlic clove, crushed

1 x 400g (14oz) tin of chopped tomatoes (in rich tomato juice)

2 tsp tomato purée

350g (12oz) broccoli, cut into small florets

100g (4oz) feta cheese

85g (3½ oz) black olives, pitted

2 tbsp chopped mixed fresh herbs (such as flat-leaf parsley and basil)

salt and freshly ground black pepper

lightly dressed mixed salad, to serve

Preheat the oven to 200°C/400°F/gas 6. To make the pancake batter, sift the flour and a pinch of salt into a bowl, then make a well in the centre. Break in the eggs and add a little of the milk. Mix the liquid ingredients together, then gradually take in the flour and beat until smooth. Finally beat in the remaining milk until you have a batter the consistency of single cream. Stir in the chives and leave to rest for 5 minutes (or up to 30 minutes covered with cling film in the fridge if time allows).

Heat a large non-stick pan and, when hot, brush with a thin film of oil and add a little of the butter. Pour a small amount of the batter into the pan and swirl it around until it evenly covers the bottom. Cook for 1 minute until the edges are curling away from the pan and the underside is golden. Flip over and cook for another minute or so. Transfer the pancake to a plate lined with a square of non-stick baking paper. Repeat until you have 8 pancakes in total, layering them up on the plate between squares of the non-stick baking paper.

Meanwhile, make the tomato sauce. Heat 1 tablespoon of oil in a frying pan. Add the onion and cook for 2–3 minutes until softened but not coloured, stirring. Stir in the garlic and cook for 30 seconds or so, then add the tomatoes and tomato purée. Season to taste. Bring to the boil, then reduce the heat and simmer for 8–10 minutes until slightly reduced and thickened, stirring from time to time.

Cook the broccoli in boiling salted water for 2–3 minutes until tender. Drain and quickly refresh under cold running water. Place in a large bowl and crumble in the feta. Stir in the olives and herbs, then fold in the tomato sauce. Season to taste.

Divide the broccoli mixture between the pancakes. Roll up to enclose the filling and then arrange in a single layer, seam-side down, in a lightly buttered ovenproof dish. Dot with the remaining butter and bake for about 5 minutes until the pancakes are heated through. Serve the pancakes straight from the dish with a large bowl of salad alongside.

AUBERGINE CAVIAR BRUSCHETTA WITH CHARGRILLED CIABATTA

217

This aubergine 'caviar' is ideal warm or cold as a dip. It is a variation on *baba ganoush*, which means 'spoilt old man' in Arabic.

Serves 2

5 tbsp olive oil

1 aubergine, peeled and finely diced

1 small red onion, finely chopped

6 thick slices ciabatta bread, cut on the diagonal

2 tbsp chopped fresh coriander

1 tbsp snipped fresh chives

sea salt and freshly ground black pepper

lime wedges, to garnish

Heat 3 tablespoons of the olive oil in a frying pan and then tip in the aubergine. Cook for about 5 minutes until just beginning to soften and colour. Season generously, add the onion, then continue to sauté for 4–5 minutes or until the onion is softened and tender, stirring occasionally.

Meanwhile, heat a griddle pan until it is smoking hot. Drizzle the remaining oil over the slices of bread, sprinkle with sea salt and toast on the griddle pan until nicely marked on both sides.

Stir the coriander and chives into the aubergine mixture and transfer to a serving bowl set on a plate. Garnish with the lime wedges and serve warm or cold with the hot, chargrilled bread.

CREAMY MUSHROOM RISOTTO

218

A risotto is not designed to be light but is a rich and deliciously creamy dish. In Italy, where it is only ever served as a starter, it is usually followed by a very simple and extremely light second course.

Serves 4

25g (1oz) dried porcini mushrooms

200ml (7fl oz) boiling water

4 tbsp olive oil

3 fresh bay leaves

6 chopped fresh sage leaves,

3 chopped fresh parsley sprigs

600ml (1 pint) water

1 vegetable stock cube

25g (1oz) butter

1 onion, very finely chopped

450g (1lb) risotto rice, such as Arborio

150ml (¼ pint) white wine

100g (4oz) fresh grated Parmesan

2 tbsp double cream

250g (9oz) chestnut or open-cup mushrooms, sliced

2 garlic cloves, chopped

2 tbsp chopped fresh parsley

salt and freshly ground black pepper

Stir the dried mushrooms into the boiling water, take off the heat and set aside to soak for 10 minutes. Drain, reserving the soaking liquid, and roughly chop the mushrooms.

Heat 2 tablespoons of the olive oil in a large pan and cook the herbs for 1 minute. Pour in the water and the reserved soaking liquid, then crumble in the stock cube and bring to the boil.

Meanwhile, melt the butter in a pan and cook the onion for 5 minutes until softened. Stir in the rice and cook for 1 minute. Add the soaked mushrooms and white wine, stirring until the liquid is absorbed. Keeping the heat fairly high, gradually add the hot stock a ladle at a time, stirring until the liquid is absorbed and the rice is tender and creamy – this process takes about 20 minutes. Stir in the Parmesan and cream and add salt and pepper to taste.

Heat the remaining olive oil in a large frying pan and cook the fresh mushrooms and garlic over a high heat for 2–3 minutes until golden brown. Stir in the chopped parsley and add salt and pepper to taste.

To serve, spoon the risotto into a large serving dish and scatter over the garlic mushrooms.

CHEESY BAKE AND SPLIT-PEA CAKES

A lot of people are wary of split peas but they're very tasty and adaptable.

Serves 4

350g (12oz) new potatoes, scraped or scrubbed and halved

5 fresh mint leaves

1 red pepper, deseeded

5 tbsp olive oil

2 onions, chopped

2 tsp wholegrain mustard

300ml (½ pint) double cream

150g (5oz) baby button mushrooms, quartered

a small bunch of fresh chives, snipped

175g (6oz) paneer cheese

1 x 400g (14oz) tin of yellow split peas, drained

100g (4oz) fresh brown breadcrumbs

25g (1oz) plain flour

1 egg, beaten

200g (7oz) fresh spinach, stalks removed

salt and freshly ground black pepper

Preheat the oven to 200°C/400°F/gas 6. Cook the potatoes and mint in boiling salted water for 10–12 minutes. Slice the pepper into 1cm (½ in) wide rings, then set them aside and roughly chop the top and bottom parts of the pepper. Heat 1 tablespoon of the olive oil in a frying pan and cook the onions and chopped pepper for 5 minutes. Stir in the mustard and season to taste.

Gently heat the cream in a small pan. Stir in the mushrooms and cook for 3–4 minutes, then the chives and seasoning. Drain the potatoes and mint and transfer to an ovenproof dish. Spoon over half the onion mixture, then pour over the creamy mushrooms. Crumble the paneer on top and bake for 8–10 minutes.

In a bowl, mix together the split peas, remaining onion mixture and breadcrumbs. Season, then gradually add enough flour and egg to bind the mixture. Shape into 4 even-sized patties and dust with a little flour. Heat 2 tablespoons of oil in a separate frying pan and gently fry for 5 minutes, turning once, until golden.

Fry the pepper rings in a separate pan in 1 tablespoon of olive oil for 5 minutes until softened. Heat 1 tablespoon of olive oil in a large pan and add the spinach. Cover and cook for 2–3 minutes, stirring occasionally until wilted. Drain well, then season. Stack the pepper rings and patties on top of the spinach, drizzle with the remaining oil and serve with the paneer gratin.

GNOCCHI WITH SAGE BUTTER

It's amazing how many delicious recipes you can make from the humble potato.

Serves 2

450g (1lb) potatoes, chopped

a good pinch of salt

50g (2oz) plain flour, plus extra for dusting

85g (3½ oz) unsalted butter

a handful of chopped fresh sage leaves

freshly grated Parmesan, to serve (optional)

Place the potatoes in a pan of boiling salted water, cover and simmer for 10–12 minutes until completely tender. Drain and return to the pan for a couple of seconds to dry out. With a wooden spoon, push the potatoes through a sieve set over a bowl. Add the salt, flour and 25g (1oz) of butter. Mix to bind.

Turn the potato mixture out onto a lightly floured work surface. Knead lightly until smooth and roll into a long sausage shape about 2½ cm (1in) in diameter. Cut into 2cm (¾ in) pieces, then press each piece with a fork to mark grooves. Dust in flour.

Add the gnocchi to a pan of simmering water a few at a time and cook gently for 2–3 minutes or until they float. Transfer to a warm dish. Melt the remaining butter in a pan with the sage leaves and cook over a very gentle heat for a couple of minutes. Pour over the gnocchi and scatter over the Parmesan to serve.

MALAYSIAN SWEET POTATO CURRY

Puréeing the onions before cooking is a popular Malay technique that gives a distinctive texture to the curry, helped by the addition of the almonds, a natural thickener.

Serves 4

1 red onion, chopped

1 garlic clove, chopped

1cm (½ in) piece of fresh root ginger, chopped

2 red bird's eye chillies, seeded and chopped

1 lemongrass stalk, outer core removed, chopped

2 tbsp ground almonds

2 tbsp sunflower oil

1 tsp each ground cumin, coriander, paprika and turmeric

500g (1lb 2oz) sweet potatoes, cut into 1cm (½ in) chunks

300ml (½ pint) vegetable stock

1 x 400g (14oz) tin of coconut milk

juice of 1 lime

salt and freshly ground black pepper

steamed Basmati rice, to serve

fresh coriander leaves, to garnish

Place the onion in a mini food-processor with the garlic, ginger, chillies, lemongrass, almonds, oil and spices. Whizz until well combined to a purée.

Heat a large pan. Add the onion paste and stir-fry for 2–3 minutes until cooked through but not coloured. Add the sweet potatoes and continue to stir-fry for another 2–3 minutes until just beginning to colour. Season generously.

Pour the vegetable stock into the pan with the coconut milk, stirring to combine. Bring to the boil, then reduce the heat and simmer for 15 minutes or until the sweet potatoes are completely tender but still holding their shape.

Stir the lime juice into the sweet potato curry and season to taste. Divide the rice among warmed serving bowls and ladle in the curry. Garnish with the coriander leaves and serve at once.

CHILLI, BROCCOLI AND MANGO NOODLE STIR FRY

To make this more substantial, mix an egg and cook like a pancake, then shred and add to the noodle mixture. (See illustration, page 2.)

Serves 2

100g (4oz) medium egg noodles

2 tbsp sunflower oil

225g (8oz) long-stemmed broccoli florets, trimmed

4 spring onions, finely chopped

1 small green mango, peeled and cut into slices

1 red scotch bonnet chilli, seeded and thinly sliced

1 tbsp chopped fresh coriander

a few drops of sesame oil

salt and freshly ground black pepper

Drop the noodles into a pan of boiling water and remove from the heat. Stir with a fork and then leave to stand for 4 minutes or according to the packet instructions until tender. Stir and drain well.

Heat a wok or large frying pan until very hot. Add the oil to the wok, swirling it up the sides, then add the broccoli. Stir-fry for 3–4 minutes until just beginning to soften.

Add the spring onions to the broccoli and stir-fry for another minute or so. Using a wooden spatula, fold in the mango slices with the drained noodles.

Add the chilli to the wok, season to taste and continue to stir-fry for another 1–2 minutes until the broccoli is completely tender and cooked through. Fold in the coriander and sprinkle with the sesame oil. Divide between warmed bowls to serve.

VEGGIE MUSHROOM BURGERS

A delicious combination of mushrooms stuffed with creamy goats' cheese, this makes a meat-free meal full of interesting flavours and textures. It's a perfect dish for the barbecue.

Serves 2

8 large flat mushrooms, stems removed, (each about 10cm/4in in diameter)

2 tbsp olive oil

225g (8oz) soft goats' cheese

1 tsp chopped fresh thyme

2 garlic cloves, crushed

salt and freshly ground black pepper

fresh flat-leaf parsley sprigs, to garnish

Heat a griddle pan until smoking hot. Trim the mushrooms to uniform shapes. Brush with some of the olive oil and place, gill-side down, in the pan. Cook the mushrooms for 5 minutes or until the gills are just tender, but do not turn them.

In a bowl, mash together the goats' cheese, thyme and garlic and season generously.

Remove the mushrooms from the heat and brush all over with the remaining oil. Fill 4 of them with the goats' cheese mixture, then place the remaining mushrooms on top to form sandwiches. Place the 'burgers' back in the pan. Cook, turning occasionally, for 3–4 minutes, or until the cheese starts to melt. Garnish with parsley sprigs to serve.

AUTUMN VEGETABLE PIE

Quick and easy, this elegant dish will prove a popular main course with vegetarians and carnivores alike.

Serves 4

200g (7oz) plain flour

100g (4oz) butter

1 small egg yolk

5 tbsp water

1 egg, beaten

FOR THE FILLING

250g (9oz) baby new potatoes, scrubbed or scraped and halved lengthways

3 carrots, sliced

350g (12oz) broccoli, cut into small florets

50g (2oz) butter

2 tbsp plain flour

450ml (¾ pint) milk

225g (8oz) freshly grated Gruyère or Cheddar cheese

1 tbsp chopped fresh dill

1 tbsp snipped fresh chives

salt and freshly ground black pepper

snipped fresh chives, to garnish

Preheat the oven to 200°C/400°F/gas 6. To make the pastry, place the flour, butter and salt in a food-processor and whizz until the mixture resembles fine breadcrumbs. Add the egg yolk and enough water to blend to a firm dough.

On a floured surface, roll out the pastry to a thickness of about 5mm (¼ in). Using a small, sharp knife, cut out 8 large leaf shapes. Transfer to a baking sheet, brush with beaten egg and bake for 10–15 minutes until golden brown.

To make the filling, cook the potatoes in a large pan of boiling salted water for 10–12 minutes until tender. Remove the potatoes from the pan with a slotted spoon and add the carrots and broccoli. Cook for 3–4 minutes until tender.

Meanwhile, melt the butter in a large pan, then stir in the flour and cook for 1 minute. Gradually beat in the milk to make a smooth sauce. Stir in the cheese, chopped herbs and salt and pepper to taste. Add the cooked vegetables, stir well and cook for a few minutes until the cheese has melted and the vegetables are heated through.

To serve, spoon the saucy vegetables onto 4 serving plates and top each plate with 2 pastry leaves. Garnish with the chives.

TILAPIA AND SWEET-POTATO GNOCCHI

Gnocchi seem to have the same mystery attached to them as soufflés, but go on and try them, you won't be disappointed.

Serves 2

2 sweet potatoes, diced

150g (5oz) plain flour

1 egg, beaten

1 tbsp chopped fresh rosemary

1 x 350g (12oz) tilapia

2 spring onions, finely chopped

1 tbsp chopped fresh coriander

3 tbsp olive oil

1 leek, thinly sliced

1 garlic clove, finely chopped

2 tbsp crème fraîche

salt and freshly ground black pepper

3 spring onions, thinly sliced, to garnish

Cook the sweet potatoes in a large pan of boiling salted water for 10 minutes until softened. Drain well and roughly mash. Mix with the flour, beaten egg, rosemary and plenty of salt and pepper. On a floured surface, roll the gnocchi mixture out into a long sausage and cut into 1cm (½ in) lengths. Cook the gnocchi in a large pan of boiling salted water for 3–4 minutes until they float to the surface of the water. Drain well.

Diagonally score the fish on both sides. Season the slashes, then pack them with the spring onions and coriander. Heat 2 tablespoons of olive oil in a heavy-based frying pan and cook the fish for 7–8 minutes, turning once, until cooked through.

Heat the remaining oil in a large frying pan and cook the leek and garlic for 5 minutes, until soft. Season and stir in the crème fraîche and the gnocchi. Cook gently until heated through. To serve, pile the gnocchi onto a serving plate and arrange the tilapia on top. Garnish with the spring onion slices.

CRISPY FRIED SOLE WITH GREEN BEANS AND AIOLI

This technique works with any type of sole that's available, or try skate wings cut into 2½ cm (1in) pieces.

Serves 2

sunflower oil, for deep-frying

2 egg yolks

2 tsp Dijon mustard

3 garlic cloves, crushed

1 tsp white wine vinegar

100ml (3½ fl oz) sunflower oil

100ml (3½ fl oz) olive oil, plus a little extra

100g (4oz) fine green beans, trimmed

1 egg white

2 tbsp double cream

4 lemon sole fillets, skinned

50g (2oz) plain flour, seasoned generously

salt and freshly ground black pepper

fresh whole chives, to garnish

Heat a deep-fat fryer or deep-sided pan one-third full of sunflower oil to 180°C/350°F. Beat the egg yolks with the mustard, garlic, vinegar, 1 tablespoon of water and seasoning, until thickened. Mix the oils together in a jug and add to the egg-yolk mixture, drop by drop, whisking constantly. After adding 2 tablespoons of oil the mixture should be quite thick. Add the remaining oil more quickly, a teaspoon at a time, whisking constantly. Season, then transfer to a plastic squeezy bottle and chill until ready to use.

Blanch the beans in boiling salted water for 3–4 minutes. Drain and refresh under cold running water. Return half to the pan and set aside. Very finely slice the other half and place in a bowl.

Add the egg white to the finely chopped beans and whisk in the cream. Pat the sole fillets dry and cut each one in half on the slight diagonal. Add to the egg white mixture and rub in well. Massage the flour into each piece of sole, coating evenly. Drop into the heated oil and deep-fry for 2–3 minutes until crisp and golden brown. Drain on kitchen paper. Add a little olive oil to the reserved beans and reheat. Arrange on warmed serving plates and pile the crispy fried sole on top. Drizzle with aioli and garnish with chives to serve.

HOT AND HERBY MACKEREL WITH SAUTÉED SWEET POTATOES

If you're looking to eat healthily, you really can't beat mackerel.

Serves 2

225g (8oz) sweet potato, peeled and sliced lengthways

1 sprig of fresh coriander

4 tbsp olive oil

2 whole mackerel, cleaned and scaled

4 red chillies, seeded and finely chopped

grated rind and juice of 1 lemon

2 tbsp chopped fresh coriander

1 tbsp chopped fresh parsley

1 tsp each chopped fresh mint, basil and tarragon

2 garlic cloves, finely chopped

½ iceberg lettuce

salt and freshly ground black pepper

2 red chillies, seeded and sliced

Preheat the grill. Cook the sweet potato and coriander sprig in a large pan of boiling salted water for 6–8 minutes until tender. Drain and pat dry; discard the coriander. Heat 2 tablespoons of the olive oil in a heavy-based frying pan and cook the sweet potato for 2–3 minutes on each side until golden brown.

Cut 4 diagonal slits, 1cm (½ in) deep, in each side of the mackerel. Mix together the chopped chillies, lemon rind and juice, herbs and garlic; season. Stuff three-quarters of the mixture into the mackerel cavities. Heat the remaining oil in a frying pan and cook the mackerel for 6 minutes, turning once, then cook under the grill for 3–4 minutes, turning occasionally.

Finely shred the lettuce and toss with the remaining herb stuffing. Pile onto a plate, top with a layer of sweet potato slices and arrange the mackerel on top. Spoon over the cooking juices. Garnish with the sliced chillies.

FRIED PLAICE WITH PEA AND MINT MASH

Any fishmonger would be happy to fillet a whole plaice for you for this recipe.

Serves 2

1 large potato, diced

225g (8oz) frozen peas

1 tbsp chopped fresh mint

25g (1oz) butter

FOR THE SAUCE

25g (1oz) butter

4 shallots

150ml (¼ pint) white wine

75g (3oz) button mushrooms, sliced

1 tbsp chopped fresh tarragon

grated rind of 1 lemon

grated rind of 1 lime

3 tbsp double cream

FOR THE FISH

3 tbsp plain flour

25g (1oz) light muscovado sugar

½ tsp ground cumin

4 boneless, skinless plaice fillets

1 tbsp olive oil

15g (½ oz) butter

juice of ½ lemon

salt and freshly ground black pepper

Cook the potato in a large pan of boiling salted water for 10 minutes. Add the peas and mint and cook for a further 3–4 minutes until softened. Drain well, then return to the pan. Mash together, then add the butter and season with salt and pepper to taste; cover and keep warm.

Meanwhile, make the sauce. Place the butter, shallots, wine, mushrooms, tarragon and citrus rind in a pan. Bring to the boil and simmer gently for 6 minutes. Stir in the cream and continue to simmer gently for a few minutes until slightly thickened.

To cook the fish, mix together the flour, sugar, cumin and a little salt and pepper. Lightly score the flesh of each plaice fillet and coat in the seasoned flour, shaking off the excess. Heat the oil and butter in a large, heavy-based frying pan and cook the fish for 3–4 minutes on each side until golden. Squeeze over the lemon juice and remove from the heat.

To serve, place a 7½ cm (3in) ring mould in the centre of two plates and fill with the mash. Place the shallots on either side of the mash and pour around the sauce. Remove the moulds and place 2 fried plaice fillets on top of each pile of mash.

BREAM WITH LANGOUSTINES

This recipe for black bream with samphire and langoustines makes a very sophisticated dish. Ask your greengrocer to get hold of the samphire for you or substitute with young, tender asparagus.

Serves 2

sunflower oil, for deep-frying

1 large potato cut into 2cm (¾ in) slices

1 tsp ground turmeric

2 tomatoes, quartered

11 tbsp olive oil

1 tsp salt

3 tsp caster sugar

2 tsp balsamic vinegar

6 langoustines

1 tsp tomato purée

1 onion, thinly sliced

1 yellow pepper, seeded and cut into 2cm (¾ in) pieces

1 tbsp snipped fresh chives

2 tsp white wine vinegar

100g (4oz) samphire

1 x 350g (12oz) black bream, filleted

4 tbsp seasoned plain flour

salt and freshly ground black pepper

Preheat the oven to 220°C/425°F/gas 7. Preheat a deep-fat fryer or fill a deep-sided pan one-third full with sunflower oil and heat to 190°C/375°F. Cook the potato slices and turmeric in boiling salted water for 10–12 minutes. Fry the tomatoes for 1–2 minutes in 2 tablespoons of olive oil in an ovenproof pan. Add salt and 2 teaspoons of sugar. Roast in the oven for 7–8 minutes, drizzle with the vinegar, cover and keep warm.

Cook the langoustines in boiling water for 1 minute, drain; peel the tails. Remove the heads and gently heat them in a pan with the tomato purée, crushing them with the back of a spoon. Add 6 tablespoons of olive oil and warm gently for 3–4 minutes. Place the onion in a sieve, sprinkle liberally with salt and set aside. Cook the pepper pieces, skin-side down over a high heat in 1 tablespoon of olive oil for 3–4 minutes; keep warm. Rinse the onions and pat dry. Deep-fry in hot sunflower oil for 2–3 minutes until crisp and golden. Drain on kitchen paper.

Strain the langoustine oil through muslin and stir in the chives, white wine vinegar, remaining sugar and seasoning. Blanch the samphire in boiling water for 1–2 minutes until tender, drain and toss with 1 tablespoon of olive oil. Dust the bream with the flour and shallow-fry over a high heat in the remaining olive oil for 1–2 minutes on each side. Stack the potatoes and bream on the samphire and arrange the tomatoes and langoustine tails to the side. Drizzle around the dressing and garnish with the onions.

HADDOCK MONTE CARLO

This dish worked a treat – wonderful served with sautéed spinach and a glass of crisp, dry white wine. (See illustration, page 122.)

Serves 2

150ml (¼ pint) milk

50ml (2fl oz) double cream

2 x 100g (4oz) haddock fillets, skinned and boned

1 small red onion, finely chopped

2 tsp olive oil

2 ripe firm tomatoes, seeded and diced

1 garlic clove, crushed

2 egg yolks

50g (2oz) freshly grated Parmesan

salt and freshly ground black pepper

Preheat the grill. Place the milk and cream in a wide pan and bring almost to the boil. Add the haddock fillets, reduce the heat and poach for 4–5 minutes until just tender. Sauté the red onion for a few minutes in the hot oil until soft but not coloured. Add the tomatoes and garlic and sauté for another 2 minutes. Season and divide between warmed heatproof plates. Remove the haddock from the poaching liquid and arrange on top of the tomato mixture; keep warm.

Season the remaining poaching liquid and whisk in the egg yolks. Continue to cook for 1–2 minutes until thickened, stirring constantly. Stir in the Parmesan and ladle over the haddock to cover completely. Place the plates directly under the grill for 1–2 minutes until bubbling and lightly golden. Serve at once.

SEARED TUNA WITH SWEET POTATO CRISPS AND PEACH SALSA

Watch the sides of the tuna steaks while they cook – when they look cooked a quarter of the way up, turn them over.

Serves 2

sunflower oil, for deep-frying

1 tsp olive oil

2 x 100g (4oz) fresh tuna steaks, each about 2½cm (1in) thick

1 orange-fleshed sweet potato (no more than 225g/8oz in weight)

1 tbsp medium curry powder

FOR THE PEACH SALSA

1 tbsp olive oil

1 tbsp balsamic vinegar

1 ripe peach, halved, stoned and diced

10 cherry tomatoes, quartered

2 tbsp shredded fresh basil

salt and freshly ground black pepper

Preheat a deep-fat fryer or fill a deep-sided pan one-third full with oil and heat to 190°C/375°F. Heat a griddle pan until very hot. To make the peach salsa, heat the olive oil and balsamic vinegar in a small pan for 2–3 minutes. Place the peach in a bowl with the cherry tomatoes and basil. Season and fold in the hot olive oil and balsamic mixture; set aside.

Drizzle the heated griddle pan with the olive oil and cook the tuna steaks for 2–3 minutes on each side, depending on how rare you like your fish.

Using a mandolin, cut the sweet potato into wafer-thin slices and deep-fry in batches for 30 seconds to 1 minute until crisp and lightly golden. Mix the curry powder in a small bowl with 1 tablespoon of salt. Tip the deep-fried sweet potato crisps onto kitchen paper and quickly and liberally dust with the curried salt. Arrange the tuna on warmed plates, spoon over the peach salsa and serve with the crisps on the side.

SCENTED SEAFOOD CURRY

Use any selection of seafood or firm-fleshed fish for this deliciously fragrant curry.

Serves 2

1cm (½in) piece of fresh root ginger, peeled and chopped

2 garlic cloves, chopped

1 mild red chilli, seeded and chopped

1 small bunch of coriander, plus extra leaves to garnish

2 tsp sunflower oil

6 tbsp vegetable stock (from a cube is fine)

6 tbsp double cream

175g (6oz) squid, cleaned and sliced

175g (6oz) raw, peeled tiger prawns, cleaned

100g (4oz) small live clams, cleaned

1 x 275g (10oz) packet of cooked Thai fragrant rice (or use leftover rice)

salt and freshly ground black pepper

Place the ginger, garlic, chilli and coriander in a mini food-processor with a splash of water. Blend to form a smooth paste, adding another splash of water if necessary.

Heat the oil in a pan and tip in the ginger paste. Heat gently for a minute or so until fragrant, then pour in the vegetable stock and allow to bubble down by half. Stir in the cream and bring to a gentle simmer. Cook for 1–2 minutes until slightly reduced and thickened.

Fold the squid, prawns and clams into the scented cream mixture and season to taste. Cover with a lid and heat gently until the seafood is cooked through and the clams have opened; discard any that do not open.

Meanwhile, heat the rice according to the packet instructions and divide between warmed plates. Ladle on the scented seafood curry and garnish with coriander leaves.

GRATIN MUSSELS

Food trends come and go but this recipe has stood the test of time. (See illustration, page 122.)

Serves 2

24 large fresh mussels, cleaned

a glug of dry white wine

25g (1oz) unsalted butter

1 garlic clove, crushed

2 slices of day-old white bread, crusts removed, diced

a pinch of finely diced red bird's-eye chilli

a small handful of fresh flat-leaf parsley leaves

salt and freshly ground black pepper

2 lemon wedges, to serve

Preheat the grill and heat a large pan until hot. Add the mussels and wine and cover tightly. Cook for 3–4 minutes, shaking half way through. All the mussels should have opened; discard any that do not. Drain them through a colander and allow to cool.

Melt the butter in a small pan and gently sauté the garlic for 1 minute without colouring. Tip into a food-processor or liquidizer. Add the bread to the food-processor with the chilli and parsley, then blitz to fine crumbs. Season to taste.

Discard the empty half shells from the mussels and arrange them in a shallow baking tin. Spoon the breadcrumbs on top to cover completely. Grill for 2 minutes until crisp and lightly golden. Arrange the gratin mussels on warmed plates with lemon wedges to serve.

HOT SQUID AND PRAWNS WITH COCONUT GRAVY

The flavours and textures in this dish are sensational. Serve it with a pile of sweet potato chips.

Serves 4

675g (1½ lb sweet potatoes, cut into thick, chunky chips

5 tbsp olive oil

4 tbsp dark soy sauce

a pinch of freshly grated nutmeg (optional)

350g (12oz) baby squid, cleaned

1 lime

1 tsp dried chilli flakes

225g (8oz) raw, peeled tiger prawns, veins removed, but with tails intact

2 tbsp madras curry paste

1 tbsp tomato purée

1 x 400g (14oz) tin of coconut milk

175g (6oz) baby spinach leaves

salt and freshly ground black pepper

Preheat the oven to 230°C/450°F/gas 8. Par-boil the sweet potatoes in boiling salted water for 4–5 minutes; drain and toss with 2 tablespoons each of the olive oil and soy sauce. Transfer to a large roasting tin; season with black pepper and nutmeg, if using. Bake for about 15 minutes until crisp and golden brown.

To prepare the squid, cut off the tentacles and set aside. Cut each squid tube open and slash into the flesh in a lattice pattern using a small sharp knife, taking care not to cut too deeply.

Squeeze the juice from half the lime into a bowl with the rest of the olive oil, soy sauce, chilli flakes and seasoning. Add the prepared squid and prawns; set aside for 5 minutes (or up to 30 minutes). Add the curry paste and tomato purée to a hot pan and fry for 30 seconds, stirring. Pour in the coconut milk and simmer for 5 minutes, stirring occasionally. Season to taste.

Heat a non-stick wok and add the squid and prawns with all their marinade. Stir-fry over a high heat for 1–2 minutes until the squid is lightly seared and just tender. Cook for another 1–2 minutes until the prawns have changed colour and are just cooked through. Finish the gravy with a squeeze of lime juice and spoon into warmed bowls. Pile a small mound of spinach leaves into the centre of each and top with the spicy squid and prawns. Serve immediately with the chips on the side.

CHICKEN AND CHICKPEA TAGINE WITH HONEY

The combination of flavours here is really successful, and it all gets cooked in one pot so there's little washing up.

Serves 2

4 large boneless, skinless chicken thighs or 2 boneless, skinless breasts

½ tsp each ground paprika, turmeric, cinnamon, ginger and cayenne pepper

1 tbsp clear honey

3 tbsp olive oil

1 small red onion, finely sliced

2 garlic cloves, finely chopped

2 ripe tomatoes, peeled, seeded and chopped

300ml (½ pint) chicken stock

1 x 400g (14oz) tin of chickpeas, drained and rinsed

juice of ½ lemon

2 tbsp shredded fresh coriander

1 tbsp shredded fresh mint

salt and freshly ground black pepper

steamed couscous, to serve (optional)

Trim down the chicken and cut into bite-sized pieces. Place in a bowl with the spices, honey and 1 tablespoon of the oil. Season generously, then stir well to combine and set aside for at least 5 minutes to allow the flavours to develop (or up to 24 hours covered with cling film in the fridge if time allows).

Heat the remaining 2 tablespoons of oil in a sauté pan with a lid, then sauté the onion and garlic for 4–5 minutes until softened and beginning to brown. Add the marinated chicken and sauté for a minute or so until just sealed and lightly browned.

Add half the tomatoes to the pan with the stock and chickpeas, then bring to the boil. Reduce the heat, cover and simmer for 8 minutes or until the chicken is completely tender and the sauce has slightly thickened, stirring occasionally; season.

Stir the remaining tomatoes into the pan and season to taste, add the lemon juice, coriander and mint. Stir to combine and arrange on warmed serving plates with the couscous, if liked.

RICH AND CREAMY CHICKEN RAVIOLI

Don't be scared to try making your own fresh pasta – once you've practised it a few times, you'll soon get to know how the dough should feel, and the results are well worth the effort.

Serves 2

225g (8oz) boneless, skinless chicken breasts

2 eggs and 1 egg yolk

300ml (½ pint) cream

a small handful of fresh basil

165g (5½ oz) plain flour, plus extra for dusting

50g (2oz) unsalted butter

1 onion, chopped

5 tbsp white wine

2 tbsp snipped fresh chives

2 carrots, cut into long, fine matchsticks

juice of ½ orange

2 courgettes

juice of ½ lemon

salt and freshly ground black pepper

snipped fresh chives, to garnish

Place the chicken breasts, 1 egg, 4 tablespoons of the cream, the basil and plenty of salt and pepper in a food-processor and whizz until smooth.

Place the flour, remaining egg and the egg yolk in a clean food-processor and whizz until the mixture comes together to form a firm dough. Tip the dough out onto a floured surface and knead for several minutes until smooth.

Roll the dough through the widest setting of a pasta machine about 5–6 times, folding the dough in half between each roll. When the dough is smooth and elastic, continue to pass through the machine, using a thinner setting each time to give a long, thin sheet of pasta. Using a 7½ cm (3in) pastry cutter, stamp out 16 circles of pasta.

Place a heaped teaspoon of the chicken mixture in the centre of 8 of the circles; dampen the edges with a little water. Use the remaining rounds to cover the filling. Press the edges together to seal but try not to trap any air inside the ravioli.

Cook the ravioli in a large pan of simmering salted water for 6–8 minutes until tender. Drain well.

Meanwhile, melt half the butter in a small pan. Cook the onion for 3 minutes until softened, then pour in the wine, the remaining cream, and salt and pepper to taste. Cook gently for 5 minutes, then stir in the snipped chives.

Meanwhile, place the carrots in a separate pan with half the remaining butter, the orange juice and seasoning. Cook for 3–4 minutes until tender. Drain well.

Using a swivel-style vegetable peeler, thinly slice the courgettes lengthways into ribbons. Heat the remaining 15g (½ oz) butter in a large frying pan and add the courgette ribbons and the lemon juice. Cook for 2–3 minutes until just tender and season to taste.

To serve, pile of courgettes into the centre of plates and place the ravioli on top. Pour over some of the cream sauce, top with the carrot, and sprinkle with the chives.

CHICKEN BREASTS WITH BACON AND MUSHROOM STUFFING

237

Don't be tempted to overfill the chicken breasts or they'll burst.

Serves 2

115g (4oz) unsalted butter, diced and chilled

6 button mushrooms, very finely chopped

2 rindless streaky bacon rashers, finely chopped

2 boneless, skinless chicken breasts

2 tbsp plain flour, seasoned

1 large egg

25g (1oz) white breadcrumbs

1 tbsp olive oil

2 tbsp dry white wine

juice of ½ lemon

120ml (4fl oz) double cream

2 tbsp chopped mixed fresh tarragon, chives and flat-leaf parsley

salt and freshly ground black pepper

steamed French beans and baby new potatoes, to serve

Preheat the oven to 200°C/400°F/gas 6. Heat a frying pan and melt half the butter. Cook the mushrooms and bacon for 3–4 minutes until lightly golden, stirring. Season and leave to cool. Using a sharp knife, cut horizontally almost all the way through each chicken breast. Stuff with the mushroom and bacon mixture and seal and secure with cocktail sticks.

Lightly whisk the egg. Heat a large ovenproof frying pan. Coat each stuffed chicken fillet in the seasoned flour, then dip in the beaten egg and coat in the breadcrumbs. Add the oil to the pan with a knob of the butter and cook the chicken for 3–4 minutes, turning once. Transfer to the oven and cook for another 6–8 minutes or until the chicken is cooked through and tender.

Place the wine and lemon juice in a small pan and cook until reduced by half. Stir in the cream and simmer for another minute or so, stirring. Add the remaining butter, a little at a time, whisking constantly until you have a smooth sauce. Season and stir in the herbs. Remove the cocktail sticks from the chicken breasts and arrange on warmed plates with the beans and potatoes to the side. Spoon around the sauce and serve at once.

SMOKED DUCK WITH POTATO SALAD AND BEETROOT RELISH

238

This salad takes no time at all to prepare.

Serves 2

175g (6oz) baby new potatoes, scrubbed

3 tbsp extra-virgin olive oil

juice of ½ lemon

1 tbsp snipped fresh chives

40g (1½oz) lamb's lettuce

100g (4oz) smoked duck breast, cut into thin slices

FOR THE BEETROOT RELISH

4 cooked baby beetroot, drained (from a jar)

2 spring onions, finely chopped

1 tsp tiny fresh dill sprigs

a pinch of sugar

salt and freshly ground black pepper

Cut the new potatoes into slices and cook in a pan of boiling salted water for about 8 minutes or until tender.

To make the beetroot relish, finely chop the beetroot and mix with the spring onion, dill and sugar in a bowl until well combined. Season with pepper.

Place the olive oil, lemon juice and chives in a large bowl. When the potatoes are cooked, drain well and then tip into the bowl, tossing until evenly coated. Season to taste, then quickly fold in the lamb's lettuce and divide between plates.

Arrange the duck on top in a fan shape and add small mounds of the beetroot relish around the edge of the plate to serve.

STUFFED PHEASANT

This dish would work wonderfully served with bubble and squeak.

Serves 2

2 pheasant breasts

1 tbsp double cream

2 tsp dry white wine

1 tsp Dijon mustard

FOR THE STUFFING

2 tbsp sunflower oil

100g (4oz) cooked chestnuts, roughly chopped

½ x 275g (10oz) tin of blackcurrants

1 tbsp redcurrant jelly

FOR THE BRANDY SAUCE

1 tbsp sunflower oil

1 small onion, finely chopped

300ml (½ pint) chicken stock

2 tbsp brandy

150ml (¼ pint) double cream

1 tbsp each chopped fresh parsley and dill

salt and freshly ground black pepper

fresh parsley and dill sprigs, to garnish

Preheat the oven to 200°C/400°F/gas 6. Heat the oil for the stuffing in a pan and stir in the chestnuts, blackcurrants and redcurrant jelly. Cook for 2–3 minutes until thick and pasty, then leave to cool.

Place the pheasant in a buttered ovenproof dish and season well. Mix together the cream, wine and mustard and spread over the pheasant breasts. Roast for 8 minutes, basting occasionally. Using a small knife; cut a pocket in each breast. Pack the cavities with the stuffing, piling any excess mixture on top, and return to the oven for 5 minutes until cooked through.

Heat the oil for the brandy sauce in a separate frying pan and cook the onion for 5 minutes until soft. Stir in the stock, brandy, cream, parsley and dill. Bring to the boil, then simmer rapidly until reduced by two-thirds; season to taste.

Serve on warm plates. Pour over the sauce and garnish with the parsley and dill sprigs.

GUINEA FOWL WITH GRAPE DRESSING

This simple but very stylish dish would serve as a lovely dinner-party main course. The dressing can be prepared in advance.

Serves 2

2 potatoes, cut into 2½ cm (1in) thick slices

3 tbsp olive oil

2 x 75g (3oz) boneless guinea fowl breasts

2 shallots, quartered

1 red pepper, cut into quarters, reserving the trimmings

FOR THE GRAPE DRESSING

25g (1oz) butter

25g (1oz) caster sugar

½ tbsp balsamic vinegar

½ tbsp red wine vinegar

a sprig of fresh basil

2 tbsp olive oil

50g (2oz) seedless green grapes, halved

salt and freshly ground black pepper

fresh basil leaves, to garnish

Preheat the oven to 200°C/400°F/gas 6. Cook the potato slices in boiling salted water for 5–8 minutes until just tender; drain. Heat 1 tablespoon of the oil in an ovenproof frying pan and cook the breasts for 4–5 minutes, turning once. Season well, then cook in the oven for 5–6 minutes until cooked through.

Heat the remaining oil in a large griddle pan or heavy-based frying pan. Cook the shallots, pepper quarters and potato slices for 4–5 minutes on each side until tender and golden brown.

Heat the butter in a frying pan and add the pepper trimmings and the caster sugar. Cook gently, stirring frequently, for 5–6 minutes until the peppers have softened and browned. Stir in the vinegars and bring to the boil, then pour the mixture into a bowl. Add the basil and olive oil and set aside to cool. Strain into a clean bowl and stir in the grapes; season to taste.

To serve, arrange the guinea fowl on top of the vegetables. Spoon a round the dressing and garnish with the basil leaves.

VENISON BURGER WITH PRUNE SALAD

Here is a simple but rather unusual way of serving venison sausages. Most supermarkets now stock them, but better still, seek out a local butcher who makes his own.

Serves 2

4 venison sausages

2 spring onions, finely chopped

1 tsp chopped fresh thyme

4 prunes, stoned and finely chopped

olive oil, for cooking

2 ciabatta rolls

FOR THE PRUNE SALAD

a handful of fresh flat-leaf parsley leaves

a handful of fresh coriander leaves

a small bunch of fresh chives, roughly sliced on the diagonal

2 spring onions, finely sliced

2 prunes, stoned and chopped

1 tsp toasted sesame seeds

½ tsp white wine vinegar

1 tbsp extra-virgin olive oil

salt and freshly ground black pepper

Preheat the oven to 200°C/400°F/gas 6 and heat an ovenproof frying pan. Split the skin on each venison sausage and place the meat in a bowl. Add the spring onions, thyme, prunes and seasoning. Mix together using your hands and then shape into 2 even-sized patties.

Add a thin film of olive oil to the heated frying pan and quickly sear the venison patties on both sides. Transfer to the oven for 5–6 minutes or until cooked through and tender.

Heat a griddle pan until hot. Split the ciabatta rolls, drizzle with a little olive oil and toast on the griddle pan.

To make the prune salad, place the parsley in a bowl with the coriander, chives, spring onions, prunes, sesame seeds, vinegar and olive oil. Mix well to combine.

Place the bottom halves of the ciabatta rolls on warmed plates and top each one with a venison patty. Pile the prune salad on top and place the tops to the side to serve.

VENISON MEDALLIONS WITH CHIVE CRUSHED POTATOES

For maximum flavour, marinate the venison, covered with cling film, in the fridge for up to 24 hours. (See illustration, page 122.)

Serves 2

2 x 100g (4oz) venison medallions

2 garlic cloves, cut into 10 slivers

10 tiny fresh rosemary sprigs

finely grated rind of 1 lemon

85ml (3fl oz) olive oil

1 large leek, sliced on the diagonal

225g (8oz) new potatoes, scrubbed

2 tbsp snipped fresh chives

salt and freshly ground black pepper

Preheat the oven to 220°C/425°F/gas 7. Make 5 small incisions around the sides of each venison medallion. Insert the garlic slivers and rosemary sprigs. Season with pepper and sprinkle over half of the lemon rind, then drizzle over a tablespoon of the olive oil. Turn to coat the medallions evenly, then set aside.

Sauté the leek in 2 tablespoons of the oil for 3–4 minutes, then push to one side and add the marinated medallions and quickly brown all over. Spread the leeks back over the bottom of the pan and sit the medallions on top, then transfer to the oven and roast for 5–10 minutes, depending on how rare you like your meat. Remove from the oven and leave to rest in a warm place.

Cook the potatoes in a pan of boiling salted water for 10–12 minutes until tender; drain and transfer to a bowl. Add the remaining olive oil and gently crush each potato until it just splits. Add the remaining lemon rind, season and then mix carefully until all the oil has been absorbed. Stir in the chives. Serve at once on warmed plates.

Bonfire Night recipe

VENISON BURGER WITH PRUNE SALAD

TOAD-IN-THE-HOLE WITH VENISON SAUSAGES AND RED SHALLOT GRAVY

Mix the batter quickly and use it immediately. It is also crucial to heat the oil in the tin until it is smoking hot.

Serves 2

2 venison sausages

4 tbsp sunflower oil

4 eggs

150ml (¼ pint) milk

300g (10oz) plain flour

1 banana shallot, finely chopped

120ml (4fl oz) red wine

150ml (¼ pint) beef stock

1 tsp tomato purée

25g (1oz) chilled unsalted butter, diced

salt and freshly ground black pepper

Preheat the oven to 220°C/425°F/gas 7 and heat a 4-hole, Yorkshire pudding tin. Twist each sausage in half and cut to make 4 small sausages. Brown in a frying pan for 2–3 minutes. Remove the tin from the oven and pour a little of the oil into each hole. Return to the oven until the oil is smoking hot. Whisk together the eggs and milk with 150ml (¼ pint) of water. Season generously. Place the flour in a bowl and make a well in the centre. Pour the egg mixture into the well and gradually whisk in the flour. Quickly remove the tin from the oven and pour in the batter. Top each one with a sausage and bake for about 15 minutes until the batter is well risen and golden brown.

Heat the remaining oil in a small pan and sweat the shallot for 3–4 minutes. Add the red wine and simmer for 2–3 minutes to reduce, then add the stock and tomato purée and simmer for 5–6 minutes until the gravy has slightly reduced and thickened. Just before serving, whisk in the butter and season. Arrange on warmed plates with the gravy poured over the top.

MINI MOUSSAKAS

Minced lamb is very good value for money and often has more flavour than minced beef.

Serves 2

1 large potato, sliced

1 tbsp sunflower oil

1 onion, chopped

1 garlic clove, crushed

225 (8oz) lean minced lamb

1 tsp ground cumin

2 tsp tomato purée

50ml (2fl oz) dry white wine

50ml (2fl oz) chicken or lamb stock

1 courgette, sliced

1 tbsp olive oil

25g (1oz) unsalted butter

25g (1oz) plain flour

300ml (½ pint) milk

½ tsp freshly grated nutmeg

1 tbsp chopped fresh flat-leaf parsley, plus extra, to garnish

4 plum tomatoes, peeled, seeded and finely diced

50g (2oz) freshly grated Cheddar

salt and freshly ground black pepper

Par-boil the potato slices in salted water for 6–8 minutes. Heat the sunflower oil in a heavy-based pan. Fry the onion for 2–3 minutes until soft, add the garlic and cook for 1–2 minutes until soft. Add the lamb and cook for 2–3 minutes until slightly browned, add the cumin, tomato purée, white wine and stock. Season and combine. Bring to a simmer, reduce the heat and bubble gently for 3–4 minutes or until thickened and dry.

Heat a griddle pan. Toss the courgette slices in the olive oil, season and chargrill for 2–3 minutes or until tender. Melt the butter in a heavy-based pan, remove from the heat and add the flour, stirring continuously. Return to the heat and cook for 1 minute, stirring, then gradually pour in the milk, stirring until smooth. Add the nutmeg, season and simmer for 2–3 minutes.

Preheat the grill. Stir the parsley into the lamb, season and divide between two ovenproof dishes or two 10cm (4in) metal cooking rings. Add a layer of courgettes, then potatoes and top with the tomatoes. Pour over the sauce and scatter over the cheese. Grill for 3–4 minutes or until golden and bubbling. Garnish with parsley.

LAMB CHOPS WITH POLENTA AND GARLIC MUSHROOMS

245

This Italian-inspired dish offers a huge range of flavours and textures – it can be simplified by omitting the mushrooms. The lamb stock adds extra flavour to the polenta, but you can use chicken stock if you prefer.

Serves 2

150g (5oz) chestnut mushrooms

4–5 tbsp olive oil

juice of 1 lemon

1 garlic clove, finely chopped

600ml (1 pint) hot lamb stock

150g (5oz) polenta

1 tbsp chopped fresh parsley

1 small onion, chopped

4 tomatoes, diced

1 tbsp tomato purée

5 tbsp water

1 tbsp chopped fresh basil

100g (4oz) French beans

4 lamb loin chops

salt and freshly ground black pepper

1 tbsp snipped fresh chives, to garnish

Preheat the oven to 220°C/425°F/gas 7. Arrange the mushrooms, stalk-side down in an ovenproof dish and drizzle over about ½ tablespoon of olive oil, the lemon juice and chopped garlic. Season well and bake for 5 minutes.

Meanwhile, place the lamb stock in a large pan and bring to the boil. Pour in the polenta in a steady stream, stirring constantly. Continue to cook and stir for 6–7 minutes until all the liquid has been absorbed and the grains are softened; season well, remove from the heat, cover and keep warm.

Turn over the mushrooms, drizzle with a little more oil and sprinkle over the parsley; return to the oven for a further 5 minutes until tender.

Heat 2 tablespoons of the oil in a frying pan and cook the onion for 5 minutes until softened. Stir in the tomatoes, tomato purée and water. Simmer gently for 3–4 minutes, then season to taste. Stir in the basil.

Meanwhile, cook the beans in a large pan of boiling salted water for 2 minutes. Drain well.

Heat about ½ tablespoon of oil in a griddle pan or heavy-based frying pan and cook the seasoned lamb for 3–4 minutes on each side until well browned but still a little pink in the centre. Remove from the pan and set aside to rest.

Toss the beans with about1 tablespoon of olive oil and add to the griddle pan. Cook for 2–3 minutes until tender but still firm.

To serve, spoon the polenta onto a plate, place the lamb on top and scatter over the beans. Spoon around the sauce and arrange the mushrooms round the edge of the plate. Garnish with the chives.

KORMA LAMB BIRYANI

This is a southern variation on the classic lamb biryani, adding some coconut along with a handful of cashew nuts and raisins.

Serves 4

350g (12oz) boneless lean lamb, cubed

1 tsp ground turmeric

2 tsp medium-hot curry powder

2 tbsp sunflower oil

3 tbsp chopped fresh coriander

25g (1oz) unsalted butter

1 onion, finely chopped

50g (2oz) cashew nuts

225g (8oz) Basmati rice

2 tbsp raisins

600ml (1 pint) hot lamb or chicken stock

25g (1oz) creamed coconut, grated

100g (4oz) frozen peas

salt and freshly ground black pepper

Toss the lamb in the turmeric, curry powder and 1 tablespoon each of the oil and fresh coriander to coat. Marinate for as long as possible (up to 24 hours, covered with cling film in the fridge).

Heat the remaining oil in a sauté pan with a tight-fitting lid, add the butter and, once it has stopped sizzling, tip in the onion. Cook for 4–5 minutes until softened and beginning to brown at the edges. Add the lamb with the cashew nuts and cook over a high heat for 2–3 minutes until the lamb is sealed. Stir in the rice and raisins and cook for 30 seconds. Pour in the stock and add the creamed coconut. Bring to the boil, stir once, reduce the heat, cover tightly and simmer for 8–10 minutes until the rice is almost tender and most of the stock has been absorbed.

Add the peas to the rice mixture, cover and cook for another 2–3 minutes or until all the stock has been absorbed and the lamb is completely tender. Fluff up the biryani with a fork, season and scatter over the remaining coriander to serve.

CURRIED LAMB CHAPPATI ROLLS

The self-raising flour in this recipe makes the bread a little lighter than usual, but you can use all plain if you prefer.

Serves 4

100g (4oz) plain flour, plus extra for dusting

2 tbsp self-raising flour

1 tsp salt

4–6 tbsp cold water

5 tbsp olive oil

1 onion, finely chopped

2 garlic cloves, finely chopped

2 cardamom pods, cracked

1½ tsp each ground cumin, ground ginger, cayenne pepper, ground turmeric and garam masala

500g (1 lb 2oz) minced lamb

100g (4oz) shredded coconut

1 x 400g (14oz) tin of chopped tomatoes

1 x 400g (14oz) tin of chickpeas, drained and liquid reserved

1 tbsp double cream

1 tbsp each chopped fresh basil and chopped fresh coriander

1 red pepper, seeded and sliced

100g (4oz) okra, halved lengthways

salt and freshly ground black pepper

Place both flours and the salt in a large bowl and gradually add the water, a tablespoon at a time, to make a firm dough. Knead on a floured surface for 2–3 minutes until smooth. Quarter the dough and roll each piece out on a floured surface into a 15cm (6in) round. Heat a griddle or large, flat frying pan and cook the chappatis for 2–3 minutes on each side until golden.

Heat 2 tablespoons of oil in a separate frying pan. Cook the onion for 5 minutes until softened, add the garlic for another 1 minute, stir in the cardamom pods and 1 teaspoon each of the cumin, ginger, cayenne, turmeric and garam masala and cook for 1–2 minutes. Add the lamb, coconut, tomatoes and the liquid from the chickpeas. Stir well, then cook gently for 6–8 minutes until the lamb is cooked through. Stir in the cream, basil, coriander and salt and pepper to taste.

Place the chickpeas in a small pan with 2 tablespoons of the oil and the remaining spices, and gently heat through. In a separate frying pan, heat the remaining oil and cook the pepper slices over a high heat for 2 minutes until starting to brown; stir into the chickpea mixture. Add the okra to the same pan and cook for 2–3 minutes; stir into the chickpea mixture and season to taste. To serve, divide the lamb curry between the chappatis and roll up. Place on plates and spoon around the chickpea curry.

FRUITY STUFFED PORK WITH PUMPKIN SAUCE

Pork and pumpkin are a delicious autumn combination.

Serves 2

75g (3oz) butter

1 onion, chopped

250g (9oz) easy-cook white rice

600ml (1 pint) boiling water

100g (4oz) sultanas

1 cooking apple, peeled and chopped

grated rind of 1 lemon

1 tbsp chopped fresh sage

1 garlic clove, finely chopped

4 x 75g (3oz) pork escalopes

1 kabocha squash or other small pumpkin, skinned, seeded and cubed

1 vegetable stock cube

4 tbsp double cream

salt and freshly ground black pepper

fresh flat-leaf parsley sprigs, to garnish

Preheat the oven to 220°C/425°F/gas 7. Melt 25g (1oz) of the butter in a pan and cook half of the chopped onion for 3–4 minutes until softened. Stir in the rice and pour over the boiling water. Cover and simmer for 10–12 minutes until tender.

Melt 25g (1oz) of the butter in a large frying pan and cook the remaining onion, the sultanas, apple, lemon rind, sage and garlic for 5 minutes until softened. Season well. Beat out the pork escalopes with a meat mallet or rolling pin until very thin. Spoon the sultana mixture on top of each escalope and roll up tightly; secure with cocktail sticks. Heat the remaining butter in an ovenproof frying pan and cook the pork rolls for 2–3 minutes, shaking the pan until well browned. Roast in the oven for 10 minutes until cooked through.

Bring a large pan of water to the boil and add the squash and stock cube. Simmer rapidly for 5–7 minutes until the squash is tender. Drain and return to the pan. Purée with a hand-held blender, then stir in the cream and season to taste. To serve, arrange the pork rolls on top of the rice, spoon around the pumpkin sauce and garnish with the parsley sprigs.

CHIPOLATAS WITH SKILLET SCONES AND ROASTED TOMATOES

The skillet scones are best eaten as soon as they come off the pan.

Serves 2

5 small vine-ripened tomatoes, halved

olive oil, for drizzling

10 chipolata sausages

FOR THE SKILLET SCONES

100g (4oz) self-raising flour, plus extra for dusting

2 tbsp finely chopped red onion

1 tbsp snipped fresh chives

1 tbsp olive oil, plus extra for cooking

100ml (3½ fl oz) milk

salt and freshly ground black pepper

butter, to serve (optional)

Preheat the oven to 200°C/400°F/gas 6. Place the tomatoes in a baking tin and drizzle over a little olive oil. Season generously and bake for 8–9 minutes until lightly charred and softened.

Heat a flat griddle or skillet pan until hot. Place the flour in a bowl with the red onion, chives and a pinch of salt. Make a well in the centre and pour in the olive oil and milk. Quickly bring the mixture together to a soft dough.

Turn the dough out onto a lightly floured board and knead lightly until smooth. Roll out to a 2cm (¼ in) thickness and stamp out 5cm (2in) circles with a fluted pastry cutter. Add a thin film of oil to the flat griddle pan and cook the scones for 2–3 minutes on each side until slightly risen and golden brown.

Cook the sausages on the griddle pan for about 6 minutes until golden brown and cooked through, turning occasionally. Split the scones and spread with butter, if liked, then arrange on warmed plates with the roasted tomatoes and chipolatas to serve.

SPICED PORK STEAKS WITH SWEET PEAR SALSA

This recipe is full of gutsy, strong flavours.

Serves 2

2 tbsp light muscovado sugar

1 tsp coriander seeds

4 whole cloves

1 tsp allspice berries

100g (4oz) ready-to-eat dried pears

2 x 175g (6oz) pork steaks

1 tsp paprika

a pinch of ground cumin

25g (1oz) unsalted butter, diced

sunflower oil, for pan frying

120ml (4fl oz) double cream

1 tsp wholegrain mustard

2 tbsp snipped fresh chives

salt and freshly ground white pepper

Preheat the oven to 220°C/425°F/gas 7. Place the sugar in a small pan with 150ml (¼ pint) of water and the coriander seeds, cloves and allspice berries. Bring to a simmer, stirring until the sugar has melted, then stir in the pears, reduce the heat and simmer gently for 10–15 minutes or until the pears are completely tender and softened.

Heat a large ovenproof frying pan until hot. Flatten the pork steaks using a meat mallet or rolling pin covered in cling film. Place the paprika in a small bowl with the cumin and season generously, then tip onto a plate and use to coat the pork steaks. Add half the butter and a little oil to the heated pan and sauté the pork for a minute or 2 on each side until well seared. Transfer to the oven and roast for another 4–6 minutes until cooked through and completely tender. Remove from the oven and leave to rest for a couple of minutes.

Drain the pears, discarding the syrup, and set aside to cool a little, then finely dice. Place the cream in a small pan, whisk in the mustard and season. Simmer to reduce by one-third, then whisk in the remaining butter and the chives; season. Serve the pork steaks with the sweet pear salsa scattered around and then spoon around the mustard and chive cream.

PORK WITH MUSHROOMS AND CIDER SAUCE

The cider sauce brings a sweet sharpness to this dish.

Serves 2

225g (8oz) pork tenderloin, sliced thinly

2 tbsp plain flour, seasoned

3 tbsp olive oil

1 onion, chopped

1 apple, cored and chopped

75ml (3fl oz) cider

100g (4oz) button mushrooms, quartered

2–3 tbsp double cream

2 tsp chopped fresh tarragon

5 drops of Worcestershire sauce

salt and freshly ground black pepper

Season the pork slices, coat them with a little flour and fry them in 2 tablespoons of oil for 5–7 minutes, turning half-way. Set aside.

Sauté the onion and apple in the remaining oil for 3 minutes. Add the cider and mushrooms. Season and cook for 5 minutes, stirring occasionally. Add the pork and stir in the cream, tarragon and Worcestershire sauce. Leave to simmer for 10 minutes.

To serve, spoon the pork and mushrooms into the centre of warmed plates with seasonal vegetables on the side.

PORK BALLS WITH RED PEPPER SAUCE

252

A little goes a long way with this richly flavoured dish. Use as many or as few dried chilli flakes as you want – they do pack a powerful punch.

Serves 4

1 large red pepper, quartered and seeded

500g (1lb 2oz) lean minced pork

50g (2oz) fresh white breadcrumbs

2 tsp ground coriander

1–2 tsp dried chilli flakes

1 egg, beaten

3 tbsp olive oil

1 large red onion, thickly sliced

1 garlic clove, crushed

1½ tsp paprika

1 tbsp tomato ketchup

1 tbsp tomato purée

300ml (½ pint) red wine

300ml (½ pint) vegetable stock

salt and freshly ground black pepper

plain boiled rice or noodles, to serve

soured cream and fresh coriander leaves, to garnish

Preheat the oven to 200°C/400°F/gas 6. Finely chop a quarter of the pepper and slice the remainder. Set the sliced pepper to one side and blend the chopped pepper with the minced pork, breadcrumbs, ground coriander, chilli flakes, egg and seasoning in a food-processor. Using wet hands, divide the mixture into 16 even-sized portions and roll into balls. Heat 2 tablespoons of the oil in a large ovenproof frying pan and fry the balls for 3–4 minutes until sealed and lightly browned, then bake in the oven for 10–12 minutes or until cooked through.

Heat the remaining oil in a large frying pan and cook the pepper slices and onion for 4–5 minutes. Add the garlic and paprika and cook for 30 seconds, stirring, then add the ketchup, tomato purée, red wine and half the stock. Bring to the boil and cook over a high heat for 5–10 minutes or until well-reduced to form a shiny, chunky sauce, adding more stock if necessary; season.

Spoon some rice or noodles onto warmed plates and top with the pork balls. Spoon over the sauce and garnish with a drizzle of soured cream and some fresh coriander leaves.

CHORIZO STEW WITH BLACK OLIVES

253

If time allows, try a buttered herby breadcrumb topping and flash under the grill.

Serves 2

1 tbsp olive oil, plus extra for drizzling

1 hot red chilli, seeded and finely chopped

1 red onion, finely chopped

2 garlic cloves, crushed, plus 1 garlic clove, halved

100g (4oz) raw chorizo, peeled and diced

2 large thick slices of rustic bread, such as sourdough

1 x 200g (7oz) tin of chopped tomatoes

1–2 tbsp tomato ketchup

400g (14oz) tin of black-eyed beans, drained and rinsed

50g (2oz) pitted black olives

salt and freshly ground black pepper

chopped fresh flat-leaf parsley, to serve

Heat a griddle pan until very hot. Heat the oil in a large pan and sauté the chilli, red onion and crushed garlic for a few minutes until softened but not coloured. Add the chorizo to the pan and season to taste. Cook for 4–5 minutes until the chorizo is sizzling and has released some of its oil.

Add the slices of bread to the heated griddle pan and cook for 1–2 minutes on each side until lightly charred. Drizzle over a little olive oil and rub with the halved garlic clove.

Pour the tomatoes into the chorizo pan with tomato ketchup to taste and the black-eyed beans and olives, stirring to combine. Cook for 1–2 minutes until heated through. Season to taste.

Divide the stew between bowls set on serving plates and scatter with parsley. Place the bruschetta on the side and serve at once.

POTIRON À LA FLAMANDE

Potiron is stuffed pumpkin. The stuffing in this dish is pork and apple in a cider sauce.

Serves 2

1 small pumpkin, about 1kg (2¼ lb)

50g (2oz) butter

2 tbsp vegetable oil

2 eating apples, peeled, cored and finely diced

1 small onion, chopped

350g (12oz) potatoes, finely diced

350g (12oz) pork loin steak, cut into 5cm (2in) squares

½ tsp paprika

salt and freshly ground black pepper

FOR THE SAUCE

300ml (½ pint) chicken stock

150ml (¼ pint) cider

150ml (¼ pint) double cream

1 tbsp Dijon mustard

Preheat the oven to 200°C/400°F/gas 6. Slice the top off the pumpkin, scoop out the seeds and most of the flesh, leaving a shell about 1cm (½ in) thick. Cut half the butter into small pieces and put them in the pumpkin shell. Place the pumpkin in an ovenproof dish and bake in the oven for 40 minutes.

Heat the remaining butter and half the oil in a frying pan, add the apples, onion and potatoes and cook gently for 10 minutes, until softened and golden brown. Season to taste. In a separate pan, heat the remaining oil, add the pork and paprika and fry for 8–10 minutes or until cooked through.

Put the stock and cider in a heavy-based pan and boil until reduced to half its original volume. Add the cream and simmer until reduced by almost half again, then stir in the mustard and season to taste. To serve, stir the apple mixture and pork into the sauce, then spoon into the pumpkin.

SMOKY SAUSAGE CASSOULET

This is a variation on sausages and onion gravy, but the addition of a stronger-flavoured sausage and the tangy tomato sauce makes it a real treat.

Serves 4

3 tbsp olive oil

1 large onion, finely chopped

100g (4oz) piece of smoky bacon, diced

6 large ripe tomatoes, roughly chopped, or 1 x 400g (14oz) tin of chopped tomatoes

1 tbsp tomato purée

1 tbsp wholegrain mustard

1 x 400g (14oz) tin of butter beans, rinsed

8 butcher's-style spicy pork sausages

2 thick slices of rustic bread, crusts removed (about 85g/ 3oz in total)

a handful of mixed fresh herbs (such as basil, flat-leaf parsley and chives)

25g (1oz) unsalted butter

50g (2oz) Gruyère cheese, finely grated

salt and freshly ground black pepper

Preheat the grill to hot. Heat 2 tablespoons of the oil in a large pan. Add the onion and bacon and cook for about 5 minutes or until the onion has softened and the bacon is cooked through.

Add the tomatoes to the pan with the tomato purée and mustard, then season, stirring to combine. Bring to a simmer and cook for about 5 minutes, stirring occasionally. Stir in the butter beans and cook for another 2 minutes until heated through.

Heat the remaining oil in a separate frying pan and cook the sausages for 6–8 minutes until tender and golden brown.

Blitz the bread in a food-processor with the herbs; tip into a bowl. Melt the butter in a small pan and stir it into the crumbs, then stir in the Gruyère to combine. Add the sausages to the tomato and bean mixture, spoon into an ovenproof dish and scatter the breadcrumb mixture on top. Place under the grill until bubbling and golden brown. Serve at once.

STEAK AND PASTA RIBBONS IN MUSHROOM SAUCE

256

The ingredients in this dish are an unbeatable combination.

Serves 2

175g (6oz) pappardelle (broad pasta ribbons) or tagliatelle

2 tbsp olive oil

25g (1oz) butter

225g (8oz) rump steak, cut into thin strips

½ onion, finely chopped

1 red pepper, seeded and diced

1 green pepper, seeded and diced

1 garlic clove, finely chopped

1 tsp Dijon mustard

1 tbsp chopped fresh parsley

a few drops of Worcestershire sauce

5 tbsp white wine

100g (4oz) mushrooms, sliced

4 tbsp double cream

salt and freshly ground black pepper

chopped fresh parsley, to garnish

Cook the pasta in a large pan of boiling salted water for 10–12 minutes until tender. Drain and toss with 1 tablespoon of the oil.

Meanwhile, heat the butter and remaining oil in a large, heavy-based frying pan and cook the steak and onion for 3–4 minutes until browned. Remove with a slotted spoon and set aside.

Add the peppers, garlic, mustard, parsley, Worcestershire sauce and wine to the same pan and bring to the boil, then simmer for 3–4 minutes. Stir in the mushrooms, cooked onions and steak, then add the cream and cook for 1–2 minutes; season to taste.

To serve, toss the pasta with the sauce and sprinkle over the chopped parsley.

TOAD-IN-THE-HOLE WITH SPICED BAKED BEANS

257

The blini pans need to be very hot for the puddings to rise quickly.

Serves 2

2 tsp sunflower oil

4 tbsp self-raising flour

a pinch of baking powder

1 egg

100ml (3½ fl oz) milk

100g (4oz) cooked cocktail sausages

½ tsp fresh soft thyme leaves

1 x 200g (7oz) tin of baked beans

a knob of butter

a splash of double cream

a pinch of medium curry powder

salt and freshly ground black pepper

Preheat the oven to 220°C/425°F/gas 7. Add a teaspoon of oil to 2 blini pans and heat in the oven.

To make the Yorkshire pudding batter, place the flour and baking powder in a large bowl with a pinch of salt. Make a well in the centre, break in the egg and gradually draw in the flour. Quickly add the milk and whisk vigorously into a smooth batter – the consistency of single cream. Transfer to a jug. Remove the hot blini pans from the oven and pour in enough batter to come half-way up the sides. Scatter the cocktail sausages and thyme over both pans, then bake on the top shelf of the oven for 8 minutes or until well risen and golden brown.

Pour the baked beans into a small pan and add the butter, cream and curry powder. Heat gently for 2–3 minutes until warmed through. Season to taste. Tip the toad-in-the-holes onto warmed plates and spoon over the spiced baked beans to serve.

ICE CREAM TOWER WAFFLES WITH PECAN PRALINE AND TOFFEE SAUCE

This recipe would also work well with ready-made Scotch pancakes or split croissants.

Serves 2

sunflower oil, for greasing

2 Belgian waffles

4–6 small scoops of vanilla ice cream

FOR THE TOFFEE SAUCE

4 tbsp maple syrup

25g (1oz) butter

2 tbsp double cream

FOR THE PECAN PRALINE

100g (4oz) caster sugar

50g (2oz) toasted pecan nuts

Preheat the oven to 220°C/425°F/gas 7. Lightly oil 3 baking sheets. Place the maple syrup, butter and cream in a pan and heat gently for 2–3 minutes until smooth. Set aside to cool.

Place the sugar in a very clean, heavy-based pan and heat gently until it has dissolved. Then bring to the boil and boil fast for a few minutes until the resulting syrup begins to turn pale brown, gently swirling the pan to ensure even cooking. When the caramel is a rich golden brown colour, dip the base of the pan into a sink of cool water to prevent further cooking. Add the toasted pecan nuts, shaking the pan to coat evenly. Pour the pecan caramel mixture onto one of the oiled baking sheets, leaving some of the caramel behind in the pan.

To make the spun sugar, take a clean, small metal spoon and a knife-sharpening steel. Dip the spoon into the remaining caramel, move the spoon up and down the steel, pulling the sugar with your fingers until a candy-floss texture is achieved. Carefully transfer the spun sugar to an oiled baking sheet and repeat with another spoonful.

Place the waffles on the remaining baking sheet and cook for 3 minutes or until completely heated through. Meanwhile, break the set pecan praline into small pieces with a rolling pin.

Place the hot waffles on warmed plates and top with the scoops of ice cream. Sprinkle over the pecan praline and drizzle the toffee sauce around. Place some of the spun sugar on the top of each dessert in a tall pile and serve at once.

PLUM TARTS WITH GREEK YOGHURT

The crisp tart, creamy yoghurt and sweet, juicy plums make
a really melt-in-the-mouth dessert.

Serves 4

175g (6oz)
strawberry jam

50g (2oz) sultanas

100g (4oz) seedless
black grapes, halved

4 tbsp damson wine
or red wine

a pinch of freshly
ground black pepper

4 tbsp Greek yoghurt

250ml (9fl oz) double
cream, lightly
whipped

25g (1oz) butter

6 plums, halved and
stoned

caster sugar, to taste

icing sugar, for
dusting

FOR THE PASTRY

25g (1oz) ground
almonds

225g (8oz) plain flour,
plus extra for dusting

100g (4oz) unsalted
butter, chilled and
diced

a pinch of salt

1 egg, beaten

Preheat the oven to 200°C/400°F/gas 6. Place the ground
almonds, flour, butter and salt in a food-processor and whizz until
you have fine breadcrumbs. Add the egg and blend until you
have a firm dough, adding a little cold water if necessary. Chill
the pastry for at least 10 minutes, preferably an hour.

Roll the pastry out onto a floured surface until 5mm (¼ in) thick
and use to line four 10cm (4in) tartlet tins. Cover each pastry
case with greaseproof paper filled with baking beans and bake
for 10 minutes. Remove the paper and baking beans and bake
for 5 minutes until lightly browned. Leave to cool on a wire rack.

Heat the strawberry jam gently in a pan, stirring occasionally
until melted. Place the sultanas and grapes in a separate pan and
heat gently for 1 minute, then add the wine and black pepper.
Simmer for 3 minutes until slightly reduced, then strain away the
juices and place in a bowl to cool. Fold in the Greek yoghurt and
4 tablespoons of the whipped cream, then add the mixture to
the jam in the pan and simmer until thickened; remove from the
heat and leave to cool. Melt the butter in a separate pan and
cook the plums for 5 minutes, turning occasionally until tender.
Add sugar to taste. Leave to cool.

Divide the fruity yoghurt mixture between the pastry cases and
arrange 3 plum halves on top of each. Pipe over the remaining
cream. To serve, place each tartlet on a serving plate and spoon
around the jam compote. Dust with icing sugar.

POACHED PLUMS WITH CHOCOLATE CREAM

This would also be delicious with some biscotti for dipping.

Serves 2

3 ripe small plums,
halved and stoned

120ml (4fl oz) red
wine

juice of 1 lemon

FOR THE CHOCOLATE
CREAM

100g (4oz) plain
chocolate, at least 70
per cent cocoa solids

1 x 250g (9oz) carton
mascarpone

2 tbsp sifted icing
sugar

Place the plums in a pan with the red wine and lemon juice.
Bring to the boil, then reduce the heat and simmer for 4–5
minutes until the plums are tender.

Meanwhile, melt the chocolate in the microwave or in a
heatproof bowl set over a pan of simmering water. Quickly beat
in the mascarpone and enough icing sugar to taste. Drain the
plums and place in the freezer for a couple of minutes to cool
down quickly.

Place a 7½ cm (3in) metal cooking ring in the centre of each
plate and fill with the chocolate cream. Heat the sides with
a mini-blowtorch and carefully remove the rings. Arrange the
cooled plums around the chocolate and serve at once.

PLUM AND ALMOND PIZZA

This is an unusual twist to a very classic combination, although almost any firm fresh or tinned fruit would work just as well.

Serves 2

50g (2oz) unsalted butter

50g (2oz) caster sugar

50g (2oz) ground almonds

1 egg

½ tbsp plain flour

1 drop almond essence

2 x 375g (13oz) packets of ready-rolled puff pastry, thawed if frozen

2 x 400g (14oz) tin of plums in syrup, drained and sliced

4 tsp demerara sugar

vanilla ice cream, to serve

Preheat the oven to 220°C/425°F/gas 7. Place the butter and sugar in a food-processor and whizz until softened. Add the ground almonds, then the egg and flour. Add the almond essence and whizz again briefly.

Place the pastry sheets on a lightly floured surface and, using a saucer as a template, cut out four 15cm (6in) rounds. Place on 2 baking sheets. Spoon about 2 tablespoons of the almond mixture into the centre of each circle and spread it out, leaving a 1cm (½ in) space around the edge.

Arrange the plums on top of the almond mixture. Sprinkle 1 teaspoon of demerara sugar over each pizza and bake for 10–12 minutes or until the pizzas are puffed up and golden around the edges. Serve with scoops of vanilla ice cream.

VANILLA-SCENTED PEARS WITH RASPBERRY ZABAGLIONE

It is crucial that the pears are covered completely with liquid while they are being poached.

Serves 2

600ml (1 pint) dry white wine

225g (8oz) caster sugar

1 vanilla pod

finely grated rind and juice of 1 lemon

2 ripe firm Comice pears, peeled and cores removed

100g (4oz) raspberries

1 tbsp icing sugar, plus extra for dusting

2 egg yolks

fresh mint sprigs, to decorate

Place 500ml (18fl oz) of the wine in a small, deep-sided pan with 175g (6oz) of the sugar, the vanilla pod and the lemon rind and juice. Bring to the boil, then reduce the heat, stirring until the sugar has dissolved. Add the pears to the pan, cover with baking paper and a lid, and poach for 10 minutes or until just tender, turning occasionally. Ensure they are constantly submerged.

Place the remaining wine and sugar in a small pan and simmer gently for a few minutes until the sugar has dissolved, stirring. Increase the heat and cook until reduced by one-third. Reserve some of the raspberries for decoration and place the remainder in a food-processor with a tablespoon of cold water and the icing sugar. Blend to a purée, then pass through a sieve into a bowl.

Place the egg yolks in a heatproof bowl and set over a pan of simmering water. Whisk in the reduced wine mixture and continue to whisk until the mixture is very light and just thick enough to leave a ribbon trail when the whisk is lifted. Remove from the heat and continue to whisk for 1 minute to stabilize the mixture. Fold in the raspberry purée.

Drain the pears on kitchen paper. Arrange upright on serving plates and spoon over the raspberry zabaglione. Decorate with the mint, raspberries and a light dusting of icing sugar.

BLACK FOREST LAYER WITH WHITE CHOCOLATE SAUCE

A classic dessert with a *Ready Steady Cook* accent. Impressive, decadent and incredibly easy to make.

Serves 2

200ml (7fl oz) double cream

4 tbsp Tia Maria

2 tbsp sifted icing sugar

2 large chocolate muffins

12 cherries preserved in brandy, drained

cocoa powder, to dust

FOR THE WHITE CHOCOLATE SAUCE

200ml (7fl oz) double cream

100g (4oz) white chocolate, broken into pieces

To make the white chocolate sauce, place the cream in a small pan and bring to scalding point (almost but not quite to the boil). Remove from the heat, stir in the white chocolate and allow to melt. Leave to cool a little.

Place the cream in a large bowl with the Tia Maria and icing sugar and whisk until soft peaks have formed. Cut each muffin horizontally into 2 even slices and use half to fill the bottom of two 10cm (4in) metal cooking rings, breaking up as necessary. Cover with half of the flavoured cream and scatter the cherries on top. Add another layer of the muffin to enclose the cherries and cream completely. Spoon the rest of the flavoured cream on top and spread evenly with a palette knife. Dust liberally with the cocoa powder and, using a blowtorch briefly around the sides to help release them, carefully remove the cooking rings. Drizzle around the cooled white chocolate sauce. Serve at once.

FRUITS OF THE FOREST SPONGE

If you make this dessert for adults only, add a splash of cassis or your favourite liqueur to the ricotta mixture.

Serves 2

1 x 300g (11oz) tin of forest fruits in light syrup

12 sponge fingers

175g (6oz) ricotta cheese

100ml (3½ fl oz) double cream

4 tbsp Greek yoghurt

½ lemon, pips removed

50g (2oz) plain chocolate, at least 70 per cent cocoa solids

icing sugar, to dust

Drain the juice from the tin of fruit into a shallow dish, reserving the fruit. Dip the sponge fingers briefly into the juice and use them to line two 10cm (4in) metal cooking rings set on plates, standing them up so the tops protrude.

Place the ricotta cheese in a bowl with the cream, yoghurt and a squeeze of the lemon juice. Add 4 tablespoons of the drained fruit juice. Whip to form soft peaks, then use to fill the sponge-lined rings, almost but not quite to the top. Spoon a couple of tablespoons of the reserved forest fruits on top of the ricotta mixture so they come to the top of the sponge fingers. Grate over the chocolate.

Blitz the remaining juice and fruit in a mini food-processor with a squeeze of lemon juice. Pass through a fine sieve into a jug and then drizzle around the plate. Carefully remove the cooking rings and dust the sponges with a little icing sugar to serve.

POACHED FIGS WITH VANILLA YOGHURT

265

Make sure you select unbruised fruit when choosing your figs.

Serves 2

1 miniature bottle of port (about 50ml/ 2fl oz in total)

finely grated rind and juice of 1 orange

1 vanilla pod, split in half and seeds scraped out

1 tbsp light muscovado sugar

2 ripe firm figs

75g (3oz) Greek yoghurt

1–2 tsp icing sugar

Place the port in a pan with the orange rind and juice, scraped-out vanilla pod and muscovado sugar. Bring to a simmer and allow to reduce for a couple of minutes.

Cut the figs into quarters and carefully add to the pan. Poach for 3–4 minutes until tender, spooning over the port liquid occasionally to ensure the figs cook evenly.

Place the yoghurt in a bowl and beat in the vanilla seeds and icing sugar to taste.

Spoon the poached figs into warmed, wide-rimmed bowls and continue to reduce the remaining poaching liquid for another couple of minutes until slightly sticky. Drizzle over the figs and add a dollop of the vanilla yoghurt to the side to serve.

FANCY FRUIT COBBLER

266

Fruit cobbler is a real heart-warming pudding and is super served with yogurt, ice cream or, best of all, lots of custard.

Serves 6

225g (8oz) plain flour, plus extra for dusting

1 tbsp baking powder

a pinch of salt

50g (2oz) caster sugar

75g (3oz) butter, chilled and diced

grated rind of ½ orange

6–8 tbsp milk

1 tbsp demerara sugar

FOR THE FILLING

50g (2oz) butter

3 pears, peeled, cored and chopped

350g (12oz) cooking apples, peeled, cored and chopped

2 tbsp demerara sugar

2 fresh rosemary sprigs

juice of ½ orange

1 x 400g (14oz) tin of apricot halves in natural juice

25g (1oz) candied stem ginger, chopped

juice of ½ lemon

icing sugar, to dust

Greek yoghurt, to serve

Preheat the oven to 220°C/425°F/gas 7. Sift the flour, baking powder and salt into a food-processor. Add the caster sugar and butter and whizz until the mixture resembles breadcrumbs. Add the orange rind then, with the motor running, gradually add enough milk to form a soft dough.

On a lightly floured surface, gently knead the dough until smooth then roll out to a thickness of 2cm (¾in) and stamp out 8–10 rounds with a 7½ cm (3in) pastry cutter. Transfer to a baking sheet and brush with a little of the milk. Sprinkle over the demerara sugar and bake for 10 minutes until well risen and golden brown.

Meanwhile, melt the butter in a large frying pan. Add the pears, apples, sugar, rosemary and orange juice and cook for 2 minutes. Add the juice from the tin of apricots and the ginger and simmer for 5 minutes. Add the apricot halves and lemon juice and simmer for 2–3 minutes until piping hot.

To serve, spoon the hot fruit into a serving dish and arrange the cobbler topping around the edge of the fruit. Dust with icing sugar and serve with the Greek yoghurt.

APPLE CRISP WITH ORANGE-SCENTED CUSTARD

This is a speedy variation on the traditional apple brown Betty.

Serves 2

40g (1½ oz) unsalted butter, plus extra for greasing

2 Granny Smith apples, peeled, cored and sliced

2 tbsp dark muscovado sugar

¼ tsp ground cinnamon

2 tbsp sultanas

150g (5oz) fresh white breadcrumbs

4 tsp clear honey

200ml (7fl oz) double cream

2 egg yolks

2 tbsp caster sugar

1 tsp finely grated orange rind

1 fresh rosemary sprig

icing sugar, for dusting

Preheat the oven to 220°C/425°F/gas 7. Melt half the butter in a sauté pan. Add the apples, toss to coat, then sprinkle with the sugar and cinnamon. Cook for 2–3 minutes until the apples are lightly caramelized but holding their shape. Stir in the sultanas and divide half the mixture between 2 lightly-buttered ovenproof dishes, transferring the remaining mixture to a bowl. In the same pan, fry the breadcrumbs in the remaining butter until golden. Sprinkle half over the apple mixture in the dishes. Spread over the remaining apple mixture and sprinkle with the rest of the breadcrumbs to cover completely. Drizzle with honey and bake for 8–10 minutes or until bubbling and lightly golden.

Warm the cream in a small pan. Whisk together the egg yolks and sugar. Pour in the heated cream, whisking continuously. Transfer to a clean pan and stir in the orange rind and rosemary sprig, then cook over a low heat until thickened, stirring with a wooden spoon. Remove from the heat, discard the rosemary and pour into a serving jug. Dust the apple crisps with icing sugar and serve the jug of orange-scented custard on the side.

APPLE STRUDEL ROLLS WITH CARDAMOM CUSTARD

Authentic Greek filo pastry is the easiest to handle and gives the best result.

Serves 2

sunflower oil, for deep-frying

50g (2oz) butter

a good pinch of ground ginger

a good pinch of ground cinnamon

finely grated rind of 1 lemon

1 apple, peeled, cored and diced

25g (1oz) sultanas

150g (5oz) filo pastry, thawed if frozen

1 egg, beaten

FOR THE CARDAMOM CUSTARD

150ml (¼ pint) milk

2 egg yolks

1 tbsp caster sugar

1 cardamom pod, split open and seeds ground to a powder

Preheat a deep-fat fryer or fill a deep-sided pan one-third full with oil and heat to 190°C/375°F. Melt the butter in a pan and set aside half. Stir the ginger into the remainder with the cinnamon, lemon rind, apple and sultanas. Cook gently for 2–3 minutes until the apples are beginning to soften.

Cut the filo into six 25cm (10in) squares. Layer up 3 squares, lightly brushing with melted butter between each one. Spoon half of the apple mixture about 7½ cm (3in) from one of the corners. Pull over the corner to enclose the filling completely, then fold in the 2 sides and roll up like a cigar, using a little of the beaten egg to seal the edges. Repeat with the remaining filo and filling. Deep-fry the rolls in the heated oil for 2–3 minutes until crisp and golden brown. Drain on kitchen paper.

Heat the milk in a small pan but don't allow it to boil. Whisk the egg yolks, sugar and cardamom until pale and fluffy. Slowly pour in the hot milk, whisking constantly. Return the mixture to a clean pan and whisk over a gentle heat until thickened. Arrange the rolls on warmed plates and spoon over the custard to serve.

INSTANT TIRAMISU

This is a fantastically simple version of a classic dessert.

269

Serves 2

250g (9oz) curd or cream cheese

2 tbsp double cream

1 vanilla pod, split in half and seeds scraped out

4 tbsp strong black coffee

25g (1oz) caster sugar

50g (2oz) sponge fingers, snapped in half

50g (2oz) mixed blueberries and raspberries

1 miniature Grand Marnier (about 50ml/2fl oz in total)

25g (1oz) plain chocolate (at least 70 per cent cocoa solids), finely grated

Whisk the curd cheese, double cream and vanilla seeds in a large bowl until thickened.

Mix the coffee and caster sugar in a shallow dish. Dip in half of the sponge fingers, then arrange in the base of individual dessert glasses.

Scatter over the blueberries and raspberries and drizzle half of the Grand Marnier on top, then cover with the creamy vanilla mixture. Scatter over half of the grated chocolate.

Repeat the layers until all the ingredients have been used up, finishing with a layer of grated chocolate. Serve at once.

FLAPJACK STACKS WITH ANGEL HAIR

Flapjacks and candyfloss are brought together here, along with caramelized apples and a fruity sauce, to make a simple but very effective dessert.

270

Serves 2

25g (1oz) butter

4 apples, peeled, cored and roughly chopped

2 tbsp caster sugar

150ml (¼ pint) double cream, whipped to soft peaks

FOR THE FLAPJACKS

75g (3oz) butter

50g (2oz) light muscovado sugar

2 tbsp golden syrup

175g (6oz) porridge oats

FOR THE FRUITY SAUCE

150ml (¼ pint) Lindisfarne Mead

50g (2oz) raisins

grated rind and juice of 1 orange

grated rind and juice of 1 lemon

grated rind and juice of 1 lime

75g (3oz) dried cranberries

½ tbsp olive oil

FOR THE ANGEL HAIR

150g (5oz) caster sugar

300ml (½ pint) water

Preheat the oven to 220°C/425°F/gas 7. Melt the butter in a pan and add the sugar, syrup and oats, stirring until the sugar dissolves. Place a 7½ cm (3in) ring mould on a lined baking sheet and spoon in 3 tablespoons of the mixture, pressing down well. Remove the ring and repeat to make 3 more rounds. Bake for 8 minutes until golden, then cool on a wire rack.

Pour the mead into a pan and stir in the raisins, citrus rind and juice, cranberries and the olive oil. Heat gently for 3–4 minutes.

Meanwhile, melt the butter in a heavy-based frying pan and stir in the apples and sugar. Cook for 7–8 minutes, stirring regularly, until the apples are tender and golden brown.

To make the angel hair, place the sugar and water in a pan and heat gently, stirring, until the sugar dissolves. Bring to the boil and simmer rapidly without stirring until the mixture turns golden brown. Using a metal spoon, quickly drizzle the caramel over the back of a wooden spoon to form fine strands; leave to cool and harden.

To serve, place 2 flapjacks on separate plates and spoon on a dollop of the whipped cream, top this with the caramelized apples. Place the remaining flapjacks on top and spoon over another dollop of whipped cream. Decorate with the angel hair and pour around the fruity sauce.

BUTTERNUT SQUASH SPONGES WITH COCONUT ICING

These moist sponges would make a perfect tea-time treat, or they could be easily transported for a picnic.

Serves 4

120ml (4fl oz) olive oil, plus extra for brushing

½ small butternut squash (about 150g/5oz in total)

100g (4oz) light muscovado sugar

2 eggs

150g (5oz) self-raising flour

½ tsp baking powder

½ tsp each ground cinnamon and ginger

150g (5oz) icing sugar

2 tbsp coconut milk

Preheat the oven to 220°C/425°F/gas 7. Brush a 4-holed Yorkshire pudding mould with a little oil. Peel the butternut squash and grate using a mandolin or a sharp knife. Place the muscovado sugar and eggs in a large bowl and use an electric beater to whisk together until light and fluffy.

Sift the flour into a bowl with the baking powder and spices. Gradually whisk the oil into the egg mixture, adding a tablespoon of flour in between each addition to prevent the mixture from curdling. Finally fold in the grated butternut squash and divide between the prepared Yorkshire pudding moulds. Bake for 10–12 minutes or until cooked through and lightly golden.

Meanwhile, sift the icing sugar into a small bowl and then beat in enough coconut milk to make a smooth icing. Remove the sponges from the oven and tip out of the moulds, then turn out on a wire rack and leave to cool a little. Drizzle the coconut icing over the sponges and arrange on serving plates.

BRANDY-SNAP BASKETS WITH FRUIT AND CHOCOLATE SAUCE

These baskets look beautiful but take only a few minutes to make.

Serves 2

FOR THE CHOCOLATE SAUCE

75g (3oz) plain chocolate, at least 70 per cent cocoa solids

85ml (3fl oz) warm water

3 tbsp double cream

50g (2oz) butter

FOR THE FRUIT BASKETS

a little lemon juice

2 small apples, cored and chopped

2 small pears, cored and chopped

3 brandy snaps

15g (½ oz) almond flakes

50g (2oz) butter

35g (1½ oz) caster sugar

1 tsp ground cinnamon

a little shredded zest of orange

a little shredded zest of lime

a little shredded zest of lemon

fresh mint leaves, to garnish

Preheat the oven to 200°C/400°F/gas 6. Squeeze a little lemon juice over the apple and pear flesh, to prevent it from discolouring. Melt the chocolate with 85ml (3fl oz) of water. When the chocolate has melted, stir in the cream and cook for 2–3 minutes. Then add the butter.

Lay a piece of baking parchment or greaseproof paper on a baking tray. Place the brandy snaps and almond flakes on this and bake in the oven for 1–2 minutes, until the brandy snaps are flat and malleable. Leave the almonds in the oven for 5 minutes longer, until they are toasted golden brown. Place the brandy snaps over upturned cups to form baskets, then leave to harden.

Caramelize the apples and pears in the remaining butter and the caster sugar. After 4 minutes, add the cinnamon and continue to cook until the fruit has turned golden.

To serve, make lakes of chocolate sauce on 2 plates. Arrange 2 brandy-snap baskets on top of each plate. Fill each basket with the caramelized fruit and toasted almonds, and garnish with the citrus fruit zest and some fresh mint leaves.

STEAMED PUDDING WITH CARAMEL SAUCE

This classic steamed pudding is made in minutes in the microwave.

Serves 4

100g (4oz) self-raising flour

50g (2oz) caster sugar

50g (2oz) butter, softened, plus extra for greasing

1 egg

4 tbsp milk

225g (8oz) fresh dates, stoned

2 tbsp flaked coconut

grated zest of 1 lemon

1 satsuma, peeled and sliced

1 tbsp clear honey

FOR THE SAUCE

5 tbsp caster sugar

1 tbsp water

150ml (¼ pint) double cream

Butter a microwave-proof 900ml (1½ pint) pudding basin or bowl. Blend the flour, sugar, butter and egg in a food-processor until you have fine breadcrumbs. With the motor still running, gradually add the milk and whizz until smooth. Chop half of the dates and stir them into the mixture with the flaked coconut and lemon zest. Line the sides of the basin with the satsuma slices and spoon the honey into the base. Carefully spoon the pudding mixture into the basin. Cover with a plate and cook in the microwave on high for 4½ minutes. Leave to rest for 5 minutes.

Gently heat the sugar in a small pan. Add the water and cook gently until the sugar has dissolved. Simmer for 2–3 minutes until the syrup turns to a golden caramel. Push the whole dates onto the ends of 4 wooden skewers and dip them in the caramel. Leave to set on baking parchment or greaseproof paper.

Stir the cream into the rest of the caramel, simmer for 2 minutes. Turn the pudding out on to a serving plate, pour the cream sauce around the base and decorate with the caramel-coated dates.

COSMOPOLITAN

This is a very potent party drink.

Serves 2

100g (4oz) cranberries, thawed if frozen

1 miniature bottle of Grand Marnier (about 50ml/2fl oz in total)

a good handful of ice cubes

finely grated rind and juice of 2 limes

4 tbsp caster sugar

Put 2 Martini glasses in the freezer. Place the cranberries in a liquidizer with the Grand Marnier, ice cubes, and half of the lime juice and sugar. Blend until smooth. Pass through a fine sieve into a jug, pressing with the back of a wooden spoon to get all the juice.

Place the remaining lime juice in one saucer, and mix the lime rind with the remaining sugar in another. Take the glasses from the freezer and dip the tops in the lime juice, then in the lime-flavoured sugar. Pour the Cosmopolitans into the frosted glasses to serve.

COINTREAU AND MANDARIN SMOOTHIE

The mandarins give this cocktail body. It's refreshing but don't get too carried away – it is easy to drink, but deceptively strong.

Serves 2

1 x 400g (14oz) tin of mandarins in light syrup

1 miniature bottle of Cointreau (50ml/2fl oz in total)

50ml (2fl oz) double cream, well chilled

2 tbsp mascarpone

a handful of ice cubes

6 cranberries

icing sugar, to dust

Place the mandarins and their syrup in a liquidizer with the Cointreau, double cream, mascarpone and ice. Blend to a frothy purée, then pour into tall glasses to serve.

Lightly crush the cranberries and decorate each glass with them. Dust with icing sugar to create a 'snowy' effect and serve immediately.

WINTER

SWEET POTATO SOUP WITH SESAME SPINACH SALAD

There are several varieties of sweet potato available, with skins ranging in colour from orange and pink to purple.

Serves 4

25g (1oz) unsalted butter

1 onion, chopped

2 tsp ground coriander

675g (1½ lb) sweet potatoes, finely chopped

1.2 litres (2 pints) vegetable stock

FOR THE SALAD

2 handfuls of baby spinach leaves, roughly shredded

1 tbsp sesame seeds, toasted

1 tsp sesame oil

1½ tsp dark soy sauce

1 red chilli, seeded and very finely chopped

salt and freshly ground black pepper

Heat the butter in a large pan. Add the onion and cook for 5 minutes until softened but not coloured. Stir in the ground coriander with the sweet potatoes and cook for 1 minute.

Pour the stock into the pan and season with black pepper. Bring to the boil and simmer for about 15 minutes or until the sweet potatoes are cooked through and tender.

Meanwhile, place the baby spinach in a bowl and add the sesame seeds, sesame oil, soy and chilli, tossing to combine. Season to taste and set aside.

Transfer the soup to a food-processor in batches and whizz until smooth, then pour back into the pan; or use a hand-held blender. Reheat gently, then season to taste. Ladle into 4 warmed bowls and top each with a generous handful of dressed spinach salad. Eat immediately.

KIPPER CHOWDER

A bowl of soup must be one of the most welcoming foods known to man. This comforting chowder always goes down well when it is bitterly cold outside.

Serves 4

600ml (1 pint) milk

1 kipper fillet (undyed, if possible)

1 bay leaf

40g (1½ oz) unsalted butter

25g (1oz) plain flour

2 tbsp white wine

225g (8oz) fresh spinach, stalks removed

100g (4oz) cooked mashed potato

50g (2oz) freshly grated Cheddar

1 garlic clove, finely chopped

50ml (2fl oz) double cream

salt and freshly ground black pepper

Gently cook the milk, kipper and bay leaf in a sauté pan for 3–4 minutes until just tender; cool slightly. Discard the bay leaf, move the kipper to a plate, then flake, discarding any skin and bone.

Strain the poaching milk into a jug. Melt 25g (1oz) of the butter in a pan, stir in the flour and cook over a low heat for 1 minute. Remove from the heat and add the poaching milk, little by little, stirring until smooth after each addition. Return to the heat for 4–5 minutes until thickened and smooth, stirring occasionally.

Heat a pan and add the remaining knob of butter. Once it stops sizzling, pour in the wine and allow it to bubble down. Tip in the spinach and cook for 1–2 minutes, keeping it moving around with a spatula. Season to taste, then drain. Tip into a clean tea towel and squeeze out the excess liquid, then roughly chop.

Mix the mashed potato into the cooked white sauce until well combined, then stir in the Cheddar and garlic. Cook for a minute or so until the cheese is melted, stirring. Stir in the spinach with the kipper flakes and cream, then cook gently until just warmed through. Season to taste and ladle into warmed serving bowls. Serve immediately.

PRAWN AND CHORIZO BROTH

Try to skim off the oil that gathers on top of the soup as it is cooking. A piece of absorbent kitchen paper laid on top will soak it up.

Serves 2

6 raw, whole king prawns (heads and shells intact)

1 tbsp olive oil

600ml (1 pint) chicken or fish stock

1 small red onion, finely diced

1 raw chorizo sausage, skinned and finely diced (about 50g/2oz in total)

1 large potato, finely diced

a pinch of dried chilli flakes

a pinch of ground turmeric

2 plum tomatoes, peeled, seeded and diced

2 tbsp chopped mixed fresh herbs (such as flat-leaf parsley and coriander)

salt and freshly ground black pepper

Heat a lidded pan. Break off the heads of the prawns, then remove the shells and veins. Add a little of the oil to the pan and tip in the prawn heads and shells. Cook for 1 minute, stirring, then pour in the stock and bring to a simmer. Reduce the heat and simmer for 10 minutes.

Heat the remaining oil in a separate pan and cook the onion, stirring, for 2–3 minutes until soft but not coloured. Tip in the chorizo and cook for another 2–3 minutes or until the chorizo is sizzling and releasing its natural oils. Add the potato and cook for another minute until well coated, then stir in the chilli flakes and turmeric and cook for 1 minute, stirring. Season generously.

Strain the prawn-infused stock through a fine sieve into the onion and chorizo mixture, stirring to combine. Return to a simmer, stir in the tomatoes, then reduce the heat and cook for another 5 minutes or so, until the potato is completely tender but still holding its shape, skimming off any excess fat.

Remove the pan from the heat, stir in the raw, peeled prawns, cover and set aside for 3–4 minutes to allow the prawns to cook and turn opaque. Stir in the herbs and season to taste.

PRAWN BISQUE

It's hard to believe a soup so rich in texture and flavour can be made in less than 10 minutes. You could replace the prawn shells with cracked lobster or crab shells.

Serves 2

a knob of butter

1 tbsp olive oil

1 shallot, finely chopped

1 celery stick, finely chopped

1 garlic clove, finely chopped

100g (4oz) shells from raw tiger prawns

2 sprigs of fresh tarragon

2 tbsp brandy

4 tbsp dry white wine

300ml (½ pint) hot chicken stock (from a cube is fine)

100ml (3½ fl oz) double cream

a pinch of paprika

a squeeze of lemon juice

½ tsp snipped fresh chives

salt and freshly ground black pepper

Melt the butter with the oil in a pan and sauté the shallot, celery and garlic for 1–2 minutes until softened but not coloured.

Increase the heat, add the prawn shells to the pan with the tarragon and cook for another minute or so, stirring. Pour in the brandy and allow to reduce right down. Stir in the wine and stock and bring to the boil, then boil fast for 2 minutes to reduce.

Transfer to a blender and blitz to a smooth purée, then strain back into a clean pan through a fine sieve, pressing down with the back of a wooden spoon. Stir in the cream and add the paprika and lemon juice. Season to taste and just heat through.

Ladle the prawn bisque into warmed bowls and add a tiny sprinkling of chives to each one. Serve at once.

PEAR AND WALNUT SALAD WITH GOATS' CHEESE

Lightly toast your walnuts if they aren't very fresh. (See illustration, page 180.)

Serves 2

2 x 50g (2oz) goats' cheese slices

2 tbsp seasoned flour

1 tbsp olive oil

50g (2oz) walnut halves, roughly chopped

1 tsp wholegrain mustard

1 large ripe pear

75g (3oz) mixed salad leaves

1 tbsp extra-virgin olive oil

1 tsp white wine vinegar

salt and freshly ground black pepper

Heat a non-stick frying pan. Coat the goats' cheese in the seasoned flour, shaking off any excess. Add the olive oil to the heated frying pan and then add the goats' cheese. Cook over a high heat for 1 minute on each side until crisp and lightly golden.

Place the walnuts and wholegrain mustard in a large bowl and combine well. Cut the pear into quarters, remove the core and chop the flesh into small pieces. Add to the bowl, along with the salad leaves.

Dress the pear and walnut salad with enough of the extra-virgin olive oil and vinegar to barely coat the leaves. Season to taste. Divide most of the salad between plates, top each one with a piece of the fried goats' cheese and finish off with the remaining salad to serve.

ROASTED PEARS WRAPPED IN BLACK FOREST HAM WITH ROCKET SALAD

This salad not only looks and tastes fabulous, it is also incredibly easy to make.

Serves 2

1 ripe firm pear

100g (4oz) thin Black Forest ham slices

25g (1oz) butter

4 tbsp brandy

25g (1oz) walnut halves, chopped

50g (2oz) wild rocket

2 tbsp snipped fresh chives

2 tbsp chopped fresh flat-leaf parsley

2 tbsp chopped fresh dill

175g (6oz) Cashel Blue cheese

salt and freshly ground black pepper

Heat a large frying pan. Peel the pear and cut into quarters, then remove the core and thinly slice. Cut the Black Forest ham into strips and quickly wrap one round each slice of pear.

Add the butter to the heated frying pan and once it is foaming, add the wrapped pear slices. Cook for 2–3 minutes until crisp, turning once. Pour in the brandy and allow to flambé. Scatter in the walnuts and continue to toss until the flames have died down and the liquid has evaporated.

Arrange the rocket on plates and scatter the chives, parsley and dill on top. Season to taste, then divide the wrapped pear slices and walnuts between them. Break up the Cashel Blue into small pieces, discarding the rind, and scatter on top to serve.

POTATO AND BACON RÖSTI WITH POACHED EGG

Crisp on the outside, soft and buttery inside, these röstis will help you get over the worst of hangovers.

Serves 4

2 x 200g (7oz) waxy potatoes, unpeeled (such as Maris Piper)

25g (1oz) unsalted butter

1 small onion, finely chopped

2 rindless streaky bacon rashers, finely chopped

1 tbsp white wine vinegar

4 large eggs

sunflower oil, for shallow-frying

2 tbsp chopped fresh flat-leaf parsley

25g (1oz) plain flour, sifted

salt and freshly ground black pepper

fresh chives, to garnish

Steam the potatoes over a pan of boiling water for 10 minutes, then remove from the heat and leave until cool enough to handle. Melt the butter in a frying pan and cook the onion for a couple of minutes until softened. Add the bacon and continue to cook until the bacon is just crisp. Remove from the heat.

Heat a large pan with plenty of salted water. Add the vinegar and bring to the boil. Break each egg into the water where it is bubbling, then turn the heat down and simmer gently for 1 minute. Remove each egg with a slotted spoon and plunge into iced water. When cold, trim down any ragged ends from the cooked egg white; return to the iced water until ready to use.

Heat enough oil to shallow-fry in a large frying pan. Peel the cooked potatoes and coarsely grate into a bowl. Stir in the onion and bacon mixture and the parsley and season generously, then add just enough flour to bind. Divide into 8 equal portions and shape each one into a pancake about 2½ cm (1in) thick. Shallow-fry for about 3–4 minutes on each side until golden brown and cooked through. Drain on kitchen paper. Return the poached eggs to a pan of boiling salted water for 30 seconds or until just heated through. Stack 2 röstis onto warmed serving plates, top with the poached eggs and garnish with fresh chives.

BUBBLE AND SQUEAK AND FRIED EGGS

Comforting yet homely, this classic bubble and squeak is lovely served with fried eggs.

Serves 2

450g (1lb) floury potatoes, cut into 2½ cm (1in) cubes (such as Golden Wonder, King Edward or Maris Piper)

100g (4oz) Savoy or York cabbage, roughly chopped

85g (3oz) unsalted butter

2 tbsp milk

2 tbsp sunflower oil

4 large eggs

salt and freshly ground black pepper

Cook the potatoes for 8–10 minutes in boiling salted water until tender but not breaking up. Plunge the cabbage into a pan of boiling salted water and cook for 6–8 minutes until tender. Drain and refresh under cold running water. Heat a large, non-stick frying pan. Drain the potatoes and return to their pan over a low heat to dry out. Mash them, then beat in half of the butter with the milk and seasoning. Fold in the cabbage.

Heat half the oil and a knob of the butter in the frying pan and swirl it up the sides. Tip in the potato mixture and cook for about 10 minutes, turning regularly.

Heat an omelette pan and add half the remaining oil and butter. Fry the eggs, 2 at a time, basting them in the hot fat until just set. Divide the bubble and squeak between warmed plates and slide the fried eggs on top.

CHORIZO AND FRIED EGG SANDWICH

284

The perfect late-night snack. The sublime spiciness of the chorizo gives an extra dimension to a fried egg sandwich.

Serves 2

olive oil, for cooking

8 thin cooked chorizo slices

4 slices of country-style white bread

2 large eggs

sea salt and freshly ground black pepper

Heat a griddle pan until hot. Heat a thin layer of oil in a non-stick frying pan over a medium-high heat. Add the slices of chorizo and cook for a minute or so on each side until sizzling and they have begun to release their own coloured oil into the pan. Remove from the pan, reserving the flavoured oil, and drain the chorizo on kitchen paper.

Add the bread to the heated griddle pan and cook for a minute or so on each side until nicely marked, then drizzle over a little olive oil.

Reduce the heat a little under the frying pan and break in the eggs. Leave them to cook for 2–3 minutes, spooning a little of the flavoured hot oil over the yolks until they are just set.

Arrange a slice of the griddled bread on each warmed plate and place a fried egg on top. Season to taste and add the crisp slices of chorizo. Cover with the remaining slices of griddled bread and cut on the diagonal to serve.

ITALIAN EGGY BREAD SANDWICH

285

For best results, use slightly stale bread. You can vary the filling for this sandwich depending on what's in the fridge – diced chorizo works well, as would Parma ham.

Serves 2

4 thick slices of country-style white bread (1 day old is best)

1 x 100g (4oz) ball of mozzarella, drained

4 tbsp freshly grated Parmesan

4 sun-dried tomatoes, finely chopped

2 tbsp shredded fresh basil

2 eggs

2 tbsp milk

25g (1oz) butter

salt and freshly ground black pepper

Heat a frying pan. Cut 4 circles out of the slices of bread using a 10cm (4in) pastry cutter. Dice the mozzarella and scatter over 2 of the circles of bread, leaving a small border around the edge.

Sprinkle over the Parmesan, sun-dried tomatoes and basil, then season with pepper. Cover with the remaining 2 circles of bread and press down lightly around the edges to seal.

Place the eggs in a shallow dish with the milk and season to taste. Soak both sides of each sandwich in the egg mixture, gently shaking off any excess.

Add the butter to the heated pan and, once it is foaming, add the sandwiches. Cook for 2–3 minutes until golden brown, then flip over and cook for another minute or so.

Cut each sandwich in half and arrange on warmed plates to serve.

PORK SPRING ROLLS WITH CHINESE DIPPING SAUCE

You could use any combination of vegetables for this dish, such as pak choi, baby corn, carrot and bean sprouts.

Serves 2

sunflower oil, for cooking

1 garlic clove, finely chopped

1 tsp freshly grated root ginger

100 g (4 oz) lean minced pork

1 x 25g (1oz) bag of stir fry vegetables

a dash of sesame oil

1 tsp dark soy sauce

10 spring roll or wonton wrappers (10cm/4in), thawed if frozen

1 egg yolk, beaten with 2 tbsp water

salt and freshly ground black pepper

FOR THE CHINESE DIPPING SAUCE

1 tbsp sesame oil

2 tsp tomato ketchup

a few drops of Tabasco sauce

1 tsp dark soy sauce

a good pinch of dried crushed chillies

1 tbsp chopped fresh coriander

Preheat a deep-fat fryer or fill a deep-sided pan one-third full with oil and heat to 190°C/375°F.

Heat 1 tablespoon of the sunflower oil in a frying pan and stir-fry the garlic, ginger, pork and seasoning for a couple of minutes until the pork is sealed and lightly browned. Add the stir fry vegetables with the sesame oil and soy sauce and continue to stir-fry for another 2–3 minutes until the pork is cooked through but the vegetables are still crunchy. Tip out onto a baking sheet and spread out to allow the mixture to cool as quickly as possible. Place 1 heaped tablespoon of the mixture near one of the corners of a spring roll or wonton wrapper. Pull over the corner to enclose the filling completely, then fold in the two sides, brush with the egg yolk mixture to seal and roll up like a cigar. Repeat until you have 10 spring rolls in total. Deep-fry the spring rolls for 1–2 minutes until crisp and golden brown. Drain well on kitchen paper.

To make the Chinese dipping sauce, place all the ingredients in a bowl and whisk to combine. Arrange the spring rolls on warmed plates. Divide the sauce between individual dipping bowls and set to the side of each plate to serve.

HOT CHEESE IN A BOX WITH GRIDDLED CIABATTA

This is a great way to use up cheese that won't ripen properly. Serve with a bitter leaf salad with a wholegrain mustard dressing.

Serves 2

1 small Camembert (in a wooden box)

olive oil, for drizzling

1 garlic clove, finely chopped

a good pinch of soft, fresh thyme leaves

1 small ciabatta loaf

salt and freshly ground black pepper

Preheat the oven to 220°C/425°F/gas 7 and heat a griddle pan until searing hot. Remove the wrapper from the Camembert and return the cheese to the wooden box. Season generously and drizzle with olive oil. Sprinkle the garlic and thyme on top and place on a baking sheet. Bake for 6–8 minutes until warmed through and bubbling.

Meanwhile, cut the ciabatta into slices on the diagonal and arrange on the heated griddle pan. Cook for a minute or so on each side until nicely marked, and drizzle with a little olive oil. Depending on the size of your griddle pan, you may have to do this in batches.

Arrange the Camembert in the middle of a large plate and pile the griddled ciabatta around the edges to serve.

CHILLI SQUID WITH MANGO SALAD

This dish has everything going for it – an excellent combination of flavours and textures and it looks fab to boot!

288

Serves 2

sunflower oil, for deep-frying

50g (2oz) plain flour

1 tsp ground cayenne pepper

a pinch of salt

200g (7oz) squid (about 3 small tubes), cleaned and cut into rings

FOR THE SALAD

1 firm ripe mango, peeled and stoned

3 limes, peeled

6 baby spring onions, halved and shredded

2 garlic cloves, crushed

2 tsp toasted sesame seeds

1 tbsp each chopped fresh coriander and mint

Preheat a deep-fat fryer or a deep-sided pan one-third full of sunflower oil to 190°C/375°F. Cut the mango flesh into julienne and place in a bowl. Cut the limes into segments and add to the mango with the spring onions, garlic, sesame seeds, coriander and mint, stirring gently to combine. Set aside at room temperature to allow the flavours to infuse.

Place the flour in a separate bowl and stir in the cayenne and salt. Use to coat the squid, shaking off any excess. Deep-fry for a minute or so until crisp and golden – you may have to do this in batches. Remove with a slotted spoon and drain on kitchen paper. Arrange mounds of the mango salad in the middle of serving plates and pile the deep-fried squid on top. Serve immediately.

SAUCY SOUFFLÉ TARTLETS

This dish should be served as soon as it is cooked. You can make the tartlet cases and red pepper dressing ahead of time.

289

Serves 4

250g (9oz) ready-made shortcrust pastry, thawed if frozen

plain flour, for dusting

2 leeks, thinly sliced

6 tbsp milk

sunflower oil, for deep-frying

2 tbsp olive oil

1 red pepper, seeded and cut into thin strips

1 tbsp chopped walnuts

1 tbsp caster sugar

½ tsp balsamic vinegar

2 tbsp seasoned plain flour

150ml (¼ pint)

FOR THE SOUFFLÉS

175ml (6fl oz) milk

100g (4oz) soft goats' cheese

2 tsp cornflour dissolved in a little water

½ tsp cayenne

3 eggs, separated

butter, for greasing

salt and freshly ground black pepper

1 tbsp snipped fresh chives, to garnish

Roll the pastry out on a floured surface to a thickness of 5mm (¼ in) and use to line four 7½ cm (3in) pastry cases. Bake blind for 12–15 minutes until crisp and golden. Meanwhile, separate the sliced leeks into rings and place in a bowl with 6 tablespoons of the milk.

Place the milk and cheese for the soufflé in a small pan and heat gently, without boiling, until the cheese melts. Stir in the slaked cornflour, cayenne and plenty of seasoning. Slowly bring to the boil, stirring until thickened. Pour the mixture into a large bowl and beat in the egg yolks and chives. In a separate bowl, whisk the egg whites until they form soft peaks and carefully fold into the cheese mixture. Pour into 4 well-buttered 7½ cm (3in) ramekins and bake for 6–8 minutes until golden and risen.

Heat the olive oil in a large frying pan and cook the pepper strips over a high heat for 4–5 minutes until beginning to blacken. Add the walnuts and cook for 1–2 minutes until golden, then stir in the sugar and balsamic vinegar. Season to taste and keep warm.

Drain the leeks and toss with the seasoned flour to coat. Deep-fry in the hot sunflower oil for 2–3 minutes until crisp and golden. Drain on kitchen paper. Turn out the soufflés into each tartlet case and arrange the crispy leeks around the edge. Pour the warm dressing over the top and garnish with the chives. Serve immediately.

SKATE WITH CAPER SAUCE AND FENNEL RÖSTI

303

Skate has a wonderful texture and flavour and tastes fantastic served with this classic caper sauce, and accompanied by fennel rösti and a warm broccoli and yellow pepper salad.

Serves 2

100ml (3½ fl oz) white wine

3 fresh thyme sprigs

1 bay leaf

6 black peppercorns

1 slice of lemon

1 tbsp white wine vinegar

300ml (½ pint) boiling water

2 x 175g (6oz) skate wings

FOR THE RÖSTI

1 large potato, coarsely grated

2 tbsp olive oil

1 fennel bulb, quartered and thinly sliced

6 black peppercorns

a pinch of dried oregano

FOR THE WARM SALAD

500g (1lb 2oz) broccoli, cut into small florets

1 tbsp olive oil

1 yellow pepper, seeded and chopped

a small handful of fresh basil leaves

FOR THE DRESSING

5 tbsp white wine

1 tbsp olive oil

1 tsp Dijon mustard

1 tbsp white wine vinegar

FOR THE SAUCE

50g (2oz) unsalted butter

2 tbsp pickled capers, well rinsed

juice of ½ lemon

salt and freshly ground black pepper

Place the wine, thyme, bay leaf, peppercorns, lemon, vinegar and boiling water in a large sauté pan, bring to the boil and simmer for 4 minutes.

Meanwhile, make the rösti. Dry the potato in a clean tea towel. Heat 1 tablespoon of the oil in a frying pan and gently cook the fennel and peppercorns for 8 minutes until the fennel is softened. Transfer to a large bowl and stir in the potato, oregano and plenty of salt and pepper. Shape the mixture into round cakes about 2cm (¾ in) thick. Heat the remaining oil in the same pan and cook the rösti for 3–4 minutes on each side until golden brown; keep warm in a low oven.

Add the skate to the pan of simmering water and cook for 10–12 minutes, turning once, until just cooked.

Meanwhile, make the warm salad. Cook the broccoli in a pan of boiling salted water for 3 minutes. Drain well and cool under cold water. Heat the oil in a wok or large frying pan and stir-fry the broccoli and pepper for 2–3 minutes until tender but still firm. Stir together the dressing ingredients and add to the pan with the basil leaves. Cook for a further minute or so, stirring, and season to taste.

To make the sauce, melt the butter in a small frying pan, stir in the capers and a squeeze of lemon juice and cook over a high heat for 3–4 minutes until the butter is dark brown – take care not to let it burn.

To serve, place the rösti on 2 plates and arrange the skate wings on top. Pour around the sauce and serve with the warm salad.

TROUT WITH FENNEL

This very modern dish cleverly pairs the delicate flavour of the fish with juicy, firm-textured fennel.

Serves 2

2 tbsp sunflower oil

1 fennel bulb, sliced

1 garlic clove, finely chopped

2 x 75g (3oz) boneless, skinless trout fillets

6 tbsp white wine

2 tsp lemon juice

4 tbsp hot vegetable stock

FOR THE SAUCE

½ cucumber, peeled and chopped

1 red onion, chopped

1 red pepper, seeded and roughly chopped

4 tomatoes, chopped

3 garlic cloves, finely chopped

5 tbsp chopped fresh basil

150ml (¼ pint) olive oil

1 tbsp tomato ketchup

5 tbsp hot vegetable stock

salt and freshly ground black pepper

fresh chives, to garnish

Preheat the oven to 200°C/400°F/gas 6. Heat the sunflower oil in an ovenproof frying pan and cook the fennel and garlic for 3–4 minutes, turning occasionally until browned.

Twist the trout fillets and place them in a small, oiled ovenproof dish. Drizzle over 2 tablespoons of the wine, the lemon juice and plenty of salt and pepper. Place in the oven for 7–8 minutes until the fish is just cooked. Pour the remaining wine and the stock into the fennel pan with a little salt and pepper and place in the oven for 15 minutes until tender.

Place the cucumber, red onion, red pepper, tomatoes, garlic, basil, olive oil, tomato ketchup, stock and plenty of salt in a food-processor and pulse to form a coarse sauce.

Spoon the sauce onto 2 plates and divide the fennel between each one, placing it on top of the sauce. Top each with a trout fillet and garnish with the chives.

SEARED SALMON WITH SWEET POTATO AND ROCKET SALAD

This is a great way to cook this succulent fish.

Serves 2

600ml (1 pint) sunflower oil

1 large sweet potato, cut into matchsticks (about 275g/10oz in total)

250ml (9fl oz) white wine

1 small onion, finely chopped

1 tsp Dijon mustard

120ml (4fl oz) vegetable stock

2 tbsp double cream

juice of 1 lemon

25g (1oz) unsalted butter, diced

2 tbsp chopped fresh chervil, plus extra sprigs, to garnish

4 tomatoes

2 tbsp olive oil

1 tbsp balsamic vinegar

250g (9oz) boneless, skinless salmon fillet, cut into 1cm (½ in) wide strips

25g (1oz) rocket

salt and freshly ground white pepper

Heat the oil in a deep frying pan to 190°C/375°F and deep-fry the sweet potatoes until crisp. Drain on kitchen paper.

Heat together the wine, half the onion, half the mustard and the vegetable stock in a small pan. Bring to the boil and simmer gently for 5 minutes, then stir in the cream and half the lemon juice. Remove from the heat and gradually whisk in the butter to give a rich, glossy sauce. Add the chopped chervil and blend until smooth. Season to taste.

Roughly chop the tomatoes and then toss in a bowl with the remaining chopped onion and mustard, 1 tablespoon of olive oil and the vinegar. Cook the salmon for 1 minute in 1 tablespoon of olive oil in a very hot frying pan. Remove with a spatula, then season with salt, pepper and a squeeze of lemon juice.

To serve, toss the rocket leaves in with the tomato salad and pile into the centre of a plate. Arrange the salmon strips on top of the salad and pile the sweet potato sticks on top. Pour around the sauce and garnish with the chervil sprigs.

SPICY MACKEREL FILLETS WITH FRUITY TOMATO CHUTNEY

When buying mackerel, freshness is the most important quality to look for, so buy from a reliable fishmonger.

Serves 2

2 tbsp olive oil

1 small onion, finely chopped

1 garlic clove, crushed

1 large apple, peeled, cored and chopped

2 plum tomatoes, peeled, seeded and chopped

1 tsp balsamic vinegar

1 tbsp dark muscovado sugar

4 tbsp plain flour

½ tsp each ground paprika, cayenne pepper and garam masala

2 fresh mackerel, filleted and boned

50g (2oz) unsalted butter

250g (9oz) fresh spinach, stalks removed

½ lemon, pips removed

salt and freshly ground black pepper

Heat 1 tablespoon of the oil in a pan and add the onion, garlic, apple and tomatoes. Cook for 5 minutes or until the mixture has started to soften, stirring occasionally. Add the vinegar and sugar and cook for another 10–12 minutes, stirring occasionally until the mixture has reduced and thickened. Season to taste.

Heat a large frying pan. Mix together the flour and spices on a flat plate. Season generously and use to coat the mackerel fillets. Add the remaining oil and a knob of butter to the pan and fry the fillets, skin-side down, over a medium-high heat for 2–3 minutes until the skin is crisp. Turn over and cook for another minute or so until just tender, being careful not to overcook.

Heat a large pan. Add a knob of butter and cook the spinach for 2–3 minutes until the leaves are just wilted. Season, drain off the excess liquid and arrange in the middle of warmed serving plates. Heat the remaining butter in a small pan until nutty-brown but not burnt and add a squeeze of lemon juice. Place 2 of the mackerel fillets on each serving of spinach, drizzle over the butter mixture, then spoon the chutney around the edge.

JERK MULLET WITH PINEAPPLE SALSA

This dish is a traditional Jamaican recipe, where the fish would be wrapped in banana leaves and barbecued. Substitute red or grey snapper, salmon, trout or even sea bass for the mullet, if you wish.

Serves 2

1 yellow pepper, halved, seeded and chopped

2 red Scotch bonnet chillies, seeded and finely chopped

1 garlic clove, roughly chopped

2½ cm (1in) piece of fresh root ginger, roughly chopped

½ tsp ground allspice

4 tbsp white wine vinegar

4 tbsp dark soy sauce

3 tbsp olive oil, plus a little extra

450g (1lb) red mullet, cleaned, scaled and fins removed

1 ripe baby pineapple

1 tbsp chopped fresh coriander

juice of 1 lime

salt and freshly ground black pepper

Thai fragrant rice, to serve (optional)

Preheat the oven to 240°C/475°F/gas 9. To make the jerk seasoning, place the yellow pepper in a food-processor with one of the chillies, the garlic and ginger and blitz until well blended. Add the allspice, vinegar, soy sauce and 1 tablespoon of the olive oil, then whizz again until smooth. Season to taste.

Cut several deep slashes into each side of the mullet and place in a lightly oiled, shallow ovenproof dish. Pour over the jerk seasoning and rub it into the fish, making sure that some of it goes right down into the slashes. Bake for 12–15 minutes, or until the mullet is completely cooked through and tender.

Meanwhile, make the pineapple salsa. Peel the pineapple and remove the core, then cut the flesh into 1cm (½ in) cubes. Place in a bowl with the remaining chilli, 2 tablespoons of the oil, the coriander and lime juice. Season generously and mix well, then set aside at room temperature to allow the flavours to combine. For maximum effect, serve the red mullet straight from the dish with separate bowls of pineapple salsa and Thai fragrant rice, if liked.

SPAGHETTI IN A BAG WITH MUSSELS

The key to this simple dish is to use good-quality pasta. Check the cooking instructions on the back of the spaghetti packet and cook it for about 4 minutes less than recommended.

Serves 2

100g (4oz) spaghetti

3 tbsp olive oil

1 small onion, finely chopped

2 garlic cloves, crushed

½ tsp dried chilli flakes

¼ tsp fresh thyme leaves

85ml (3fl oz) dry white wine

50ml (2fl oz) fish stock

1 x 400g (14oz) tin of chopped tomatoes (in rich tomato juice)

1 tbsp tomato purée

2 tbsp chopped mixed fresh herbs (such as basil, flat-leaf parsley and chives)

450g (1lb) large, fresh mussels, well cleaned

salt and freshly ground black pepper

Preheat the oven to 220°C/425°F/gas 7. Cook the spaghetti in boiling salted water for 8 minutes until almost tender.

Heat a sauté pan. Add 2 tablespoons of the oil and cook the onion for 2–3 minutes until softened, stirring occasionally. Add the garlic, chilli flakes and thyme and cook for another minute, stirring. Pour in the wine and allow to bubble down, then add the stock, tomatoes and tomato purée. Season to taste and bring to the boil, then reduce the heat and simmer for 5 minutes or until slightly reduced and thickened, stirring occasionally.

Cut out two 38cm (15in) squares of non-stick baking paper and crumple into small balls, then open them out again. Drain the spaghetti and tip into the tomato sauce with the fresh herbs. Stir to mix, then spoon half onto each square of paper. Insert the mussels into the pasta and drizzle over the remaining olive oil.

Lift up opposite sides of the paper square and fold together, twisting and tucking the other ends to form a secure parcel. Place on a baking sheet and bake for 6–8 minutes until the bag has ballooned, all the mussels have opened (discard any that do not) and the spaghetti is completely tender. Arrange on warmed serving plates and serve immediately.

LINGUINE WITH CLAMS

There is a wide array of clams now available from good fishmongers. Look out for amandes de mer, palourdes and tellines, or experiment with a mixture.

Serves 2

175g (6oz) linguine pasta

1 tbsp olive oil

1 small red onion, finely chopped

2 garlic cloves, finely chopped

85ml (3fl oz) dry white wine

1 ripe tomato, diced

a good pinch of dried, crushed chillies

225g (8oz) live clams, well cleaned

1–2 tbsp extra-virgin olive oil

1 tbsp chopped fresh flat-leaf parsley

salt and freshly ground black pepper

Cook the linguine in boiling salted water for about 8 minutes until al dente, or according to the packet instructions.

Meanwhile, heat the oil in a large pan. Add the red onion and garlic and sauté for 2–3 minutes until softened but not coloured.

Pour the wine into the pan and allow to reduce right down, then tip in the tomato and add the crushed chillies. Bring to a simmer and boil fast for 1–2 minutes until slightly reduced. Season.

Tip the clams into the pan, then cover with a tight-fitting lid and steam for 2–3 minutes, shaking the pan occasionally until all the clams have opened. Discard any that do not.

Meanwhile, drain the linguine. When the clams are cooked, add the linguine to the pan with a good glug of extra-virgin olive oil and toss until well combined. Divide between warmed. wide-rimmed bowls, scatter over the parsley and serve.

PASTA WITH POACHED SMOKED HADDOCK AND BAKED TOMATOES

This creamy pasta made with gently poached smoked haddock and served with baked tomatoes makes a lovely mid-week supper.

Serves 4

350g (12oz) rigatoni pasta

1 onion, chopped

1 garlic clove, crushed

4 tbsp olive oil

50g (2oz) fresh white breadcrumbs

juice of ½ lemon

2 tbsp chopped fresh parsley

10 small tomatoes

75g (3oz) freshly grated Double Gloucester

300ml (½ pint) milk

225g (8oz) boneless, skinless smoked haddock

4 tbsp white wine

150ml (¼ pint) double cream

2 tbsp chopped fresh dill

225g (8oz) spinach, stalks removed

salt and freshly ground black pepper

Preheat the oven to 190°C/375°F/gas 5. Cook the pasta in a large pan of boiling salted water for 10 minutes until tender. Fry half the onion and the garlic for 5 minutes in 2 tablespoons of the oil. Stir in the breadcrumbs, lemon juice, parsley and seasoning. Cut off the tops and deseed 8 of the tomatoes. Spoon in the breadcrumb mixture and place in an ovenproof dish. Sprinkle over half the cheese and bake for 10 minutes.

Heat the milk gently in a shallow pan. Add the fish and poach for 6–8 minutes until just cooked. Heat the remaining oil in a separate pan and cook the reserved onion for 5 minutes until softened. Chop the remaining 2 tomatoes and add to the onion pan with the wine, cream and dill. Season and simmer gently for 5 minutes. Flake the haddock and stir into the sauce.

Cook the spinach for 3–4 minutes in a pan until wilted. Drain the pasta and place in a heatproof dish, pour over the cream sauce and sprinkle with the remaining cheese. Grill for 3–5 minutes until bubbling and golden. Arrange the spinach around the edge and serve with the baked tomatoes.

NATURAL OYSTERS WITH CHILLI SHALLOT VINEGAR

An oyster knife is a good investment – make sure you buy one with a guard, and use a tea towel to protect your hand.

Serves 2

12 oysters (native, if possible)

FOR THE CHILLI SHALLOT VINEGAR

100ml (3½ fl oz) red wine vinegar

1 shallot, very finely diced

½ mild red chilli, seeded and very finely chopped

1 tbsp snipped fresh chives

freshly ground black pepper

Combine the ingredients for the chilli shallot vinegar in a small bowl and season with pepper to taste. Set aside to allow the flavours to develop.

Scrub the oyster shells then place one, wrapped in a clean tea towel, on a firm surface with the flattest shell uppermost and the hinge pointing towards you. Gripping the oyster firmly, insert an oyster knife into the gap in the hinge and twist to snap the shells apart.

Slide the blade along the inside of the upper shell to sever the muscle that holds it together. Lift the lid off the top shell, being careful not to spill any juices. Carefully clean away any broken shell and finally run the knife under the oyster to loosen it. Repeat until all the oysters are opened and then arrange on plates.

Spoon a little of the chilli shallot vinegar onto each oyster and serve at once.

ROAST GOOSE WITH SEASONAL VEGETABLES

Goose is less fashionable these days, but it makes a very impressive centrepiece for Christmas lunch.

Serves 2

1 goose breast, trimmed (skin on)

2 x 225g (8oz) potatoes

1 large parsnip, diced

175ml (6fl oz) red wine

120ml (4fl oz) chicken stock

grated rind of 1 orange

a pinch of ground mixed spice

50g (2oz) chilled unsalted butter, diced

8 large Brussels sprouts, trimmed and grated

1 garlic clove, crushed

120ml (4fl oz) double cream

1 tbsp fresh thyme leaves

salt and freshly ground black pepper

Preheat the oven to 200°C/400°F/gas 6. Heat an ovenproof frying pan. Score the skin of the goose breast with a sharp knife and then add to the pan, skin-side down. Cook for a few minutes until lightly golden, then turn over and cook on the other side for 1–2 minutes until well sealed. Transfer to a wire rack and set over the frying pan in the oven to catch the fat. Bake for 10–15 minutes or until the goose is tender and cooked through.

Cut each potato into 8 wedges and place in a pan of boiling salted water. Cover and cook for 6–8 minutes until just tender. Place the parsnip in a separate pan of boiling salted water and cook for 10–12 minutes until tender. Place the wine in another pan with the chicken stock, orange rind and mixed spice and boil fast until reduced by half. Heat half the butter in a small wok and add the Brussels sprouts and garlic. Stir-fry for 2–3 minutes until just tender, then stir in half of the cream and warm through. Season to taste.

Remove the goose from the oven, drain the excess fat into the pan and transfer to a warm plate to rest for at least 5 minutes. Drain the potatoes and tip into the hot pan of goose fat. Add the thyme and cook for 3–4 minutes on each side until lightly golden. Season to taste.

Drain the parsnips and place in a food-processor with the remaining cream. Whizz until blended and season to taste. Carve the goose breast into slices and divide between warmed serving plates. Add dollops of the parsnip purée and serve with the creamed, stir-fried Brussels sprouts and potato wedges on the side. Whisk the remaining butter into the reduced wine mixture to warm through, then drizzle the sauce around the plates to serve.

TANDOORI-STYLE CHICKEN WITH BUTTERED RICE

313

This may not be an authentic Indian-style tandoori but the results are incredibly good, particularly served with the buttery rice.

Serves 2

4 tbsp Greek yoghurt

1 tsp tomato purée

2 garlic cloves, crushed

3 cardamom pods, lightly crushed

1 tsp ground ginger

2 tsp medium curry powder

2 x 150g (5oz) skinless chicken fillets, cut into cubes

2 tsp sunflower oil

FOR THE BUTTERED RICE

25g (1oz) butter

1 small onion, finely chopped

1 x 250g (9oz) packet of cooked basmati rice (or use leftover rice)

4 tbsp hot chicken stock (from a cube is fine)

salt and freshly ground black pepper

chopped fresh coriander, to garnish

Preheat the oven to 200°C/400°F/gas 6 and heat an ovenproof frying pan. Mix the yoghurt, tomato purée, garlic, cardamom, ginger and curry powder in a bowl. Add the chicken and stir until well coated. Add the oil to the hot frying pan and quickly sauté the chicken for 1 minute to seal, then transfer to the oven and cook on the top shelf for 6–8 minutes until completely tender and lightly charred.

Melt half the butter in a pan and sauté the onion over a high heat for 1–2 minutes until soft. Add the rice to just warm through, then sprinkle over the stock, tossing the pan constantly. Season to taste. Generously grease six 150ml (¼ pint) metal dariole moulds with the rest of the butter. Divide the rice among them and arrange on a baking sheet. Cover each one tightly with foil. Cook on the second shelf in the oven for 2–3 minutes until all the stock has been absorbed.

Turn out 3 dariole moulds onto each plate and pile the tandoori-style chicken alongside. Garnish with the coriander.

CHICKEN PARCELS WITH JERUSALEM ARTICHOKE PURÉE

314

Chicken and Jerusalem artichokes are a perfect flavour marriage.

Serves 2

225g (8oz) Jerusalem artichokes, peeled and thinly sliced

600ml (1 pint) vegetable stock

1 red onion, chopped

1 tsp dried thyme

a pinch of grated nutmeg

4 boneless, skinless chicken thighs

50g (2oz) butter

100g (4oz) button mushrooms, quartered

juice of ½ lemon

1 tbsp chopped fresh parsley

225g (8oz) spring greens, tough stalks removed, but leaves kept whole

6 tbsp Greek yoghurt

salt and freshly ground black pepper

In a large pan, bring to boil the Jerusalem artichokes, stock, a quarter of the onion, ½ teaspoon of thyme and the nutmeg, and simmer for 15 minutes. Season the chicken and cook in half the butter in a large frying pan for 15 minutes, turning once, until golden brown. Place the mushrooms, half the remaining onion, ½ teaspoon of thyme, half the remaining butter, the lemon juice, parsley and 2 tablespoons of water in a small pan and cook gently for 10 minutes. Season to taste.

Add 4 spring green leaves to the pan of artichokes and cook for 2–3 minutes until tender. Set aside to cool. Shred the remaining greens into 1cm (½ in) ribbons. Set the chicken aside to rest. Stir-fry the shredded greens and remaining onion in the chicken pan with the remaining butter and 4 tablespoons of stock from the Jerusalem artichoke pan for 3–4 minutes until tender; season. Drain the artichokes and blend with 2 tablespoons of the Greek yoghurt until smooth.

Top each chicken thigh with 1 tablespoon of yoghurt and wrap in a cooked cabbage leaf to make 4 parcels. Spoon the artichoke purée onto a plate and arrange the chicken parcels on top. Drizzle with mushroom sauce and serve the greens on the side.

CHICKEN AND SPICY SAUSAGE

315

This is real comfort food and an explosive combination of flavours.

Serves 2

1 egg

250g (9oz) fusilli tricolore (multi-coloured pasta spirals)

4 tbsp olive oil

25g (1oz) butter

3 tbsp sunflower oil

100g (4oz) boneless, skinless chicken breasts, cut into bite-sized pieces

1 onion, finely chopped

100ml (3½fl oz) white wine

1 x 400g (14oz) tin of cherry tomatoes

½ tsp Worcestershire sauce

5 tbsp double cream

a few drops of Tabasco sauce

1 slice of white bread, crusts removed, diced

50g (2oz) piece of raw chorizo, diced

1 tbsp white wine vinegar

½ tsp Dijon mustard

2 Little Gem lettuces

2 tbsp freshly grated Parmesan or Pecorino

salt and freshly ground black pepper

snipped fresh chives, to garnish

Place the egg in a pan of boiling water and cook for 10 minutes. Drain well and cool under cold water. Cook the pasta in a large pan of boiling salted water for 12–15 minutes, until tender. Drain and toss with 1 tablespoon of the olive oil; keep warm.

Heat the butter and 1 tablespoon of the sunflower oil in a wok and stir-fry the chicken for 4–5 minutes until well browned; set aside. Add the onion to the pan and cook for 1 minute. Stir in the wine, tomatoes and Worcestershire sauce and simmer rapidly until the liquid has reduced by half. Stir in 3 tablespoons of the cream, the Tabasco sauce, and salt and pepper to taste.

Heat 1 tablespoon of sunflower oil in 2 separate frying pans. Cook the diced bread in one pan for 3–4 minutes, shaking until crisp and golden brown. In the second pan, cook the chorizo for 2–3 minutes until the edges begin to brown. Stir the chicken and chorizo into the tomato sauce with the remaining 2 tablespoons of cream. To make the dressing, whisk together the remaining olive oil, the wine vinegar and mustard; season to taste.

To serve, place the lettuce leaves on a plate. Coarsely grate over the hard-boiled egg, drizzle with the dressing and scatter over the croûtons. Turn the pasta into a large serving bowl and pour over the chicken and chorizo sauce. Sprinkle with Parmesan or Pecorino and garnish with the chives.

LEMON CHICKEN WITH THYME TATTIES

316

If you're someone who thickens their sauces with flour, cornflour or reduced cream, here's a great alternative that makes a rich, creamy sauce that tastes wonderful and is incredibly easy to make.

Serves 2

2 large, unpeeled potatoes, diced

275g (10oz) boneless chicken, cut into bite-sized pieces

1 tbsp vegetable oil

2 tbsp chopped fresh tarragon

150ml (¼ pint) white wine

250ml (9fl oz) hot chicken stock

juice of 1 lemon

3 egg yolks

1 tbsp olive oil

25g (1oz) butter

2 fresh thyme sprigs

salt and freshly ground black pepper

Cook the potatoes in a boiling salted water for 15 minutes; drain well. Meanwhile, season the chicken pieces and cook in the oil in a large pan for 5 minutes, turning frequently until well browned. Drain off any excess fat and stir in the tarragon and white wine; simmer rapidly until the liquid is reduced by half. Pour in the stock and cook for a further 2–3 minutes until cooked through.

Whisk together the lemon juice and egg yolks and add to the chicken, stirring continuously. Cook for 3–4 minutes, stirring to produce a smooth, thickened sauce; season.

Heat the olive oil and butter in a large frying pan and add the drained potatoes, thyme and a little seasoning. Cook for 5 minutes until tender and golden brown. To serve, pile the sautéed potatoes onto a plate and spoon over the chicken.

TEX MEX TURKEY

No need to travel down Mexico way for this freestyle
interpretation of Mexican burritos.

Serves 2

1 tbsp sunflower oil

15g (½ oz) butter

2 spring onions,
sliced

½ green pepper,
seeded and chopped

1 x 200g (7oz) tin of
chopped tomatoes

1 tbsp tomato purée

225g (8oz) turkey
breast stir-fry strips

1 tsp ground cumin

¼ tsp hot chilli
powder

1 tsp dried oregano

½ tsp cocoa powder

3 tbsp double cream

2 tsp lemon juice

salt and freshly
ground black pepper

FOR THE REFRIED BEANS

40g (1½oz) butter

1 x 400g (14oz) tin of
kidney or pinto beans

1 tsp ground cumin

¼ tsp hot chilli
powder

6 soft flour tortillas

150g (5oz) Greek
yoghurt

1 tbsp chopped,
pickled, green
jalapeño chillies

fresh flat-leaf parsley
sprigs, to garnish

To make the refried beans, melt the butter in a heavy-based
frying pan and add the kidney beans. Mash with a potato
masher to form a coarse purée. Stir in the cumin, chilli powder
and salt and pepper to taste. Cook gently for 10 minutes, stirring
occasionally, until piping hot.

Meanwhile, make the chilli filling. Heat the oil and butter in a
separate, heavy-based frying pan and cook the spring onions and
pepper for 2 minutes. Stir in the chopped tomatoes and tomato
purée, then push the mixture to one side of the pan. Add the
turkey to the other side of the pan and stir in the cumin, chilli,
oregano, cocoa powder and salt and pepper. Cook for 2–3
minutes, then stir together the turkey and vegetables and cook
for a further 8 minutes until the vegetables are tender and the
turkey is cooked through. Stir in the cream and lemon juice and
cook for 1 minute.

Heat the tortillas, one at a time, in a hot, dry frying pan for
1–2 minutes, turning once. To serve, mix together the yoghurt
and chopped chillies and spoon into a small serving bowl. Fold
2 of the tortillas into quarters and place them on the side of a
serving plate. Roll up another tortilla and place this in the centre
of the plate. Spoon half of the turkey chilli over the central tortilla
and spoon 2 piles of refried beans next to the quartered tortillas.
Repeat for the second plate. Garnish with the flat-leaf parsley.

TURKEY STROGANOFF WITH HERB RICE

For evenings when you want instant comfort food, you can't go
far wrong with this variation on an old favourite.

Serves 2

100g (4oz) quick-cook
long-grain rice

1 small red onion

2 tbsp olive oil

2 x 75g (3oz) turkey
breast steaks

1 tsp hot paprika,
plus extra for dusting

50g (2oz) button
chestnut mushrooms,
thinly sliced

a good glug of dry
white wine

50ml (2fl oz) double
cream

2 tbsp chopped mixed
fresh herbs (such as
chives, basil and flat-
leaf parsley)

a knob of butter

2 tbsp Greek yoghurt

salt and freshly
ground black pepper

Cook the rice in a pan of boiling salted water for 8–10 minutes
until tender. Thinly slice the onion, then fry in the oil for 1–2
minutes until softened, stirring constantly. Slice the turkey into
strips and toss in the paprika, then add to the pan. Cook for
another few minutes until sealed and lightly golden.

Tip the mushrooms into the pan and continue to cook for
1 minute, tossing until well combined. Pour in the wine and
allow it to bubble down, then add the cream, stirring to
combine. Season and simmer for another minute or so until
thickened and reduced. Drain the rice and return to the pan,
then stir in the herbs and butter. Divide the rice between
warmed plates, spoon over the stroganoff and add a dollop
of yoghurt and a dusting of paprika to serve.

CORONATION-STYLE TURKEY WITH PARSNIP CHIPS

Add wafer-thin slices of cucumber and finely sliced spring onions to the shredded lettuce if you've got them to hand.

Serves 2

3 tbsp Greek yoghurt

2 tbsp mayonnaise

1 tsp mild curry paste

1 garlic clove, crushed

finely grated rind and juice of ½ lemon

1 tbsp chopped fresh coriander

225g (8oz) cooked turkey breast

4 ready-to-eat, dried apricots, finely diced

1 Little Gem lettuce

FOR THE PARSNIP CRISPS

sunflower oil, for deep-frying

1 parsnip

1 tbsp plain flour

a good pinch of curry powder

sea salt and freshly ground black pepper

chopped fresh flat-leaf parsley, to garnish

To make the parsnip crisps, preheat a deep-fat fryer or fill a deep-sided pan one-third full with oil and heat to 190°C/375°F. The oil should be hot enough so that when a bread cube is added, it browns in 40 seconds. Cut the parsnip into wafer-thin slices. Place the flour on a plate and season generously, then add the curry powder and mix to combine. Dust the parsnips in the flour, shaking off any excess, and deep-fry for 1–2 minutes until crisp and lightly golden. Drain on kitchen paper and repeat until all the crisps are cooked. Pile into a warm bowl and season with salt.

Combine the Greek yoghurt in a bowl with the mayonnaise, curry paste, garlic, lemon rind and juice and coriander. Shred the turkey and fold into the Greek yoghurt mixture with the apricots; season to taste. Spoon the coronation-style turkey into the centre of a small platter. Shred the lettuce and arrange around the edge. Garnish with the parsley and serve at once with the bowl of parsnip crisps.

TURKEY CLUB SANDWICH

320

The club sandwich is an American restaurant speciality. There are numerous variations and you can create your own combination.

Serves 2

6 thin, rindless pancetta slices (Italian streaky bacon)

6 thick slices of white bread

25g (1oz) crisp lettuce, finely shredded

1 ripe tomato, sliced

2 tbsp snipped fresh chives

175g (6oz) cooked turkey, cut into thin slices

1 tsp chopped fresh flat-leaf parsley

FOR THE MUSTARD MAYONNAISE

2 egg yolks

1 tbsp white wine vinegar

1 tbsp Dijon mustard

1 garlic clove, crushed

200ml (7fl oz) olive oil

salt and freshly ground black pepper

Preheat the grill and cook the pancetta for 3–4 minutes until crisp and lightly golden, turning once. Drain on kitchen paper.

Place the egg yolks in a bowl with the vinegar and mustard. Add the garlic and season to taste, whisking to combine. Gradually drizzle in the olive oil, whisking continuously. After a minute or so you will notice the mixture beginning to thicken. When this happens add the oil a little faster, but not too fast or the mixture will suddenly curdle.

Toast the bread under the grill and spread with the mustard mayonnaise. Divide half the lettuce between 2 slices of the toast, scatter over the tomato slices and half the chives. Season.

Cover the tomato and chive layer with the turkey and place a slice of toast on top, mayonnaise-side up. Add the remaining lettuce followed by the crispy pancetta with the rest of the chives. Cover with the remaining slices of toast and press down lightly. Arrange on plates and scatter over the parsley to serve.

Chinese New Year recipe

ORIENTAL-STYLE SESAME DUCK SALAD

ORIENTAL-STYLE SESAME DUCK SALAD

321

The duck here is served quite pink due to time constraints, but you could always increase the time by a couple of minutes if you prefer yours more well done.

Serves 2

1 small duck breast fillet, well trimmed (about 100g/4oz)

2 tbsp clear honey

1 tbsp toasted sesame seeds

100g (4oz) baby spinach leaves

salt and freshly ground black pepper

FOR THE DRESSING

1 tbsp olive oil

1 tsp sesame oil

1 tbsp toasted sesame seeds

1 tsp dark soy sauce

juice of ½ lime

1 tsp clear honey

1 tbsp chopped fresh flat-leaf parsley

Preheat the oven to 200°C/400°F/gas 6. Heat a heavy-based, ovenproof frying pan. Score the skin on the duck breast, rub all over with the olive oil and add to the pan, skin-side down, for 5 minutes until the skin is golden brown.

Meanwhile, whisk together all the ingredients for the dressing in a large bowl. Pour off the excess fat produced by the duck, then turn over and drizzle the honey and the sesame seeds on top. Transfer to the oven and cook for another 2–3 minutes until just tender. Remove from the oven and leave to rest as long as time allows, then slice into thin strips on the diagonal.

Season the dressing and toss in the spinach leaves until well coated. Arrange the duck slices in a fan shape in the centre of each plate and divide the salad between them to serve.

GLAZED DUCK WITH ONION RINGS

322

The onion rings in this dish are made using a traditional recipe. They would be great snacks to serve before a barbecue or at a party.

Serves 2

vegetable oil, for deep-frying

100g (4oz) couscous

4 tbsp chopped fresh herbs, such as mint, coriander, chives and parsley

300ml (½ pint) boiling water

2 x 225g (8oz) duck leg portions, boned

1 tsp ground ginger

1 tsp ground cumin

juice of 2 limes

1 tbsp clear honey

50g (2oz) ready-to-eat dried apricots, roughly chopped

3 tbsp olive oil

4 tbsp pumpkin seeds, toasted

1 onion, sliced into rings

150ml (¼ pint) milk

4 tbsp plain flour

1 garlic clove, crushed

100g (4oz) green beans, halved

salt and freshly ground black pepper

Preheat the oven to 200°C/400°F/gas 6. Preheat a deep-fat fryer or a deep-sided pan one-third full of vegetable oil to 190°C/375°F. Place the couscous and herbs in a large bowl and pour over the boiling water. Set aside for 10 minutes until the grains have absorbed the water.

Score the duck skin and sprinkle with the ground ginger, cumin and seasoning. Heat a heavy-based frying pan and cook the duck skin-side down, for 5 minutes until browned. Transfer to an oven-proof dish and roast for 5 minutes, baste with the pan juices and return to the oven for 5 minutes. Drizzle over a quarter of the lime juice and the honey and return to the oven for a further 5–10 minutes until cooked through. Cover and set aside to rest.

Stir two-thirds of the remaining lime juice, the chopped apricots, 2 tablespoons of the olive oil and 1 tablespoon of the pumpkin seeds into the couscous. Dip the onion rings into the milk and then the flour, then repeat the process twice, until the rings are well coated. Deep-fry in the hot oil for 5 minutes until crisp.

Heat the remaining olive oil in a frying pan and stir-fry the garlic and beans for 2 minutes. Stir in the remaining pumpkin seeds and stir-fry for a further 2 minutes until the beans are tender. Stir in the remaining lime juice, and season to taste. To serve, arrange the glazed duck on the couscous and garnish with the stir-fried beans and the crispy onion rings.

PEKING-STYLE DUCK WITH PANCAKES

This dish normally takes days to prepare, but this is a quick version created on the show.

323

Serves 2

4 tbsp clear honey

juice of ½ lime

1 tbsp dark soy sauce

2 duck breasts, skinned

85g (3oz) plain flour

2 eggs

3 tbsp sunflower oil

2 tsp sesame oil

1 small red onion, finely chopped

¼ tsp dried chilli flakes

50g (2oz) light muscovado sugar

1 tbsp white wine vinegar

1 bunch of spring onions, cut into fine matchsticks

½ cucumber, seeded and cut into fine matchsticks

salt and freshly ground black pepper

To prepare the marinade, place the honey in a shallow, non-metallic dish and add the lime juice and soy sauce, stirring to combine. Cut the duck breasts in half horizontally, then cut into strips and prick with a fork. Stir into the marinade, season with pepper and set aside for 5 minutes (or up to 24 hours, if time allows).

To make the pancakes, place the flour in a bowl with a good pinch of salt. Make a well in the centre and gradually beat in the eggs with 1 tablespoon of the sunflower oil and about 50ml (2fl oz) of cold water to make a smooth creamy batter. Allow to rest for 5 minutes (up to 2 hours in the fridge is perfect, if possible).

Heat a non-stick wok over a medium heat until searing hot. Add the marinated duck, reserving the marinade, and stir-fry for 6–8 minutes until cooked through and caramelized, adding a few drops of water to the pan occasionally if the mixture starts to catch and burn. Remove from the heat and pile into a warmed serving dish. Set aside for a few minutes to allow the duck to rest.

Meanwhile, heat a heavy-based, non-stick frying pan. Add a thin film of sunflower oil to the pan and then add a small ladleful of the pancake batter. Swirl around to form a pancake that is no more than 13cm (5in) in diameter. Cook for a minute or so until just set and lightly golden, then flip over and cook for another 30 seconds. Transfer to a warmed serving plate and continue until you have 10 pancakes.

Heat the sesame oil in a small pan. Add the onion and chilli flakes, then cook for 2–3 minutes until softened, stirring. Sprinkle over the sugar, tossing to combine, and as the sugar begins to melt, stir in the vinegar and the reserved marinade. Cook gently for 3–4 minutes or until the sauce has thickened and become slightly sticky. Remove from the heat and pour into a serving bowl.

Serve the Peking duck with a stack of the pancakes, the bowl of caramelized red onion sauce and separate dishes of the spring onion and cucumber to serve. Let your guest take a pancake, smear on a small spoonful of sauce and top it with some of the vegetables and Peking duck before rolling it up to eat.

GOURMET SAUSA[GE]

Gamey-type sausages, such
very well with the sweetnes
in this strapping dish.

Serves 4

8 venison or wild
boar sausages,
(about 450g/1lb)

1 tbsp sunflower oil

450g (1lb) new
potatoes, scraped or
scrubbed

300ml (½ pint) red
wine, plus 3 tbsp

½ lamb stock cube

90g (3½ oz) butter

1 red onion, chopped

1 red pepper, seeded
and diced

2 tbsp wild rowan or
redcurrant jelly

1 tbsp red [wine]
vinegar

2 tbsp chop[ped]
coriander

1 small Sav[oy]
cabbage, sl[ed]

1 garlic clo[ve]
crushed

2 tbsp olive

10 juniper b[erries]
crushed

2 tbsp snip[ped]
chives

salt and fre[shly]
ground blac[k]

SAUSAGES AND [MASH]
WITH ONION GR[AVY]

This is comfort food at its be[st]
to prepare. (See illustration, [p.])

Serves 2

sunflower oil, for
brushing

6 pork and leek
sausages

25g (1oz) butter

1 red onion, thinly
sliced

85ml (3fl oz) red
wine

FOR THE MAS[H]

25g (1oz) b[utter]

1 small oni[on]
chopped

1 x 400g (1[4oz])
butter bean[s drained]
and rinsed

2 tbsp hot c[hicken]
stock (from [a cube if]
fine)

a splash of [double]
cream

salt and fre[shly]
ground blac[k]

PLUM DUCK

The combination of duck with fruit is a classic, but the recipes
are usually complicated. This recipe, however, is for an effortless,
elegant dish simply cooked in one pan on top of the stove.

Serves 4

700ml (1¼ pints) hot
vegetable stock

200g (7oz) easy-cook
long-grain rice

grated rind of
1 orange

2 tbsp olive oil

2 x 350g (12oz) duck
breasts

½ tsp ground
cinnamon

1 bunch of spring
onions, chopped

350ml (12fl oz) red
wine

3 red plums, chopped

1 tbsp demerara
sugar

2 tbsp self-raising
flour

¼ tsp salt

½ tsp bicarbonate of
soda

4 tbsp milk

1 egg, beaten

1 tbsp chopped fresh
parsley

100g (4oz) asparagus
tips

100g (4oz) baby corn

salt and freshly
ground black pepper

In a large pan, bring the stock to the boil and stir in the rice
and orange rind. Bring back to the boil, then simmer for
12–15 minutes until the rice is tender. Drain and keep warm.

Heat ½ tablespoon of olive oil in a heavy-based frying pan and add
the duck, skin-side down. Sprinkle over the cinnamon and a third
of the spring onions. Cook for 10 minutes, then turn. Add the red
wine and the plums, then sprinkle over the sugar and a little salt
and pepper. Cover and cook gently for 10 minutes until the duck
is cooked through.

Sift the flour, salt and bicarbonate of soda into a bowl. Whisk
in the milk and beaten egg to make a smooth batter, then stir in
the remaining spring onions and the parsley. Heat ½ tablespoon
of olive oil in a large frying pan and cook the pancake batter, a
tablespoonful at a time, for 2–3 minutes on each side until
golden brown. Drain on kitchen paper. Cook the asparagus and
baby corn for 2–3 minutes in the remaining oil.

Place the pancakes on a plate and spoon over the vegetables.
Top with the duck breasts and serve the rice on the side.

SPATCHCOCKED QUAIL AND COUSCOUS

This spectacular recipe brings together all kinds of different
ethnic influences. The quails cook to perfection under the grill,
but taste even better when cooked on the barbecue.

Serves 2

2 quails

juice of 1 lime

1 tbsp soy sauce

1 tbsp clear honey

1 tbsp sesame oil

a few drops of
Tabasco sauce

2 garlic cloves,
crushed

1 onion, chopped

2 celery sticks,
chopped

2 tbsp sunflower oil

600ml (1 pint)
chicken stock

4 tomatoes, each cut
into 8 wedges

50g (2oz) sultanas

25g (1oz) butter

175g (6oz) couscous

salt and freshly
ground black pepper

snipped fresh chives,
to garnish

Preheat the grill to medium. Using kitchen scissors, cut along
both sides of the backbone of each quail and remove them.
Open out the quails and flatten them with the heel of your hand.
Push two 20cm (8in) skewers diagonally through each one. (If
using bamboo skewers, soak in hot water for 30 minutes
beforehand to stop them burning.)

Mix together the lime juice, soy sauce, honey, sesame oil,
Tabasco and half the garlic. Season to taste, brush onto the
quails and grill for 12–15 minutes, turning once and basting
occasionally with any remaining mixture, until cooked and well
browned. Fry the onion, celery and remaining garlic in the
sunflower oil for 3 minutes until softened. Stir in 150ml (¼ pint)
of the stock, the tomatoes, sultanas, 3 drops of Tabasco and
seasoning. Bring to the boil, then simmer for 5 minutes. Melt the
butter in a pan and stir in the couscous, remaining stock and
seasoning. Bring to the boil, then simmer for 3–4 minutes until
the couscous grains are light and fluffy. Spoon the celery mixture
onto plates, place the couscous on top, and the grilled quail over
that. Garnish with the chives.

WINTER | Poultry and Game   **215**

FRUITY RABBIT

This delicious and rather u
a very underestimated me
chicken very successfully.

Serves 2

100ml (3½ fl oz)
white wine

1 red-skinned potato,
diced

1 parsnip, diced

100g (4oz) butter

juice of 1 orange

4 tbsp olive oil

75g (3oz) fine green
beans

2 tsp granulated
sugar

2 tbsp w

2 tbsp w
vinegar

3 tbsp d

50g (2oz
ready-to-

350g (12
cut into
pieces

1 onion,

1 garlic
crushed

salt and
ground b

BRAISED GUINE/
WITH CHESTNU

Guinea fowl is much easie
It tastes like a really flavou

Serves 2

25g (1oz) unsalted
butter

1 small onion,
chopped

4 streaky bacon
rashers (rindless),
roughly chopped

2 skinless guinea
fowl breasts, cut into
2cm (¾ in) pieces

¼ tsp dried sage

200ml (7
white wi
Chardon

10 tinne
packed v
chestnut

2 tbsp d

1 tbsp sr
chives

salt and
ground b

seasonal
boiled, to

CHOCOLATE ORANGE CHEESECAKES

These cheesecakes are very easy to make and just take a little
chilling time in the fridge to set.

Serves 4

sunflower oil, for
greasing

100g (4oz) digestive
biscuits, crushed

grated rind of 1
orange

½ tsp each mixed
spice and ground
cinnamon

50g (2oz) unsalted
butter, melted

225g (8oz) plain
chocolate (at least 70
per cent cocoa solids)

3 tbsp milk

3 tbsp brandy

225g (8oz) full-fat
soft cheese

150ml (¼ pint) double
cream

1 tbsp caster sugar

cocoa powder,
to dust

Lightly oil four 10cm (4in) cooking moulds and place on an oiled
baking sheet. Place the biscuits in a bowl and add the orange
rind, mixed spice and cinnamon. Stir in the melted butter and
divide between the 4 moulds, pressing down with the back of
a spoon to form a base. Chill.

Melt the chocolate in a heatproof bowl set over a pan of
simmering water. Transfer half into a separate bowl, set aside
and allow to cool a little. Stir the milk and 1 tablespoon of the
brandy into the remainder. Leave to cool.

Beat together the cream cheese, double cream, sugar and
remaining brandy until smooth and holding its shape, then fold
in the cooled, melted chocolate. Spoon onto the chilled biscuit
bases and level with a palette knife that has been briefly dipped
in water. Chill for at least 5 minutes (or up to 24 hours is fine).

Remove the moulds by warming the sides with a cloth that
has been dipped in hot water and squeezed dry. Dust the
cheesecakes with cocoa powder and arrange on serving plates.
Pour around the chocolate sauce to serve.

CHOCOLATE ORANGE MOUSSE

A little indulgence is a wonderful thing and good-quality chocolate
makes all the difference in this recipe, so try to get chocolate with
a minimum of 70 per cent cocoa solids.

Serves 2

50g (2oz) plain
chocolate (at least
70 per cent cocoa
solids), broken into
squares

1 orange

200ml (7 fl oz) double
cream, well chilled

2 tbsp sifted icing
sugar, plus extra for
dusting

cocoa powder,
for dusting

Melt the chocolate in the microwave on high for 2 minutes or set
over a pan of simmering water for 3 minutes. As soon as it has
melted, transfer to a cold bowl with a spatula to help it cool
down as quickly as possible.

Finely grate the rind from the orange and set aside. Using a very
sharp knife, remove any remaining skin and all the white pith,
then carefully cut into segments and reserve to decorate.

Whip the cream with the icing sugar and orange rind in a large
bowl until soft peaks have formed. When the melted chocolate
has cooled sufficiently, fold it into the cream mixture to achieve
a rippled marble effect.

Set a 10cm (4in) metal cooking ring on each plate and fill with
the chocolate orange mousse. Quickly and carefully, use a
blowtorch to warm each ring before removing it again. Decorate
the plates with the orange segments and add a light dusting
of the icing sugar and cocoa powder to serve.

AMARETTI CHEESECAKE WITH CARAMELIZED WALNUTS

A dessert with an unusual flavour combination, which looks spectacular but involves little effort – what could be better?

Serves 2

150ml (¼ pint) double cream

finely grated rind of 1 lemon

4 tbsp ricotta cheese

a few drops of vanilla extract

100ml (3½ fl oz) dry white wine

75g (3oz) amaretti biscuits

2 ripe figs

icing sugar, to dust

FOR THE CARAMELIZED WALNUTS

50g (2oz) caster sugar

50g (2oz) walnut halves

Heat the caster sugar in a heavy-based frying pan, without stirring, until it dissolves. Increase the heat and cook for another few minutes until a light caramel colour is achieved. Add the walnuts, shaking the pan to coat evenly, then spoon them onto non-stick parchment paper and leave to cool and harden.

Whisk the cream until soft peaks have formed. Fold in the lemon rind, ricotta and vanilla extract. Place a 10cm (4in) metal cooking ring on each of 2 plates. Pour the wine into a small bowl. Dip the amaretti biscuits in the wine, then arrange them in the bottom of the cooking rings, slightly crushing to fit. Spoon half of the cream mixture on top and level with the back of a spoon. Add another layer of the dampened, lightly crushed amaretti biscuits, and cover with the rest of the cream mixture, smoothing across the top with a palette knife.

Cut each fig into thin slices and arrange in a fan shape over each cheesecake, covering the cream completely. Dust liberally with icing sugar and flash with a blowtorch until lightly caramelized. Briefly heat the sides of the cooking rings with a blowtorch to remove them easily. Decorate with the caramelized walnuts.

LITTLE CHOCOLATE CHILLI POTS

These little custard pots cook very well in the microwave. Just be careful not to overcook the mixture or the eggs will scramble, ruining the smooth, creamy texture.

Serves 2

4 egg yolks

50g (2oz) caster sugar

1 vanilla pod

150ml (¼ pint) double cream

50ml (2fl oz) milk

1 tsp ground cinnamon

1 tsp chilli powder

25g (1oz) cocoa powder, plus extra for dusting

Whisk the egg yolks and caster sugar until light and fluffy using an electric beater or by hand with a wooden spoon. Set aside.

Cut the vanilla pod in half with a sharp knife, then scrape out the seeds and place in a pan. Add the cream and milk, then whisk in the cinnamon, chilli and cocoa powder. Slowly bring to the boil, whisking continuously.

Gradually pour the cream mixture into the egg yolks and sugar, beating constantly to combine. Divide between two 120ml (4fl oz) ramekins, cover with cling film and pierce a couple of times with a sharp knife. Cook in the microwave on high for 2 minutes, then leave to rest for 2 minutes before cooking on high again for 1 minute or until almost set.

Remove the ramekins from the microwave and allow to sit for 1 minute, then take off the cling film and dust with a little extra cocoa powder. Serve warm set on serving plates, or cold – they will keep happily in the fridge for up to 24 hours.

LEMON CAKE WITH PINEAPPLE

This cake is best eaten just warm and not long out of the oven. It's a wonderfully indulgent dessert, perfect for a tea-time treat or as a dinner-party finale.

344

Serves 4–6

100g (4oz) unsalted butter, softened, plus extra for greasing

100g (4oz) caster sugar, plus extra for dusting

2 eggs, beaten

finely grated rind of 1 lemon

1 tsp ground ginger

100g (4oz) self-raising flour

2–3 tbsp milk

1 ripe pineapple, peeled, cored and thickly sliced

1 tbsp clear honey

juice of ½ orange

100ml (3½ fl oz) double cream

150g (5oz) thick Greek yoghurt

1–2 tbsp icing sugar to taste, plus extra for dusting

Preheat the oven to 200°C/400°F/gas 6. Grease two 20cm (8in) non-stick sandwich tins and lightly dust with caster sugar, shaking out the excess. Set aside.

Blend the butter and sugar in a food-processor. Pour in the eggs through the feeder tube, then add the lemon rind and ginger. Tip in the flour and milk, then pulse briefly to combine. Divide between the tins and bake for 12–14 minutes until well risen.

Cook the pineapple slices on a hot griddle pan for 4–5 minutes, turning half-way through. Remove the pan from the heat and allow to cool slightly. Mix together the honey and orange juice and pour over the pineapple in the warm pan, turning to coat. Lightly whip the cream and fold it in with the yoghurt and the icing sugar to taste.

When the cakes are baked, turn them out onto a wire rack and leave to cool a little, then spread the cream filling over each half. Top one half with half of the pineapple slices, and sandwich the two halves together. Arrange the rest of the pineapple slices on top, dust with icing sugar, then cut into slices.

UPSIDE-DOWN PINEAPPLE SPONGE WITH CARAMEL SAUCE

This was a real experiment, but the result was a knockout.

345

Serves 2

100g (4oz) unsalted butter, softened, plus extra for greasing

100g (4oz) caster sugar

1 egg

100g (4oz) self-raising flour

1 tbsp clear honey

4 slices pineapple, drained if from a tin

FOR THE CARAMEL SAUCE

50g (2oz) unsalted butter

50g (2oz) caster sugar

2 tbsp clear honey

Cream the butter and sugar together in a large bowl until pale and fluffy. Beat in the egg and then fold in the flour.

Grease a 1.2 litre (2 pint) microwavable pudding basin with butter and drizzle with the honey. Arrange the pineapple slices around the inside of the bowl and spoon in the sponge mixture. Cover with cling film, pierce with a fork and microwave on high for 6 minutes until well risen and lightly golden.

Meanwhile, make the caramel sauce. Melt the butter in a pan and add the sugar and honey. Heat gently for 3–4 minutes until slightly reduced and thickened.

Remove the pineapple sponge from the microwave and turn out onto a plate. Drizzle over the caramel sauce and serve at once.

WINTER BERRY SPONGE AND CUSTARD

346

This microwaved version of a steamed pudding is nursery food at its best. It has a lovely dense, moist texture. Be warned – there will be requests for second helpings.

Serves 2

100g (4oz) frozen mixed berries

150g (5oz) caster sugar

100g (4oz) self-raising flour

1 tsp baking powder

100g (4oz) butter, plus extra for greasing

3 large eggs

1 vanilla pod, split in half and seeds scraped out

2 tbsp red wine

FOR THE CUSTARD

50ml (2fl oz) milk

100ml (3½ fl oz) double cream

1 vanilla pod, split in half and seeds scraped out

3 large egg yolks

50g (2oz) caster sugar

Defrost the berries in the microwave; drain and reserve the juice. Blend the fruit in a food-processor with 100g (4oz) of the sugar, the flour, baking powder, butter, eggs and vanilla seeds. Butter a 1.2 litre (2 pint) microwavable pudding basin and spoon in the sponge mixture – it should be no more than two-thirds full to give the pudding room to rise. Cover with cling film, pierce the top once or twice with a sharp knife and then cook on high for 8 minutes until well risen and cooked through.

Place the milk, cream and vanilla seeds and pod in a small pan and bring up to simmering point; set aside to infuse. Whisk the egg yolks and 50g (2oz) of the sugar until soft and fluffy. Remove the vanilla pod from the heated milk mixture and discard, then gradually add the milk to the whisked egg yolks and sugar. Pour back into a clean pan and cook gently for about 5 minutes until the custard coats the back of a wooden spoon, stirring regularly.

Place the reserved berry juice – you should have about 4 tablespoons in total – in a small pan with the remaining sugar and the red wine. Bring to the boil and boil fast for 2 minutes until slightly reduced and thickened, stirring occasionally. Remove the sponge from the microwave and turn out onto a plate. Pour over the fruit syrup and allow it to soak in. Serve with a jug of the custard to allow people to help themselves.

HOT AND STEAMY PUDDING WITH RASPBERRY CREAM

347

If the microwave has a place in the kitchen, it's for this dish and any other 'steamed' pudding.

Serves 4

50g (2oz) mixed dried fruit, such as prunes, figs and apricots, chopped

1 x 300g (11oz) tin of raspberries in apple juice, strained and juice reserved

50g (2oz) butter, softened, plus extra for greasing

100g (4oz) light muscovado sugar

2 eggs, beaten

100g (4oz) self-raising flour

2 tbsp milk

2 tbsp golden syrup

300ml (½ pint) double cream

Soak the dried fruit in the fruit juice reserved from the tin of raspberries. Beat together the butter and sugar until pale and fluffy. Gradually beat in the eggs, then fold in the flour. Drain the soaked fruit and stir into the sponge mixture with the milk.

Pour the golden syrup into a buttered 1.2 litre (2 pint) microwave pudding basin. Spoon over the sponge mixture and cover with microwave film. Microwave for 4 minutes on high. Leave to stand for 5 minutes.

Meanwhile, make the raspberry cream sauce. In a large bowl, mash the raspberries with a fork. Stir in the cream, then whisk until the mixture forms soft peaks. To serve, turn out the pudding and serve with swirls of the raspberry cream.

RHUBARB AND STEM GINGER CRUMBLE

348

A little indulgence is a wonderful thing and it doesn't come much better than this. The ultimate comforting dessert made from start to finish in under ten minutes – not bad.

Serves 2

2 rhubarb stalks, trimmed and finely chopped

50g (2oz) caster sugar

4 knobs of crystallized stem ginger, drained and finely chopped

2 tsp cornflour

50g (2oz) oatmeal biscuits

25g (1oz) butter, chilled and diced

25g (1oz) macadamia nuts

2 scoops of vanilla ice cream, to serve

Preheat the oven to 200°C/400°F/gas 6. Combine the rhubarb, sugar, ginger and cornflour in a microwavable bowl. Cover with cling film. Microwave on high for 3 minutes until the rhubarb is cooked through but still holding its shape.

Meanwhile, place the biscuits, butter and macadamia nuts in a food-processor and whizz until just broken down – it's important the mix has a coarse texture. Set aside.

Divide the cooked rhubarb mixture between two 200ml (7fl oz) ramekins and sprinkle the crumble mixture on top. Arrange on a baking sheet and bake for about 5 minutes until the topping is crisp and golden brown.

Place the ramekins on plates and add a scoop of ice cream on top to serve.

MUFFINS WITH ZESTY CRÈME FRAÎCHE

349

Muffins are so quick and easy to make yet they pop out of the oven perfect every time.

Makes 12

225g (8oz) plain flour

2 eggs

2 tsp baking powder

100g (4oz) caster sugar

3–4 tbsp milk

6 tbsp vegetable oil

1 tbsp demerara sugar

FOR THE ZESTY CRÈME FRAÎCHE

200ml (7fl oz) crème fraîche

grated rind of 1 lemon

grated rind of 1 lime

juice and grated rind of 1 orange

1 tbsp Greek yoghurt

1 tsp caster sugar

Preheat the oven to 220°C/425°F/gas 7. Place the flour, eggs, baking powder, caster sugar, milk and vegetable oil in a large bowl and beat well with a wooden spoon. Spoon the mixture into a non-stick, 12-hole muffin tin and sprinkle over the demerara sugar. Bake for 14 minutes until well risen and golden brown.

Meanwhile, make the zesty crème fraîche. Mix together the crème fraîche, citrus rind, orange juice, Greek yoghurt and caster sugar until well blended.

Serve the muffins warm or at room temperature with a generous dollop of crème fraîche.

PANETTONE BREAD AND BUTTER PUDDING

If you don't have panettone, which is a sweet Italian Christmas bread, good-quality raisin bread makes an excellent alternative.

Serves 2

300ml (½ pint) milk

4 egg yolks

2 tbsp caster sugar

a few drops of vanilla extract

50g (2oz) unsalted butter

175g (6oz) piece of panettone, cut into triangles

icing sugar, to dust

double cream, to serve (optional)

Preheat the oven to 220°C/425°F/gas 7 and heat a large frying pan.

Scald the milk in a small pan until almost boiling. Whisk the egg yolks, sugar and vanilla extract in a large bowl, then gradually whisk this mixture into the scalded milk in the pan. Cook for a few minutes until the mixture begins to thicken and coats the back of a wooden spoon.

Melt half the butter in the frying pan and quickly fry half the panettone triangles unti lightly golden. Arrange in an overlapping layer in a small ovenproof dish and repeat with the rest of the butter and panettone. Pour over the custard, pressing down gently with a fish slice. Place on a baking sheet and bake in the oven for 4–5 minutes until the custard is almost, but not quite, set.

Remove the pudding from the oven, dust with icing sugar and flash with a blowtorch until lightly caramelized. Serve at once with cream, if liked.

CARAMELIZED GROUND RICE PUDDINGS ON A BED OF EXOTIC BANANA

351

This is a lovely fruity, creamy pudding that will really warm you up on a cold winter's night.

Serves 4

FOR THE PUDDINGS

65g (2½ oz) dried fruit (such as apricots, prunes and peaches), finely diced

450ml (¾ pint) milk

100g (4oz) ground rice

25g (1oz) caster sugar

300ml (½ pint) double cream

2 egg yolks

butter, for greasing

50g (2oz) soft brown sugar

FOR THE SAUCE

3 oranges

75g (3oz) butter

75g (3oz) soft brown sugar

3 large bananas, diced

3–4 tbsp rum, to taste

2 tbsp honey

1 papaya, peeled, seeded and diced

Preheat the oven to 200°C/(400°F/gas 6. Soak the fruit in hot water for 5–10 minutes; drain and pat dry. Heat the milk in a pan until almost boiling, add the ground rice, caster sugar and half the double cream. Bring to the boil, stirring continuously, and cook gently for 2 minutes, then whisk in the egg yolks. Take off the heat and stir in the dried fruit, then spoon the mixture into 4 greased 7½ cm (3in) ramekins. Place in a roasting tin with 2½ cm (1in) of water and bake for about 5 minutes, until set.

Remove the rind from one of the oranges and set aside. Peel the oranges, removing all the white pith, and cut out the segments. Melt 50g (2oz) each of the butter and sugar in a frying pan, add the bananas and rum and allow to bubble for 1–2 minutes until the bananas are cooked through, but still retain their shape. Stir in the orange rind. In a separate pan, melt the remaining butter and 25g (1oz) sugar. Stir in the orange segments and honey and cook until caramelized. Stir in the papaya and heat through gently.

Turn each pudding out onto a baking tray, sprinkle with brown sugar and place under a hot grill until caramelized. Whip the remaining cream. Spoon the banana sauce onto plates, with the puddings on top. Arrange the caramelized oranges and papaya around and top with the whipped cream.

BANANA SOUFFLÉ WITH WALNUT BUTTERSCOTCH

352

The secret to a good soufflé is to butter the moulds well and not to over-whisk the egg whites.

Serves 2

a knob of butter, for greasing

2 egg whites

1 tsp fresh lemon juice

1 ripe banana

1 egg yolk

2 tbsp ready-made custard

icing sugar, to dust

FOR THE WALNUT BUTTERSCOTCH

25g (1oz) walnut halves

50g (2oz) demerara sugar

25g (1oz) butter

85ml (3fl oz) double cream

1 vanilla pod, split in half and seeds scraped out

Preheat the oven to 200°C/400°F/gas 6. Roast the walnuts for about 5 minutes until lightly toasted. Grease two 120ml (4fl oz) ramekins with butter. Place the egg whites and lemon juice in a large bowl and whisk to soft peaks. Mash the banana in a separate bowl and mix in the egg yolk and custard. Carefully fold in the egg whites. Divide the soufflé mixture between the ramekins and place on the top shelf in the oven for 8 minutes until well risen and lightly golden.

Gently heat the sugar in a heavy-based pan with the butter, cream and vanilla seeds until the sugar has dissolved, stirring occasionally. Increase the heat and cook for another couple of minutes until you have a thick, smooth sauce. Finely chop the roasted walnuts and stir them in at the end; keep warm. Remove the soufflés from the oven and dust with icing sugar. Arrange on plates with jugs of the walnut butterscotch to serve.

SNAPPY SYLLABUB AND LYCHEES

This spectacular dessert may seem a little fiddly but in fact only takes minutes to prepare – and everyone will be very impressed that you have made the ginger biscuits yourself.

Serves 2

1 x 400g (14oz) tin of lychees in syrup, drained

4 pieces of stem ginger in syrup, drained and quartered

FOR THE BISCUITS

100g (4oz) golden syrup

75g (3oz) butter

1 egg

225g (8oz) self-raising flour

2 tsp ground ginger

a pinch of salt

FOR THE SYLLABUB

150ml (¼ pint) double cream

2 tsp caster sugar

1 tbsp grapefruit juice

3 tbsp sweet dessert wine, such as muscat

1 meringue nest, crumbled

2 pieces of stem ginger in syrup, drained and finely chopped

½ pink grapefruit, cut into segments

Preheat the oven to 200°C/400°F/gas 6. Stuff the lychees with the quarters of stem ginger and set aside.

To make the biscuits, place the golden syrup, butter and egg in a food-processor and whizz until well blended. Add the flour, ground ginger and salt and blend again. Drop teaspoonfuls of the mixture, spaced well apart, on a non-stick baking sheet and cook for 5–6 minutes until golden brown.

Meanwhile, make the syllabub. Whip together the cream, sugar, grapefruit juice and 1 tablespoon of the wine until the mixture forms soft peaks. Stir the meringue and chopped stem ginger into the whipped cream mixture.

To serve, place 4 or 5 stuffed lychees in 2 tall wine glasses, drizzle over the remaining wine then spoon over the cream mixture. Place the glasses on 2 serving plates and decorate the edges with stuffed lychees, grapefruit segments and ginger biscuits.

SNAPPY GINGER BISCUITS

These home-made ginger biscuits knock spots off the shop-bought variety and they're incredibly simple to make. Make the mixture ahead of time and store in the fridge for up to 24 hours.

Makes 20

100g (4oz) unsalted butter

100g (4oz) caster sugar

½ tsp ground ginger

175g (6oz) self-raising flour

juice of ½ orange

Preheat the oven to 180°C/350°F/gas 4. Place the butter, sugar, ground ginger and flour in a food-processor and blend until the mixture forms coarse crumbs. With the motor running, slowly pour in enough orange juice to bind the mixture into a soft dough.

Place teaspoons of the mixture, well spaced, on a baking sheet and flatten each with a fork. Bake for 10–12 minutes until golden brown, then transfer to a wire rack to cool.

GINGER SPONGE PUDDING WITH CUSTARD AND NUT BRITTLE

355

Use a large enough pudding basin for the sponge to expand during cooking. (See illustration, page 180.)

Serves 2

100g (4oz) unsalted butter, plus extra for greasing

100g (4oz) self-raising flour

100g (4oz) caster sugar, plus a little extra

50g (2oz) crystallized ginger, finely chopped (from a jar)

1 tsp baking powder

2 eggs

FOR THE CUSTARD

150ml (¼ pint) milk

100ml (3½ fl oz) double cream

1 vanilla pod, split in half and seeds scraped out

2 egg yolks

25g (1oz) caster sugar

FOR THE NUT BRITTLE

100g (4oz) caster sugar

25g (1oz) Brazil nuts

Grease a 1.2 litre (2 pint) microwavable pudding basin with butter and sprinkle lightly with caster sugar, knocking out any excess. Blend the butter, flour, sugar, crystallized ginger and baking powder in a food-processor with the eggs. Transfer the mixture to the pudding basin – it should be no more than two-thirds full to allow the pudding to rise. Cover tightly with cling film. Pierce a couple of times with a sharp knife, then cook on full power for 5 minutes until well risen and cooked through.

Place the milk, cream, scraped-out vanilla pod and seeds in a small pan and bring to a simmer. Remove from the heat and set aside while you beat the egg yolks and sugar in a large bowl. Remove the vanilla pod from the milk mixture and gradually whisk into the egg mixture. Pour back into a clean pan and stir over a gentle heat for a couple of minutes until the custard has thickened and coats the back of a wooden spoon.

Place a small frying pan over a high heat. Add the caster sugar and Brazil nuts and heat until the sugar caramelizes, shaking the pan occasionally to ensure even cooking. When the caramel reaches a deep, rich amber colour, remove from the heat and pour onto a cold, non-stick baking sheet. Wait for a minute or so and then shatter with a rolling pin.

Remove the cling film from the sponge pudding and leave to rest for 1 minute before turning out onto a warmed plate. Decorate with the nut brittle and serve the custard in a jug on the side.

CRANACHAN

356

St Andrew's Day recipe

This is a very traditional dessert made with oats, cream and whisky – but there are many ways to adapt it – try it with fresh pineapple, Kirsch and toasted flaked almonds!

Serves 2

50g (2oz) Scottish porridge oats

150ml (¼ pint) double cream

2 tbsp whisky

1 tbsp clear honey

1 x 290g (11oz) tin of Scottish raspberries, drained

fresh mint leaves, to decorate

Dry-fry the oats in a non-stick pan for 4–5 minutes until golden. Transfer to a plate and leave to cool.

Whip the cream until it forms soft peaks. Using a large metal spoon, fold in the whisky, honey, raspberries and cooled oats. Spoon into 2 glasses and chill until ready to serve. Decorate with mint leaves before serving.

PANCAKES WITH LEMON SYRUP

This is a variation on an all-time classic – crêpes Suzettes. Brilliant for last-minute entertaining as these are ingredients most of us have to hand.

Serves 2

50g (2oz) plain flour

a pinch of salt

1 egg

150ml (¼ pint) milk

sunflower oil, for shallow frying

50g (2oz) butter

50g (2oz) caster sugar

finely grated rind and juice of 2 lemons

Greek yoghurt, to serve

fresh mint sprigs, to serve

Heat a heavy-based frying pan. Sift the flour and salt into a bowl and make a well in the centre. Add the egg and whisk vigorously with a balloon whisk. Gradually beat in the milk, drawing in the flour from the sides to make a smooth batter.

Put a little oil in the hot frying pan. Pour in just enough batter to thinly coat the base. Cook over a medium to high heat for about 1 minute until golden brown. Turn and cook on the other side for another 30 seconds or so – you'll need 4 in total. When the pancakes are cooked, fold each one in half and then in half again.

Meanwhile, heat the butter and sugar in a separate heavy-based pan until thick and syrupy. Add the lemon rind and juice and allow to warm through. Add the pancake triangles to the pan and spoon over the lemon syrup to coat evenly. Arrange the pancakes with the lemon syrup on warmed plates and spoon a dollop of Greek yoghurt on top. Decorate with mint sprigs.

COFFEE AND CARDAMOM MUSHROOMS

This spectacular dessert may seem a little fiddly but in fact it takes minutes to prepare. The tuiles and custard can both be kept until the next day, for a repeat performance.

Serves 6

1 x 500ml (18fl oz) carton of coffee ice cream

250ml (9fl oz) double cream

50g (2oz) caster sugar

2 cardamom pods, split

4 egg yolks

2 tbsp softened unsalted butter

50g (2oz) icing sugar, sifted

1 egg white

2 tbsp plain flour

100g (4oz) milk chocolate, grated

sifted cocoa powder and icing sugar, to decorate

Preheat the oven to 220°C/425°F/gas 7. Line a baking tray with parchment paper and mark out six 10cm (4in) circles. Line six 120ml (4fl oz) dariole moulds with cling film and fill with the ice cream. Place in the freezer to refreeze.

Bring the cream, caster sugar and cadamom pods to the boil in a small pan. Remove from the heat and slowly add the egg yolks, then return to the heat and cook gently until the mixture coats the back of a spoon. Strain through a sieve into a jug; allow to set in the fridge.

Blend the butter and icing sugar in a food-processor until softened. With the motor running, slowly add the egg white, then the flour. Place a little of the mixture in the centre of each circle on the baking sheet and spread out thinly to cover. Bake the tuiles for 2–3 minutes or until lightly coloured, then immediately remove the paper with a spatula and mould them over egg cups. Leave to set.

Sprinkle the grated chocolate around the edges of the serving plates. Turn out an ice cream into the middle of each plate. Spoon around the cardamom custard and place a shaped tuile upside-down on top of the ice cream. Dust with cocoa powder and icing sugar.

BANANA AND CHOCOLATE MILKSHAKE

359

This rich drink is more like a dessert. It is likely to be a hit with children and adults alike, so be prepared to make double the quantity.

Serves 2

75g (3oz) milk chocolate, broken into squares

2 tbsp double cream

a knob of butter

2 ripe bananas

2 scoops of vanilla ice cream

300ml (½ pint) milk, well chilled

Melt the chocolate with the cream and butter in the microwave on high for 2 minutes, or over a pan of simmering water for 3 minutes. As soon as the mixture has melted, use a spatula to transfer it to a fresh, cold bowl set over a dish of ice to cool it down.

Once the chocolate mixture is cool, place it in a liquidizer. Peel and slice the bananas, then add to the liquidizer with the ice cream and milk. Blend until smooth, then pour into tall tumbler glasses. Serve with a straw.

HOT MARZIPAN MILKSHAKE

360

This is a brilliant way of using up a leftover piece of marzipan at Christmas.

Serves 2

2 vanilla pods

600ml (1 pint) milk

100g (4oz) marzipan

4 scoops of vanilla ice cream

cocoa powder, to dust

Cut each vanilla pod in half and, using a teaspoon, scrape out the seeds. Place the seeds in a pan with the milk and marzipan and cook for 2–3 minutes until heated through, stirring occasionally.

Transfer the marzipan mixture to a liquidizer and blend until smooth. Pour into tall glasses and top each one with 2 scoops of ice cream. Dust with cocoa powder and serve at once.

HOT CHOCOLATE WITH MARSHMALLOWS

361

This is hot chocolate for grown-ups. Go for a rich Belgian chocolate, which is heavier in fats and cocoa solids than most British varieties. (See illustration, back cover.)

Serves 2

100g (4oz) Belgian plain chocolate, broken into squares

450ml (¾ pint) milk

85ml (3fl oz) double cream

a good handful of tiny marshmallows

Melt the chocolate in a non-metallic bowl on high in the microwave for 2 minutes, or set over a pan of simmering water for 3 minutes.

Place the milk and cream in a small, heavy-based pan. Add the melted chocolate, stirring with a spatula to combine. Heat gently for a few minutes, stirring continuously until piping hot but not boiling.

Pour the hot chocolate into large cappuccino cups or bowls and scatter the marshmallows on top to serve. Yummy!

BOOZY COFFEE TODDY

This is a special treat. There's nothing nicer after a hard day's work.

362

Serves 2

1 x sachet of freshly ground coffee (for a 2-cup cafetière)

50ml (2fl oz) double cream, well chilled

1 x miniature bottle of white rum (about 50ml/2fl oz in total)

2 tsp light muscovado sugar

25g (1oz) plain chocolate (at least 70 per cent cocoa solids), grated, plus extra squares to serve

Make enough coffee to fill a small cafetière (2-cup size). Place the cream in a bowl and lightly whip.

Pour 2 tablespoons of the rum into each coffee cup, add a teaspoon of muscovado sugar to each, top up with hot coffee and stir.

Carefully pour a layer of cream onto each cup, over the back of a spoon, and sprinkle with the grated chocolate. Serve immediately with a square or 2 of chocolate on the side.

Hogmanay recipe

BOOZY COFFEE TODDY

CHOCOLATE EGGNOG WITH BRANDY

Eggnog is a classic Christmas tipple.

Serves 2

400ml (14fl oz) milk

400ml (14fl oz) double cream

2 eggs

50g (2oz) caster sugar

75g (3oz) plain chocolate (at least 70 per cent cocoa solids), broken into squares

1 x miniature bottle brandy (about 50ml/2fl oz in total)

Place the milk, cream, eggs and sugar in a small, heavy-based pan and heat gently for 6–8 minutes or until the mixture is thick enough to coat the back of a wooden spoon.

Meanwhile, melt the chocolate in a non-metallic bowl in the microwave on high for 2 minutes, or set over, but not touching, a pan of simmering water for 3 minutes.

Drizzle the melted chocolate around the inside of 2 tall glass and leave for a minute or so to set. Pour the brandy into the bottom of the glasses and top up with the eggnog to serve.

ORANGE DAIQUIRI

This cocktail is very easy to make. It is a refreshing thirst-quencher and could be made with a can of pineapple chunks in natural juice instead of the oranges. (See illustration, page 180.)

Serves 2

4 oranges

3 tbsp double cream

1 x miniature bottle light rum (about 50ml/2fl oz in total)

a good handful of ice cubes

Cut the peel and all the white pith from 2 of the oranges and then cut the flesh into segments. Place in a liquidizer and squeeze in the juice from the 2 remaining oranges.

Add the cream, rum and ice cubes to the liquidizer and blend until the ice is crushed. Pour into tall cocktail glasses to serve.

MULLED WINE

The perfect drink for any winter celebration – this is a great way to warm people as they come in from the cold.

Serves 2–4

4 oranges

600ml (1 pint) red wine

2 tbsp caster sugar

1 cinnamon stick

6 whole cloves

1 lemon

Cut 3 of the oranges in half and squeeze out the juice. Place in a pan with the red wine and sugar.

Break the cinnamon stick in half and add to the pan with the cloves. Heat gently for about 5 minutes to allow the flavours to combine, stirring occasionally until the sugar has dissolved.

Cut the remaining orange and the lemon in half and then cut into slices. Ladle the mulled wine into heatproof glasses and add a couple of orange and lemon slices to each one to serve.

INDEX